Tattooed Bodies

Tattooed Bodies

Subjectivity, Textuality, Ethics, and Pleasure

Nikki Sullivan

Westport, Connecticut
London

Library of Congress Cataloging-in-Publication Data

Sullivan, Nikki, 1962–
    Tattooed bodies : subjectivity, textuality, ethics, and pleasure / Nikki Sullivan.
      p. cm.
    Includes bibliographical references and index.
    ISBN 0–275–96675–5 (alk. paper)
    1. Tattooing. 2. Body, Human—Social aspects. 3. Body, Human—Symbolic aspects.
    I. Title.
    GN419.3.S85   2001
    391.6′5—dc21   00–049181

British Library Cataloguing in Publication Data is available.

Copyright © 2001 by Nikki Sullivan

Library of Congress Catalog Card Number: 00–049181
ISBN: 0–275–96675–5

First published in 2001

Praeger Publishers, 88 Post Road West, Westport, CT 06881
An imprint of Greenwood Publishing Group, Inc.
www.praeger.com

Printed in the United States of America

The paper used in this book complies with the
Permanent Paper Standard issued by the National
Information Standards Organization (Z39.48–1984).

10 9 8 7 6 5 4 3 2

For my father, whose being and whose passing have marked me in immeasurable ways.

It is so simple, the tattooer said. Little scars that carry you along, that leave you beautiful. This, you will never lose. (Andrea Cohen, *Story of the Tattoo*)

Contents

Acknowledgments

This book derives from my personal and professional interests, and thus is a record not only of the past few years of my life, but, as importantly, of the generosity of others. I would like to thank my family and friends whose emotional and practical support, and whose tolerance when the going got tough, made the completion of this task possible. I am indebted to Nicole Anderson, Liz Diprose, Nick Mansfield, Linnell Secomb, Elizabeth Stephens, Terry Threadgold, and Wendy Waring for their astute comments on earlier drafts of this text, and for their encouragement, enthusiasm, patience, and unwaivering belief in the project. I am particularly beholden to Rosalyn Diprose whose own work, generous spirit, support, and encouragement have inspired and sustained me. My colleagues and students at Macquarie University have also provided invaluable feedback and taught me much and for this I am grateful. Thanks also goes to the Australian Federation of University Women (AFUW SA Inc.) for their generous financial assistance in the form of the Thenie Baddams Bursary. *Tattooed Bodies* would not be what it is without Amanda James' photographic images, that provide a provocative pictorial commentary on the themes discussed. Last, but by no means least, I want to thank Kellie Greene for her incalculable commitment to my life—of which this project is just one aspect. Many people have contributed to my thoughts on the subjects discussed throughout this book, not least those to whom tattooing is a remarkable and passionate venture. They have all marked me, and for this I am eternally grateful.

Introduction

According to Catherine Grognard, "the tattoo[ed body] is a unique object—a naive and provocative moving fresco" (Grognard, 1994, 131). Such a proposition is not uncommon. Indeed, it is probably not unrealistic to claim that, in our culture at least, the tattooed body is a spectacle that incites a plethora of responses, but rarely indifference. As Grognard puts it:

One can be hypnotized by the splendour of these mobile canvasses . . . or one can . . . be shocked by the bewildering strangeness of these decorations and the monstrous metamorphosis which they represent. But one can also try to understand. . . . Hasn't man always tried to unravel the mystery of destiny in order to master it? (131)

Like Grognard, I too am intrigued by tattooed bodies: often seduced by their aesthetic charm, sometimes alarmed by their seemingly threatening connotations, but, more particularly, curious as to why tattooed bodies, including my own, engender such effects. Whilst this book is an attempt to explore what I and many others find provocative—the affectivity of tattooed bodies—its aim is not to satisfy curiosity, at least not in any definitive way. Unlike Grognard, I do not want to unravel the mystery of the tattooed body in order to master it, nor do I believe such a task is either possible or profitable. Consequently my book differs considerably from the majority of analyses available, which, driven by a desire to understand the tattooed body, presume a necessity to seek out and grasp that which it is assumed "stands under": the essence of the subject in/of tattooing[1].

For example, Grognard claims that "tattooing is more than a simple decoration . . . it is a cry of the soul which tears the skin" (16). Tattooing, as the subtitle of her book suggests, is a kind of "graffiti for the soul", and Grognard is of the opinion that "[t]he very soul can be read on the open page of the [tattooed] skin" (15). Similarly, Margot Mifflin states that "tattooing is a way of cutting into nature to create a living, breathing autobiography. Written on the skin . . . tattoos are diary entries and protective shields, conversation pieces and countercultural totems, valentines to lovers and memorials to the dead" (Mifflin, 1997, 178). Tattooing, then, is understood by these writers as both the external expression of an inner essence, and a (potential) source of knowledge, of mastery, and thus of freedom. As Octavio Paz puts it, "the pilgrimage by way of the canvas or the body tattooed with signs, leads to an image that, as it vanishes, opens doors to us. . . . it is a path, a freedom" (Paz, cited in Hardy, 1992, 16). As a result of assumptions such as these, Grognard's examination of tattooing constitutes an attempt to understand what she sees as the question of the human condition.

Like many other writers fascinated by the phenomenon of tattooing, Grognard provides a cross-cultural mapping of bodily inscription that dates back to prehistoric times[2]: from the cave paintings of Lascaux to the flashes that adorn the walls of urban parlours; from the priestess of Hathor to Cher; from the Picts to punks; from Maori chiefs to modern primitives; from the Yakusa to the Hell's Angels.[3] What emerges from the picture Grognard affectionately and somewhat sentimentally paints is the sense of a universal and transhistorical "brotherhood", of an innate human compulsion to write (on or with) the self; to express the self, and thus to free the soul from the bounded space of the body. And in peeling away—metaphorically speaking—the illustrative skin of both the subject and the world, Grognard discovers the soul, knowledge, the key to mastery and freedom. Or does she?

In *Language, Counter-Memory, Practice*, Foucault speaks of the body as "the inscribed surface of events . . . a body totally imprinted by history" (Foucault, 1977, 148). As Foucault sees it, the inscriptive processes of enculturation, of systems of power/knowledge—which are always socially and historically specific—morphologically (trans)form flesh into *a body*, a text, the incarnation of social fictions that can then be read as "truth". It is my contention that tattooed bodies literalise such a phenomenon. I want to argue that bodily inscription, as Foucault envisages it, is no less permanent, changeable, or constitutive than tattooing, although of course it could be said to be less visible and therefore less easily definable or readable. But having made this claim I do not intend to proceed to read the marked body as signifying the truth of human being, nor do I want to celebrate, as do Grognard, Mifflin, and Paz, the supposedly subversive or liberatory potential of tattooing as a counter-ideological path to knowledge and freedom. For as Foucault convincingly demonstrates in *Discipline and Punish: The Birth of the Prison,* "it is not the activity of the subject of knowledge that produces a corpus of knowledge, useful or resistant to power, but power/knowledge, the processes and struggles that traverse it and of which it is made up, that determines the forms and possible domains of knowledge" (Foucault, 1979, 28). Given this, my aim, unlike Grognard's, is not to ask what does the tattooed body (as text) *mean,* or what does it tell us, in a universalizing sense, about the "human condition". Rather, I want to explore *how* the subject in/of tattooing exists in contemporary Western culture; what it *does.*

Whilst the aims and objectives of the approach exemplified by Grognard may, in one sense, be admirable, I am left feeling rather sceptical as to whether such accounts do in fact constitute—as they claim to—a challenge to so-called normative discourses and discursive practices. Analyses such as Grognard's are informed by a particular understanding of subjectivity, textuality, ethics, pleasure, and power. And these concepts reinforce one another, and operate in conjunction with one another, to reaffirm discourses and discursive practices that might loosely be called liberal humanist ones. My misgivings stem, then, from the absence of a lucid account of how identity, or subjectivity, and difference are constituted and maintained within, and as an effect of, discursive practices and systems of power/knowledge, and from the uncritical use of concepts such as ethics and pleasure. But having said this, my intention is not to prove Grognard's thesis wrong. Rather I want to suggest that her analysis—and others like it—is symptomatic of the ways in which bodies are inscriptively constituted, that is, read and written, in and through dominant social fictions that make possible specific forms of knowledge and particular subjectivities or subject positions that operate within *and* against those forms of knowledge.

Given this, the tattooed body will function throughout this text as the discursive or inscriptive site of dominant social fictions and as that which provides poignant theoretical insights into a complex constellation of concepts—namely, subjectivity, textuality, ethics, pleasure, and power/knowledge. Insofar as the sheer physicality of the tattooed body refuses to be suspended, it could be said to literalize the possibility of a hermeneutics of reading and writing subjectivity, and at the same time to performatively affect the poststructuralist insistence on reading/writing as what Bill Readings calls "a crisis of judgement" (Readings, 1991, 128). Given this, my aim is to demonstrate that the tattooed body provides a possibly unique opportunity to (re)read and (re)write subjectivity, textuality, ethics, pleasure, and the relations between them, and simultaneously to explore the ways in which subjectivity, textuality, ethics, and pleasure generate various modes of (re)writing and (re)reading bodily being.

Chapter One provides an analysis of the limitations of counter-cultural, psychological, and criminological accounts of the subject in/of tattooing, and the normative assumptions, which, despite claims to the contrary, such approaches share. My examination of these texts reveals, for example, a reliance on a depth model of subjectivity that assumes a distinction, and simultaneously a causal connection, between interiority and exteriority, mind and body. In each case the body is seen simply as an inscriptive surface, the significance of which lies in its ability to provide access to that which grounds it, namely, the psyche, soul, or consciousness. Consequently, the role of the "dermal diagnostician" is characterised in these works by a movement from surface to depth, from the material to the immaterial, from the fleshly to the conceptual. The body comes to matter in these accounts only insofar as its carnal specificity or materiality is veiled over in and through the extraction of abstract and essentially immaterial truths.

Coextensive with such a model of subjectivity is a mimetic theory of textuality that reaffirms the traditional distinction between reality and representation. Again, the tattooed body as text is taken to be a "ready-made veil, behind which lies, more or less hidden, meaning, (truth), [the Author]" (Barthes, 1975, 64). Moreover, we find in these works a reliance on an expression-reception model of communication that assumes that both meaning and identity are decipherable and definable. In each case, the marked body is taken to be a text that, when read accurately, tells of the individual's essence, character, allegiances, and intentions. But given that communication is assumed to be a straightforward process of expression and reception, it seems strange that, on the one hand, the tattooed body signifies (according to psychologists and criminologists), personality disorder and a propensity to crime, whilst, on the other hand, it is read by counter-culturalists as the hallmark of a healthy form of self-determination.

On close examination, what these seemingly polarized analyses offer us is not so much true or erroneous accounts of the subject in/of tattooing, but rather examples of the ways in which the body-subject is marked, that is, read and written, in culturally and historically specific ways, in and through processes of confession, interpretation, and evaluation. Drawing on Michel Foucault's genealogical examination of medical and juridical discourses, and the popular perceptions to which they give rise, I argue that the body is not a pre-social *tabula rasa* upon which the subject who inhabits it, expresses him- or herself—intentionally or otherwise—through processes of inscription such as tattooing. In other words, I disagree with the assumption made by the theorists discussed in Chapter One that the body is a natural object that pre-exists cultural representation and/or inscription. Alternatively, I demonstrate through my critique of the criminological, psychological, and counter-cultural texts that the body-subject is both an agent and effect of systems of power/knowledge that, in and through processes of inscription, morphologically (re)write and (re)read bodies in accordance with normative values and conventions. Insofar as the works of the theorists outlined in this chapter draw uncritically on a representational economy of the body-subject, their analyses of the subject in/of tattooing reaffirm, rather than contest, normative discourses and discursive practices. Whilst this may not pose a problem for the criminologists and psychologists whose aim is not necessarily to challenge the status quo, it is a problem for counter-cultural theorists whose theses are explicitly intended to counter normative ways of being and of thinking "on the eve of the millennium" (Mifflin, 1997, 178).

Given the limitations of a representational economy of the tattooed body-subject, Chapter Two harkens to the call made by Foucault in the closing pages of *The History of Sexuality Volume One,* for a different economy of bodies and pleasures not founded on a hermeneutical model of the subject (Foucault, 1980b, 157). The aim of this chapter is to assess the extent to which Foucault's works could be said to elaborate the possibility of a different economy of bodies and pleasures, and how useful these formulations might be for any attempt to rethink the subject in/of tattooing. I first provide a detailed exegesis of the Foucauldian axiom that systems of power/knowledge construct bodies in and through technologies of self-formation such as confession, interpretation, and classification or evaluation. What becomes apparent is that identity or subjectivity is not a pre-social essence that is *repressed* by rigid social mandates, but rather that the body-subject is written and read as a text, and is fictionalized and positioned within dominant social myths that create "a particular kind of 'depth-body' or interiority, a psychic layer the subject identifies as its (disembodied) core" (Grosz, 1990a, 65). Foucault's conception of the soul as "the effect and instrument of a political anatomy . . . the prison of the body" (Foucault, 1979, 30), not only substantiates this claim, but also provides a means of critically engaging with Grognard's assumption that the soul can be read on the open page of the tattooed skin, without suggesting that such a claim is nonsensical or simply erroneous. For, as Foucault says:

It would be wrong to say that the soul is an illusion, or an ideological effect. On the contrary, it exists, it has a reality, it is produced permanently around, on, within the body by the functioning of a [disciplinary] power. . . . This real, non corporal [*sic*] soul is not a substance; it is the element in which are articulated the effects of a certain type of power and the reference of a certain type of knowledge, the machinery by which power relations give rise to a possible corpus of knowledge, and knowledge extends and reinforces the effects of this power. (Foucault, 1979, 29)

Consequently, my discussion of Foucault's analysis of the relation between systems of power/knowledge and the constitution of particular forms of subjectivity serves as a critical ontology of the diagnoses of the subject in/of tattooing outlined in Chapter One. Foucault conceives of a critical ontology not as "a permanent body of knowledge that is accumulating", but rather as "an *ethos*" (Foucault, 1991b, 50), and this allows me to elaborate, following Rosalyn Diprose, an understanding of ethics as the study and practice of that which simultaneously constitutes and problematizes the subject's embodied place in the world, and his or her relations with others.

The remainder of Chapter Two is divided into three sections, each of which focuses on the ways in which the relation between subjectivity, ethics, and pleasure is configured in a number of Foucault's later works. These include his analysis of bucolic or polymorphous pleasures and their function in the lives of Jouy and Herculine Barbin; the notion of ethical self-fashioning as it is discussed in *The Use of Pleasure* (1987); and comments made in various interviews and articles on sadomasochism as a strategic practice of self-(trans)formation through the use of pleasure. Whilst for Foucault each of these examples potentiates, to varying degrees, a different economy of bodies and pleasures that moves beyond the limitations of a universalizing hermeneutics of subjectivity, I remain unconvinced that this is in fact the case. Indeed, I argue that in each of the aforementioned texts, the practice of ethical self-(trans)formation as a relationship of the self to the self remains firmly entrenched in a politics of subjectivity: a politics that is both individualistic and detrimental to others insofar as the necessary structural exclusion of the other—in particular women—is seen as an omission that could supposedly be rectified without posing a threat to the ethical system Foucault appears to promote. Thus I conclude that despite the fact that in *The History of Sexuality Volume One* subjectivity is clearly shown to be constituted in and through relations with others and with a world, Foucault fails, in his later works, to provide a substantial starting point from which to begin to imagine a different economy of bodies and pleasures. And this shortcoming, I argue, stems from an inadequate account of the production of identity and difference, or of self-other relations.

Since one of the fundamental problems identified in the analyses of the subject in/of tattooing in Chapter One, and the ethical practice of self-(trans)formation in Chapter Two, consists of an inability to (re)think identity and difference beyond what Irigaray calls an "Economy of the Same", my aim in Chapter Three is to develop a critique of the dualist model of self-other relations. In turn, this critique may allow for the possibility of a different economy of bodies and pleasures. This chapter juxtaposes two models of self-other relations, namely, those elaborated by Sigmund Freud and Emmanuel Levinas, and examines the notion of the oceanic feeling as paradigmatic of this relation and the way in which it is understood by each of the theorists discussed. For Freud, the oceanic feeling represents the subject's contradictory desire for oneness with the universe and, simultaneously, for absolute autonomy. In effect, the oceanic feeling is both a product and paradigm of a self-other relation founded on complementarity or opposition. For Levinas, however, the self-other relation is founded in and through alterity, and thus the oceanic feeling could be said to *figure*—rather than represent—that which precedes and exceeds (or generates the grounds of possibility of) self and other, of existents and existence, but never in absolute terms.

Through an analysis of the Levinasian account of the face to face relation, I demonstrate that the "I" (or subjectivity) is affected in and through the relation with the Other[4]. Here (the face of) the Other is not simply an object of the self's perceiving consciousness, but rather it overflows or exceeds the idea of the Other in me, and thus generates an irreducible relation of difference that both founds the self and simultaneously calls the self's sovereign authority into question. In effect, then, this account of self-other relations functions as a critique of the attempts made by the theorists discussed in Chapter One to define the (tattooed) other, and thus to reaffirm the self as the subject of knowledge. Moreover, insofar as the face to face relation delineates a metaphysics of intersubjectivity which Levinas calls ethics, then this model also provides a means of moving beyond the limitations outlined in my analysis of Foucault's notion of ethical self-(trans)formation, which, as I said, overlooks or disavows the role of the Other and of alterity in the constitution of the self.

Chapter Three also raises the question of the relation between particular forms of subjectivity and normative notions of knowledge or meaning through an analysis of Levinas' account of the Saying (*le dire*) and the Said (*le dit*). Just as ontology, as an attempt to comprehend or grasp the Other or meaning, presupposes metaphysics or alterity, Levinas argues that the Saying as a condition for all communication precedes and exceeds the Said as the meaningful content of the Saying. Like Self and Other, the Saying and the Said are not considered by Levinas to be distinct or disparate entities, but rather are at once mutually constitutive and incommensurable. The one cannot exist without the other, nor can either term be reduced to an Economy of the Same since both exist in and through the relation to, or with, alterity. Given this, my analysis provides a critique of the expression-reception model of communication at work in the analyses of the subject in/of tattooing examined in Chapter One, and offers an explanation as to why the techniques of interpretation and evaluation discussed in Chapter Two ultimately fail to "concretize" being. This chapter, then, occasions a move away from the question of meaning or intention which dominates analyses of the subject in/of tattooing, and toward the notion of an affective encounter with alterity, in and through which Self and Other are inextricably bound and irreducible to an Economy of the Same. Bodily inscription—marking and being marked—becomes what Levinas calls a trace of the-Other-in-me, which precedes and makes (im)possible the reading of the textual body of the Other as an object of knowledge.

Insofar as Levinas' work is more concerned with alterity than with subjectivity *per se*, and coextensively with the *signifiance* of signification (the Saying) than with ontological accounts of the signified (the Said), it could be said to provide a fertile starting point from which to begin to imagine a different economy of bodies and pleasures. However, Levinas makes little or no mention of the notion of pleasure, and how this might be conceived in relation to the intextuation[5] of bodies, or how the corporeal specificity of pleasure may be experienced ontologically. Consequently, Chapter Four takes up the question of (textual) pleasure as affect, and examines its performative function in the (re)reading and (re)writing of corporeality through an examination of Roland Barthes' later works. First, drawing on Barthes' "The Death of the Author", I develop a critique of the assumed distinction between the subject who reads and the written text (or body) as object, and formulate an alternative understanding of readers, writers, texts, and the relation between them that, following Barthes, I call intertextuality. An encounter between my "self", Barthes' *The Pleasure of the Text* (1994), and Beverley D'Angelo's *Marks* is performatively evoked in order to illustrate this claim. Here I demonstrate that the body is one that "does I" or performs its identity in and through its relations with others, and that both marks and is marked—*ad infinitum*—in and through these affective dramatizations of (inter)subjectivity or (inter)textuality. Thus I invoke the image of the body as a map that does not simply reproduce a tracing of interiority, but more importantly performs infinite (dis)connections with other textual bodies that are never entirely separate from itself. Such an undertaking functions as a critique of the hermeneutical attempt to understand the essence of the subject in/of tattooing, and at the same time extends Levinas' notion of an ethics of alterity to show how the inte(rte)xtuation of bodies and pleasures problematizes Foucault's account of ethical self-(trans)formation as a relation of the self to itself.

Finally, Barthes' formulation of an ethics of enunciation is examined via his notion of "writing aloud", in order to (re)consider the Levinasian configuration of the Saying and the Said in relation to the corporeality of reading and writing. From this I conclude that bodily inscription is not so much a writing with or on the body (both of which assume a body-subject that pre-exists writing), but rather it is an infinite (re)writing and (re)reading of the body-subject in and through its relations with the carnal sensuosity of the Other and the world, and with culturally and historically specific social fictions. Reading and writing become, as Jean-Luc Nancy puts it, "matters of tact" (Nancy, 1993, 198) in and through which "a body is traced, is the tracing and the trace" (198). In effect, I argue against the claim made by the theorists discussed in Chapter One that the tattooed body as text is definable, and against what might be called a hyper-postmodern position that would suggest that it is absolutely indefinable, by demonstrating that writing-aloud *figures* the relation of alterity as the sensuous precondition of the (im)possibility[6] of meaning.

The limitation of Barthes' notion of writing-aloud is that insofar as it is formulated through an analysis of the voice and of music, there is an implied privileging of the audible—as that which at once generates and ceaselessly escapes or overflows meaning—that could be said to replicate (rather than challenge) phallogocentrism's problematic scopophilic obsession. Moreover, there is a tendency in Barthes' later works to focus on the possibility of a writing that is nonexpressive, noninstrumental, nonrepresentational, and plural at the expense of developing a detailed examination of the ways in which *meaning* is (inter)textually generated. Whilst I do not want to suggest that Barthes' work is utopian in the sense that it romanticizes a future liberated from the constraints of meaning, I nevertheless feel it is necessary to draw out the implications of his insights through an exploration of the subject's participation in the production of meaning and knowledge in order to consider what the inducement for such participation might be, and how it might function.

The final chapter takes up this question via Moira Gatens' notion of imaginary bodies, social imaginaries, and the relations between them. I begin with the adage that "every picture tells a story", and draw on a novel by Michael Westlake entitled *Imaginary Women* (1989), in order to consider the stories that the tattooed body of the novel's heroine, Molly, might possibly be said to tell. Insofar as Molly is the embodiment of social fictions, or, as Foucault would put it, an agent and effect of systems of power/knowledge, her picturesque body can be read as symptomatic of the ways in which social imaginaries (in)form imaginary bodies: their desires, their capacities, and their very materiality. But at the same time, following Gatens, I argue that Molly's imaginary body as the inscriptive site of social fictions bears the trace of something else: of alterity. And this "something else", this story that can be sensed but that cannot be made to make sense, is what makes possible and impossible meaning and identity. Thus ethical self-(trans)formation is shown to be affected in and through an encounter (which is never simply intentional) with the carnal sensuosity of the Other and the world, rather than, as Foucault formulates it, as a relation of the self to itself.

Drawing on Alphonso Lingis' analysis of "savage" bodies, I argue that the notion of bodily inscription as significatory presupposes the palpability of corporeality. As my analysis of Levinas' account of the face to face relation suggests, the encounter with the marked body of the Other—which has always already taken place in a pre-original and anarchial *passed*—affects exposure. And this sensuous contact with alterity is the grounds of possibility for the production and circulation of meaning, but, at the same time, it disallows the concretization of meaning and of being(s). Bodily inscription, Lingis argues, creates an erotogenic surface, the body as a map, in and through the codification of libidinality; it is the trace of the Other-in-me, as Levinas puts it. But insofar as bodily inscription is the culturally and historically specific codification of libidinality, it can be said to effectuate the int(ert)extuation of the corporeal substance as that which both signifies and exceeds signification. Thus I demonstrate that what the theorists discussed in Chapter One offer us is a tracing that does not reproduce the map(ping) of the marked or tattooed body, but rather, through an "artificial" process of selection, translates the mapping into an image—a map of the body-subject—that is in fact nothing more than a reproduction of itself (Deleuze and Guattari, 1987, 13).

Jean-Francois Lyotard's configuration of the relation between discourse (as the condition of representation to consciousness by a rational ordering of concepts) and figure (as that which functions within and against discourse) is drawn on to substantiate this claim. Lyotard suggests that discourse and figure are necessarily and impossibly co-present as constitutive and disruptive of representation. Given this, I argue that the tattooed body as text is duplicitous. Like all imaginary bodies, it (re)tells the social fictions of which it is both an agent and an effect, and at the same time it affectively evokes—albeit "silently"—the trace of the Other, the figural that discourse cannot speak. This raises the question of whether the tattooed body could or should be viewed as transgressive, as a site of (at least potential) political import.

Through an examination of Janice McLane's analysis of "self-mutilation"[7] as the creation of a voice on the skin, a voice that speaks what the actual voice of the abuse survivor has been forbidden to tell (and which therefore it is assumed has political and/or liberatory import), I demonstrate that there is a tendency for politics to become a metalanguage that functions to authoritatively determine the literal meaning of the marked body-subject by seemingly rendering audible that which discourse cannot speak. Thus I conclude that what is needed if one is to provide an analysis of the subject in/of tattooing that moves beyond the limitations of a hermeneutics of subjectivity, is not so much a politics of subjectivity—the ultimate possibility of which is questionable—but an ethics of reading and writing (embodiment): an ethics that may at least potentially forge an idea of the tattooed body as "the site of an aporetic clash of incommensurable languages, a site that has the performative effect of provoking further discussion" (Readings, 1991, 37).

Perhaps one more preliminary remark is in order here. It concerns the aim of provoking further discussion rather than providing answers that seemingly effect closure. For the most part, analyses of the subject in/of tattooing presume that "the skin may be thought of as a sort of message centre or billboard" (Favazza, 1996, 148), and that the marked body as a surface of signs is decipherable: the exterior is taken to be the expression of an interior. Hence the one who reads the marked body of the other performs the role of the canny detective who, despite sniffing out a few red herrings, or following paths of inquiry that turn out to lead nowhere, will ultimately find his or her way through the labyrinth and discover absolute truth. The race is run, the trophy seized: victory = knowledge, and there can only be one winner.

The path that such thought inscribes is one of vertical descent, and the journey itself is simply the means to a predetermined destination. Somewhat lacking in competitive spirit, and being more interested in the sites/sights along the way than in the idea of a final destination, I found—whilst writing this book—that my journey into the world(s) of tattooed bodies did not, and would not, allow me to (re)present the illustrated skin as a premise, and the knowledge of what (in)forms it as a conclusion. As a consequence, the structure of this text performatively evokes what Deleuze and Guattari refer to as "lines of flight"[8], rather than following or reinscribing the well-trodden paths of scientific or philosophical discovery; paths that are littered with the bodies of the victor's adversaries. I cannot draw the (tattooed) Other "with a borrowed stencil", to borrow a phrase from Jeanette Winterson (Winterson, 1993, 414). My aim, rather, is to seduce, to affect, the reader and to open up the possibility of diverse and infinite voyages to destinations that are beyond the scope of my imagination and this book, rather than to convince the reader, through traditional means of argument, that knowledge is possible, and that since I have discovered it, all that is left is for you to do is to witness the truth of my claims and decree "victory to the critic" (Barthes, 1990a, 117).

NOTES

1. I use this configuration ("the subject in/of tattooing") to connote tattooing as a practice that is subject to, and a subject of, cultural interpretation and evaluation, and also the subjectivity of the tattooed person or persons that is inscribed in and through the interpretation and evaluation of tattooing as a practice. In other words, I am implying that it is impossible to theorize about tattooing as a practice without simultaneously theorizing about subjectivity. Whilst this may seem like an obvious point to make, it is surprising how often descriptions or analyses of tattooing overlook or disavow the ways in which such discourses (re)constitute embodied being.

2. See, for example, Hanns Ebensten (1953); R. Scutt & C. Gotch (1974); Andre Virel (1980); Robert Brain (1979); Michelle Delio (1993); Jeff Jaguer (1990); and W. D. Hambly (1925).

3. See the section of Grognard's text entitled "The History of Tattooing", 19–27.

4. Following Levinas I use the term "Other" rather than "other" here to indicate the metaphysical notion of alterity, of an otherness that cannot be reduced to an object of the self's perceiving consciousness.

5. This is a term used by John Fiske, following de Certeau, to describe the processes of social inscription in and through which bodies are written and read, that is, are textualized. See Fiske (1989).

6. My use of this term is an attempt to gesture toward the simultaneous possibility and impossibility of the production of meaning.

7. This is the term used by McLane to cover a range of practices (including tattooing) that mark the body.

8. Lines of flight, as Deleuze and Guattari see it, are multiplicitous, nomadic, and affect both deterritorialization and reterritorialization. A concise analysis of this concept can be found in Deleuze and Guattari's "Concrete Rules and Abstract Machines" (1984).

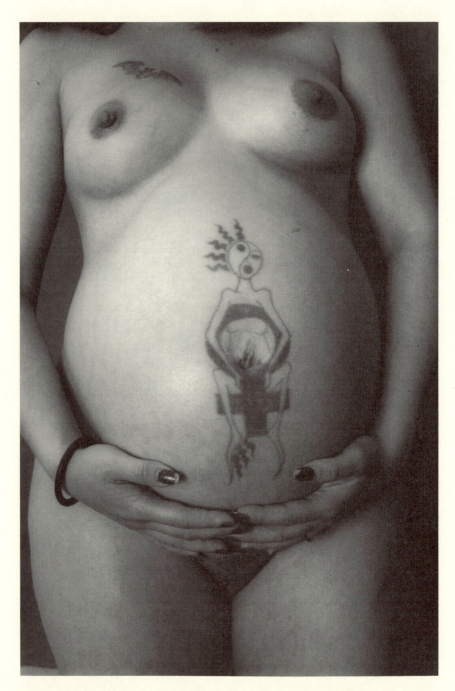

Lolly-pop and Xavier at home, 1999. Photo copyright ©Amanda James Photography

Chapter One

The Subject In/Of Tattooing

The notion that individuals identified as socially deviant are somatically different from "normal" people is a peculiarly recurring idea that is deeply rooted in Western scientific and popular thought, but one that takes many forms in relation to particular historical and political contexts. (Terry and Urla, 1995, 1)

This chapter examines the ways in which the subject in/of tattooing is understood, or more precisely discursively (re)produced, in a number of contemporary discourses. The works discussed have been chosen because they are representative of particular fields of inquiry, namely, psychiatry and/or psychology, criminology, and counter-culturalism. Moreover, each approach shares assumptions with the other, and with the broader social context that informs them and that they inform.

BY THIS MARK YOU SHALL KNOW HIM

In a fairly representative article published in 1963, Yamamoto et al. pose the question, "who is the tattooed man"?; this is a question that exemplifies the desire to discover the truth of the subject in/of tattooing. The most likely answer to this question is, according to the three researchers, "an ex-sailor who was tattooed whilst drunk; a psychopath; a schizophrenic; or a permanent juvenile delinquent" (Yamamoto et al., 1963, 365). The "tattooed man", it seems, is something of an aberration.

This classification of individuals is based on a study undertaken by the authors of 433 male patients at the Okalahoma City Veterans Administration Hospital, sixty-five of whom were tattooed. The conclusions drawn from the investigation (which included the administration of the Minnesota Multiphasic

Personality Inventory) are as follows: The tattooed man "shows definite personality deviations from his contemporaries" (367). He[1] is more likely to be immature and impulsive, to be psychopathic, to aspire to be more "masculine" than his fellow patients[2], to have a criminal record, and to be something of a liability to society (367). In short, Yamamoto and his fellow researchers ascribe to the assumption identified by Terry and Urla that socially deviant individuals "are somatically different from 'normal' people" (Terry and Urla, 1995, 1). The tattoo in this case functions as a source of diagnostic information insofar as it is read as a somatic sign of deviance, decipherable by those with expertise in scientific or psychiatric research methods. Or as Terry and Urla put it, "[i]n the process of this moral and somatic surveillance, the soul of the deviant is both exteriorized to the body's surface and annexed to its various recesses where only men of science can peer" (11).

Similarly, Gittleson et al. (1969), drawing on the work of Lander and Kohn (1943), Ferguson-Rayport et al. (1955), and Yamamoto et al., and undertaking a study of sixty-seven psychiatric patients, posit a connection between tattoos and what is enigmatically referred to by the authors as "personality disorder". Their analysis differs from that of Yamamoto et al. only insofar as they undertake a comparative study of single versus multiple tattoos. Gittleson et al. conclude that within the tattooed group studied the 49 percent who had been tattooed on more than one occasion were significantly more likely to be diagnosed with a personality disorder, to have been convicted of law breaking, to have been first tattooed at an earlier age, and to have their tattoos visible while wearing normal clothing than the 51 percent who had been tattooed on one occasion only (Gittleson et al., 1969, 1253). Whilst Yamamoto et al. posit a distinction between the marked/tattooed body and the unmarked body that correlates with an understanding of deviance/normality, Gittleson et al. develop an expanded version of this thesis through the positing of a further distinction between single versus multiple tattoos. Thus it seems that the more marked a body is, the more deviant the subject is likely to be[3].

Despite the fact that an indexical relation is implied between the interior person and the somatic exterior in both of the above-mentioned articles, neither explore in any depth the question of *why* such individuals might choose to be tattooed. This question of motivation or intentionality is taken up by Edgerton and Dingman in an article entitled "Tattooing and Identity", published in 1963 in *The International Journal of Social Psychiatry*. As the choice of journal seems to imply, the primary focus of this article is not so much on the individual psyche itself as on the relation between the subject in/of tattooing and the broader social context.

Edgerton and Dingman identify what they see as five main reasons for the preponderance of tattooing in contemporary Western culture. They are as follows:

1. Ornamentation: The desire to beautify or adorn the body.
2. Eroticism: The sexual significance of the process of tattooing [4].
3. Demonstration of socially valued characteristics: For example, the ability to endure
      pain and thus the desire to signify to others courage, masculinity, the achievement
      of adulthood, and so on.
4. Magico-religious: The desire for talismanic protection.
5. Establishment of Identity: Tattooing as a practice of self-definition[5].

Since for Edgerton and Dingman, the establishment of identity is the most prevalent motivation for tattooing in contemporary American society, this becomes the focus of their research. They claim that "a tattooed person is identifying himself to himself and to others; he is communicating something about a relationship with other persons or things that he believes he possesses, or wishes to possess, or wishes others to believe he possesses" (Edgerton and Dingman, 1963, 145). On the one hand, then, it could be said that Edgerton and Dingman share an understanding of tattooing as a form of nonverbal communication with Yamamoto et al., and Gittleson et al., but whereas for Edgerton and Dingman tattooing is understood in terms of individual intention and the volitional establishment of social relations, for Yamamoto et al. and Gittleson et al. it functions as something closer to an unwitting "mark of Cain". In other words, not only do Edgerton and Dingman accredit the tattooed subject with some agency, but their approach also attempts to move beyond a simple inside-outside model of the subject that asserts the primacy of an autonomous psychical interior. Consequently, it may appear at first glance that Edgerton and Dingman theoretically are better equipped to take into account the role of the other, and of society, in the constitution of subjectivity.

Following on from the claim that the tattoo is a sign of the establishment of self-identity, and of one's relations with others, Edgerton and Dingman identify four types of tattoos that exemplify these functions in varying ways. First, there are tattoos that signify a relationship with a group or category—for example, gang emblems such as those worn by members of the Hell's Angels, military insignia worn by servicemen, or tattoos such as Moko, which symbolises (Maori) cultural heritage. The second group of tattoos signify a relationship with another individual, such as "Mother", the name or portrait of a lover, friend, family member, or a celebrity one admires. The third type embodies the name or description of the self—for example, "John", "Bobby's Girl", "Rebel", "Killer", and so on. And fourth there is the enigmatic or idiosyncratic symbol that has import for the self alone. Such idiosyncratic tattoos are, according to Ferguson-Rayport et al., most often found amongst schizophrenics[6].

However, considering that such information regarding the self can be, and is, communicated through more "socially acceptable" and less permanent means, such as material possessions, clothing, hairstyles, rings, vocations, living arrangements, and official documents, the question remains as to why some people would choose tattooing as a means of self-expression. Whilst there may be a number of possible responses to this question, Edgerton and Dingman maintain that the most likely reason is that insofar as some people are "relatively deprived of the opportunity to acquire and display the usual and desirable symbols of the self" (146), they are likely to turn to more "subversive" means. They argue that this claim is validated by statistical data that suggest that tattoos are most commonly found amongst "enlisted military men, criminals, juveniles in general, inmates of total institutions such as prisons and mental hospitals, ethnics of low social status, and persons of low socio-economic status in general" (146), all of whom have, to varying degrees, been stripped of their individual identity, are in transitional states of being, are relatively deprived of autonomy, and are reacting against systems of authority that they perceive to be repressive or restrictive (146–47)[7]. In other words, the tattooed subject, according to Edgerton and Dingman, is opposed to and excluded from the position of citizen proper. And his failure to demonstrate the characteristics of autonomy, freedom, self-determination, rationality, and unification, inherent in the liberal (notion of the) subject, is both a cause and an effect of this exclusion. The question I want to raise here is whether Edgerton and Dingman's research simply describes an inequitable state of affairs, or whether, uncritically relying as it does on a liberal model of subjectivity and social relations, their work discursively (re)produces the subject in/of tattooing as deviant other. Let us take a closer look.

In an attempt to validate their thesis Edgerton and Dingman undertake a study of "mentally retarded"[8] patients in a large state hospital (an example of what they call a total institution). Their research involves the classification of 195 tattooed inmates as either "mildly retarded" or "severely retarded"[9]. Moreover, through an analysis of tattoo types, they conclude that those whose tattoos signify a relation to a group or category (30 percent), a relationship with another individual (40 percent), or a description of the self (10 percent), are less emotionally disturbed than those whose tattoos are idiosyncratic (20 percent). Their thesis then not only reasserts the connection made a decade earlier by Ferguson-Rayport et al. between schizophrenia and idiosyncratic tattoos, but also reaffirms the claim made by Yamamoto et al., that the tattooed wo/man is psychosomatically aberrant. Whilst, on the one hand, Edgerton and Dingman appear to suggest a positive link, by way of tattooing, between attempts by a particular "class" of people (i.e. "the marginalised") to establish identity and "successful" social integration, on the other hand, they rely on a system of classification and evaluation in which identity and difference can only be understood in dichotomous hierarchized terms. One is marked or unmarked, mildly retarded or severely retarded, and so on.

What is never questioned in works such as those discussed so far is the role of the researcher in the constitution of identity and difference[10]. The failure to question this role allows the researcher to categorize the tattooed subject as deviant other, and at the same time to at least implicitly reassert an understanding of him- or herself as "normal"—a claim that will be discussed in more depth in Chapter Two. Consequently, I would argue that even though Edgerton and Dingman's work appears, at first glance, to be more promising than that of their predecessors in that it attempts to take into account the social aspects of identity formation, it nevertheless ultimately serves to perpetuate "the notion that individuals identified as socially deviant are somatically different from 'normal' people" (Terry and Urla, 1995, l).

The failure to question their assumptions and research methods renders Edgerton and Dingman's work somewhat contradictory. Whilst they display some sympathy for those whom they describe as socially disenfranchised, they simultaneously demonstrate an inability to represent the tattooed body as anything other than a self-defeating response to inegalitarian systems of social stratification; systems that ironically their work ultimately serves to perpetuate. One possible way around this dilemma would be to extend the study of tattooed subjects beyond the realm of "total institutions" in which the subject is always already classified as deviant[11].

Despite a decrease in the number of psychological works published on the subject in/of tattooing in the last couple of decades, the available articles nevertheless continue to analyze the tattooed body in qualitatively similar ways to Yamamoto et al., Gittleson et al., and Edgerton and Dingman. One such example is a paper by Gerald Grumet published in 1983 and entitled "Psychodynamic Implications of Tattoos". The stated aim of Grumet's work is to assist the clinician in the task of what he calls "dermal diagnosis"; that is, "in the appropriate understanding of the significance of tattoos" (Grumet, 1983, 482). Grumet's thesis is predicated upon two interrelated beliefs: first, that "the human flesh has proven itself a suitable canvas on which to portray psychologically relevant themes" (482); and second, "that tattoos are a form of non-verbal communication that can often be deciphered" (489). Like his predecessors, then, Grumet embraces an inside-outside model of the subject, and at the same time unquestioningly accepts a simplistic notion of communication as a relatively straightforward process of expression and reception.

Grumet, like Edgerton and Dingman, claims that of the various motives for tattooing, the quest for personal identity is central. Insofar as he draws on the work of Freud to explain the development of ego identity as bodily, Grumet's thesis may at first appear to offer a level of theoretical sophistication lacking in the work of those discussed thus far. However, his positing of a distinction between what he terms "low barrier types" and "high barrier types" is indicative of an inability to move beyond the fundamental shortcomings of his predecessors. For Grumet the difference between the two is that the latter "are able to function in a more independent and realistic manner" (482) than the former, who, as we might have expected, are more likely to be tattooed. According to Grumet, the reason for the preponderance of tattoos amongst "low barrier types" is that "the tattoo [is] an artificial embellishment of the body boundary, [and] can be viewed . . . as a prosthetic attempt to strengthen one's ego definition" (483). Citing the findings of Edgerton and Dingman (1963), and Hamburger (1966), Grumet proceeds to develop a typically circular logic of cause and effect, whereby the desire for such prosthetic devices as tattoos stems from feelings of inferiority, alienation, insecurity, and displacement, which are at once both the cause and effect of an underdeveloped ego—the fundamental characteristic of all "low barrier types".

So far it seems there have been few, if any, theoretical advances made in the psychiatric analysis of the subject in/of tattooing in the two decades that have lapsed since the publication of Edgerton and Dingman's thesis. However, what is of interest to me regarding Grumet's article, and my reason for discussing it here, is his articulation of an extremely elaborate set of considerations aimed at assisting the would-be dermal diagnostician.

The first thing to be considered by the dermal diagnostician is the patient's emotional reaction to his or her tattoo(s). This, according to Grumet, serves as an indication of self-esteem "as tattoos represent earlier efforts to galvanize an identity and consequently symbolize the self" (489). Thus, for example, embarrassment on behalf of the subject indicates that he or she has since outgrown the need for such prosthetic devices, and has consequently undergone an evolution in psychic terms. The second factor that Grumet claims needs to be considered is the number and sequence of tattoos. From these, he says, it is possible to elicit a "tattoo history", an "archaeological unearthing of emotional relics" (490), which is tantamount to a psychic map. Further, the number of tattoos can also signify a pattern of "tattoo addiction", "an expression of personal incompleteness tied to a perennial but elusive quest for that one further design that will make [the tattooed subject] feel complete" (490). Third, recommends Grumet, the dermal diagnostician should take into account the circumstances of tattoo acquisition. This includes considerations such as whether the subject was alone or with a group at the time of procuration; whether he or she was intoxicated; and whether or not he or she was incarcerated. In this sense, tattoos can be read as indicators of a rebellious adolescence or a criminal past. Grumet also claims, citing Ferguson-Rayport et al., that the psychotic person is more likely than the average individual to have visited the tattooist alone. Fourth, it is expedient, according to Grumet, to note the location of tattoos. Drawing on the findings of Gittleson et al., Grumet claims that those with criminal tendencies are more likely to be tattooed on areas of the body that are visible in everyday clothing, such as the hands, neck, and face. Likewise, "tattoos imprinted on . . . the genitals have sexual implications and are found with some frequency in prostitutes and sexual perverts" (490)[12]. Fifth, the quality, symmetry, and size of tattoos needs to be taken into consideration. Here Grumet posits a differentiation between what he calls "artistic" or professional tattoos and "jailhouse" tattoos, which are most often self-inflicted[13], or at best inflicted by others who have no access to professional equipment. The latter, believed to be most prevalent amongst delinquent youth, signify, according to Grumet, both a "sense of reckless disregard for the future", and an "autoaggressive response to feelings of frustration, boredom and anger" (488)[14]. On the other hand, "non-criminals are more likely to have professional tattoos showing greater restraint in design, location, and number" (490)[15]. The final consideration is tattoo content. Here Grumet expounds on what he calls the "love/hate ratio", whereby it is possible to measure the proportion of "violent" tattoos such as "ferocious animals, daggers and skulls" against "friendly motifs" such as "hearts, flowers, butterflies" (490) in an attempt to glean clues as to the bearer's temperament, and in some cases to unearth "the evolution of character development" (490)[16].

Grumet's discussion of the love-hate ratio contains a provocative remark, the implications of which the author tellingly fails to consider. Reporting on the case of one individual, on whose knuckles the letters H-A-T-E supposedly tell of a delinquent past and an anti-social temperament, but for whom such letters now mean "happiness all through eternity", Grumet states that "the objective meaning of the tattoo does not [always] coincide with the private meaning for its bearer" (490–91). In as much as the meaning of this tattoo has changed for its bearer, it could be said to support Grumet's claim that tattoos can provide a pictorial history of character development. However, at the same time this example functions to undermine Grumet's model of dermal diagnosis for a number of reasons.

Insofar as the meaning of this tattoo has changed, at least for its bearer, whilst the graphic itself has remained the same, the implication is that tattoos neither contain nor represent a fixed referential reality, or, to put it another way, the relation between signifier and signified is unstable. It demonstrates that the tattoo is not simply reducible to a symbolic representation of the truth of the subject, but rather that the tattoo is inseparable from the subject and can be understood as a process (rather than an object) in and through which the ambiguous and open-ended character of identity and of meaning is constantly (re)negotiated in and through relations with others and with a world. Further, the disjunction that Grumet mentions in the above example between the "objective meaning of the tattoo" and the "private meaning for its bearer" (490–91) points to a problem inherent in the process of interpretation and evaluation that informs not only medical discourse[17], but social relations more generally. The tattoo will generate different meanings depending on the embodied history of the subject who interprets, and also on the relationship between him or her and the tattooed person. For example, if one was to come across a person with H-A-T-E tattooed on his or her knuckles, it is most likely that if they shared the same language, the tattoo would be unquestioningly interpreted as having threatening connotations. However, if one discussed the tattoo with its bearer (as Grumet does), and was told that its meaning was "happiness all through eternity", perhaps one's initial response would be modified. Nevertheless, this example challenges Grumet's system insofar as it implies an insurmountable gap between the so-called objective meaning for the subject of interpretation, and the private meaning for the tattooed individual. It is this gap, or site of excess, that affects and is affected by both change and alterity, a claim that I will go on to discuss in due course. Following on from this point is the implication that some kind of feed-back loop exists whereby the subject of interpretation may effect the private meaning of the tattoo for its bearer. For example, the fact that the individual mentioned earlier who bears the letters H-A-T-E on his knuckles is in a situation in which his character is being interpreted and evaluated by a member of the psychiatric profession would have some bearing on his response to the questions asked of him. Perhaps he has historically suffered various forms of prejudice as a result of his tattoos, in which case the simplest way to represent himself as a "respectable citizen" would be to provide the kinds of answers that he assumes the subject of interpretation would find most palatable. This is not to suggest that the tattooed subject would simply "lie" about the meaning of his tattoos, but rather, that the responses of others to his tattoos will inform the ways in which he both understands and experiences them. Thus the supposed distinction between objective meaning and subjective meaning, between the subject and the object of interpretation, is far from clear.

To conclude this section I will briefly outline my concerns regarding the theses discussed thus far, but first it is important to note that whilst it is perhaps possible to identify minor differences between the work of Yamamoto et al., Gittleson et al., Edgerton and Dingman, and Grumet, it is my contention that these analyses of the subject in/of tattooing are nevertheless founded on a number of shared assumptions. What we find in these works is a complex cluster of inextricably interrelated ideas regarding subjectivity, textuality, ethics, and pleasure that functions in accordance with what could be loosely termed liberal humanism. Given this, it is necessary to critically analyse not only each "theme", but also the relations between them if a reconfiguration of the subject in/of tattooing is to be possible. This is the task that the book attempts to undertake, but for the moment I will merely gesture toward my overall aim by critically engaging with each of the themes mentioned as they are formulated—either explicitly or implicitly—in the previously discussed works.

First, all four articles are founded on a depth model of the subject that assumes a distinction between inside and outside, self and other. For example, there is a failure to question the ways in which the dermal diagnostician's subjectivity is constituted in and through his or her relation to the tattooed other, since it is believed that the subject is autonomous and that his or her relations with others are secondary. This allows the researchers to maintain a dichotomous understanding of identity and difference that functions solely in terms of complementarity and/or opposition. Insofar as this is the case, it seems unnecessary for the dermal diagnostician to concede his or her complicity in the inscriptive processes of identity formation, and thus to critically analyse his or her research methods, or sense of self as the subject of knowledge.

Second, it is assumed that the tattoo is a form of nonverbal communication. Communication, according to this model, is understood as the expression (whether conscious of unconscious, it makes little or no difference) of a sign designating the truth of an innate "I", and the ensuing reception of this sign by another subject. This promotes a method of textual analysis that embraces the assumption that both the text—in this case the tattooed body—and the author "behind it", are transparent to others, and thus are simply open to interpretation, and consequently reaffirms the liberal notion of the subject discussed briefly above. However, this poses something of a problem for the critic, who, if he or she is to position him- or herself, and be positioned by others, as the heroic detective in the hierarchical order of things, must demonstrate that his or her skill in unearthing deeply buried truths is not one common to all. Consequently, we witness the elaboration of increasingly complex methods of dermal diagnosis not necessarily available to the unauthorised layperson, as my mapping of the previously discussed works has demonstrated. For instance, in the article by Yamamoto et al., the distinction posited is simply between the tattooed subject and the nontattooed subject. Gittleson et al. extend this thesis by drawing a distinction between single and multiple tattoos, whereas Edgerton and Dingman focus on other-oriented versus idiosyncratic tattoos. By the 1980s, if we accept Grumet's work as exemplifying a trend toward increasingly sophisticated classificatory methods, we find an incredibly complex inventory of procedures for reading the tattooed body. What this mapping of the development of psychological analyses of the subject in/of tattooing highlights is a trend that parallels the growth of what Foucault calls governmentality, that is, systems of power/knowledge that produce "individuals" in and through a proliferation of medical or psychiatric normalizing discourses and procedures of surveillance developed in Western culture from the early nineteenth century onwards[18], a point I will return to in due course.

Third, whilst a notion of pleasure is not discussed explicitly in these works, it is nevertheless apparent at an implicit level. For example, the association between tattooing and masculinity suggests that the demonstration of socially valued characteristics, such as strength, bravery, and the ability to endure pain, produces feelings of pleasure in the (male) subject since they reaffirm his sense of self and his position in the hierarchical order of things[19]. As Samuel Steward, a dubious and somewhat misogynistic academic-turned-tattoo-artist, tells it, the concept of the "hero as warrior" has been destroyed in the United States by feminism, women in general, and technology, and thus the young American male is increasingly impelled to find ways to reclaim his position as hero and warrior. Hence the sign on the wall of Steward's parlour reads: "Depressed? Downhearted? A good tattoo may make you feel like a man again" (Steward, 1990, 45). Pleasure in this sense is concomitant with the reaffirmation of the subject as subject. Likewise, the pleasure of dermal diagnosis (at least for the diagnostician) could be said to be experienced in and through the production of knowledge as truth, and the coextensive construction of the diagnostician as the author(itative) Promethean figure. In effect, then, pleasure is understood solely as the result of activities that function to reaffirm the self in accordance with particular social values. In other words, pleasure is understood implicitly as a normalizing process in these accounts of the subject in/of tattooing. But what happens when a conflict of interest arises, when what signifies manliness to one person signifies pathological tendencies to another, when what could be read as signs of pleasure are interpreted as signs of stigmatization? As the theses discussed throughout this section demonstrate, this contradiction can only be overcome, or more precisely be veiled over, if one unquestioningly maintains the conceptual split between self and other, subject and object, that informs the notions of textuality, pleasure, and ethics at work in these analyses.

Finally I want to consider the notion of ethics that again functions implicitly, at least in lay terms, in these works. Ethics is most commonly understood as a set of standards by which a group or community regulates its behaviours, distinguishes between what is legitimate or acceptable and what is not. It refers, according to the *Pan Dictionary of Philosophy,* to "standards of morality that apply to men [*sic*] not simply in virtue of their particular roles but in respect generally to their being men who live among other men" (Flew, 1984, 112). Insofar as we all could be said to be wo/men who live among other wo/men this definition suggests the logical possibility of universally applicable principles. But as Rosalyn Diprose argues in her critique of this tendency, "[i]n focusing on moral principles and . . . judgements the assumption is that individuals are present as self-transparent, isolated, rational minds and that embodied differences between individuals are inconsequential" (Diprose, 1994, 18)[20]. I will examine this claim, and Diprose's alternative notion of ethics in the following chapter, but for the moment suffice it to say that insofar as the works of the theorists discussed formulate difference in terms of *in*difference, they implicitly reaffirm a universalist notion and code of ethics in which they are situated in the position of ethical subject. This is achieved in part by positioning the tattooed other as unethical, or as an object rather than a subject of ethics, and as a threat to the moral order. Consequently, the tattooed other must be rehabilitated or quarantined, in short, reduced to an Economy of the Same through a process of recontainment and disavowal. The role of the ethical subject then—in this case the dermal diagnostician—is to scrupulously and unfailingly scour the textual body of the other for external signs of an unethical innate interiority that poses a virulent threat to the health of the body politic. In doing so, the subject reaffirms his or her sense of self and his or her position as ethical subject against the body of the other in accordance with the ethical criteria he or she assumes.

It seems that psychiatric analyses of the subject in/of tattooing repeat the tendency identified by Terry and Urla to identify somatic differences in terms of normalcy and deviance, and moreover to (re)produce the body of what is "strange" as a source of mastery that must be conquered but never entirely annihilated. In this sense, the body of the deviant other is both a structural necessity and a threat. In the following section, I will examine the works of a number of criminologists in order to explore in more detail the ways in which the tattooed body-subject is read and written in accordance with systems of power/knowledge that inform juridical and criminological discourse and construct identity and difference in culturally and historically specific ways, and more particularly in terms of normalcy and delinquency.

TATTOOING AND CRIMINALITY: SYNONYMIC TERMS?

At the turn of the century, the Italian criminal anthropologist Cesare Lombroso played a significant role in the formation of what has become known as the "Positive School" of criminology, which distinguished itself from the "Classical School" through a shift in focus from crime to the figure of the criminal. Such a shift is critically analysed by Foucault in *Discipline and Punish: The Birth of the Prison,* in which he argues that the changes that took place in European jurisprudence at this time, reflect a change in the discursive production of subjectivity. He says:

[p]sychiatric expertise, but also in a more general way criminal anthropology and the . . . discourse of criminology . . . provide the mechanisms of legal punishment with a justifiable hold not only on offences, but also on individuals; not only on what they do, but also on *what they are, will be, may be.* . . . The judges have gradually . . . taken to judging something other than crimes, namely, the "soul" of the criminal. (Foucault, 1979, 18–19, my emphasis)

Foucault goes on to develop the notion of bio-power in order to analyse the relations between systems of punishment and the production of certain political economies of the body. He claims that "the body is . . . directly involved in a political field; power relations have an immediate hold upon it; they invest it, *mark it,* train it, torture it, force it to carry out tasks, to perform ceremonies, *to emit signs*" (25, my emphasis). Or as Grosz puts it, "[t]he subject is *named* by being tagged or branded on its surface, creating a particular kind of 'depth-body' or interiority, a psychic layer the subject identifies as its (disembodied) core" (Grosz, 1990a, 65). And as we shall see, the body-subject (re)produces this fiction in and through his or her relation with subjects who interpret or read and write the textual body of the other *as other*.

The work of Lombroso occupied a central position in the development of special techniques for reading the body and the signs it "emits" and made possible both an exegesis and a diagnosis of criminality[21]. In *Polemica in Difesa Della Scuola Criminale Positiva* (1886), which he co-authored with Ferri, Garofalo, and Fioretti, Lombroso identifies the body as a "palimpsest in reverse" (Lombroso, 1886, 8), a surface of overlaid inscriptions that, when read correctly, reveals buried truths. And in a later work that lists the characteristics of the "criminal man"[22] he suggests that for criminologists reading books in libraries is a fool's errand, and should be replaced by a close scrutiny of the living "documents" incarcerated in prisons. Lombroso's approach to the textual body, what is known as anthropometry, involved the measurement of anatomical parts and dimensions, and the categorisation of individuals according to these scientific indexes. In short, Lombroso claimed that the criminal was identifiable by regressive features such as a small skull or large jaws and secondary characteristics such as tattoos, all of which signify atavism, and a retarded developmental association between criminals and species of a "lower order". This is elucidated in the following passage in which Lombroso describes his excitement at "discovering", during an autopsy performed on a criminal, a formation commonly found in rodents.

This was not merely an idea, but a revelation. At the sight of that skull, I seemed to see all of a sudden, lighted up as a vast plain under a flaming sky, the problem of the nature of the criminal—an atavistic being who reproduces in his person the ferocious instincts of primitive humanity and the inferior animals. Thus were explained anatomically the enormous jaws, high cheek-bones, prominent superciliary arches, solitary lines in the palms, extreme size of the orbits, handle-shaped or sessile ears found in criminals, savages, and apes, insensibility to pain, extremely acute sight, tattooing, excessive idleness, love of orgies, and the irresistible craving for evil for its own sake, the desire to not only extinguish life in the victim, but to mutilate the corpse, tear its flesh, and drink its blood. (cited in Lombroso-Ferrero, 1972, xxiv–xxv)

Although a century later we may like to imagine it possible to dismiss Lombroso's somewhat disturbingly rapturous proselytizing with a mere shake of the postmodern head, the fact remains that his ideas still resonate throughout the majority of criminological and psychological analyses of the subject in/of tattooing, and, in part, in society more generally. For example, his claim that "great care must be taken to ascertain whether the [criminal] subject is tattooed . . . [since] tattooing often reveals obscenity, vindictiveness . . . and violence of character" (232, 45–48) is reiterated, albeit less floridly, in the work of theorists such as Yamamoto et al. discussed in the previous section. Moreover, the association he posits between, for example, pederasts and tattooed portraits "of those with whom they have had unnatural commerce" (232) suggests that it is not enough to simply note the presence of tattoos, but that the diagnostician must, as Grumet suggests, consider factors such as the number, location, size, design, and content of tattoos, as, of course, should the layperson if he or she is to protect him- or herself from falling victim to the lethal proclivities of the deviant and seemingly vampiric other.

It is interesting to note that for Lombroso the impulse and ability to identify deviant bodies are not the sole possession of the criminal psychologist. In a number of his works he claims that members of the "lower classes" and even children are often instinctively repulsed by the appearance of the "criminal type". This supposedly validates his thesis that deviance is an innate characteristic that expresses itself in and through the exteriority of the body, since even the "least educated" amongst us are able to intuitively perceive the mark of Cain and its significance. Given this, it seems that one can identify, or be identified as, a threat to society prior to the committing of a crime, since criminality is understood as an innate characteristic externalised through bodily signs, rather than as an act that a particular society deems illegitimate or aberrant. As Adolf Loos, a contemporary of Lombroso, rather pointedly puts it, "[t]hose who are tattooed but are not imprisoned are latent criminals. . . . If a tattooed person dies at liberty, it is only that he died a few years before he committed a murder" (Loos, 1908, 100). There is no consideration given in either Lombroso's or Loos' work to the possibility suggested by Foucault that the discursive production of identity and difference involves the embodiment of social beliefs and values, and that our reading and writing of the textual bodies of others may constitute an unconscious reiterative performance of particular codes and practices, rather than an intuitive process of the recognition of innate truths. Consequently, the social construction of the problem of criminality as it is elaborated by Lombroso generates an increase in practices of surveillance of both the self and others, which, as Foucault argues, aid and abet techniques of identity formation that function in conjunction with disciplinary power.

Whilst the problems and oversights that I have identified in the work of both Lombroso and Loos may be understandable, perhaps even forgivable, given the epoch in which they were writing, it is less easy to dismiss the theses posited by the theorists discussed earlier as thoroughly outmoded and therefore of little or no consequence. Indeed, when we consider the extent to which analyses of the subject in/of tattooing remain firmly founded, despite the passing of a century, on a number of problematic assumptions regarding subjectivity, textuality, and what is ethically "proper", the similarities between these earlier and later works become frighteningly evident. So let us skip a few decades and examine an article by Richard S. Post published in the late 1960s in the *Journal of Criminal Law, Criminology, and Police Science* in order to evaluate to what extent Lombroso's mode of analysis of the subject in/of tattooing remains apparent in criminological research.

Post's article, which uncritically draws on the works of a number of the researchers discussed or mentioned earlier (including Lombroso), begins with the following hypothesis: "[T]he presence of ornamental body tattoos could serve to indicate the presence of personality disorders which could manifest themselves in criminal behaviour" (Post, 1968, 516). The motive for proving this hypothesis, at least as Post sees it, is that "the establishment of a correlation between the presence of a tattoo and social deviancy would be most beneficial in that it could be a readily discernible mark of predisposition toward such conduct" (516). In other words, the tattoo could function as a form of stigmatization that would enable the justifiable exclusion of tattooed wo/men from all walks of life to which they may be seen to present a potential threat regardless of whether they have actually committed "deviant" acts. Post goes on to cite the findings of Youniss' research undertaken at the Naval Research Laboratory in Connecticut in 1959, the Selective Service Board findings of Lander and Kohn's 1943 study of armed servicemen, and the Cincinnati Police Department's policy not to recruit candidates who are tattooed as evidence of a likely correlation between tattoos and deviancy, and as providing a defensible means of exclusion. Unlike Lombroso, Richard Post is not in the business of measuring skulls, but he nevertheless assuredly reiterates the findings of psychologists and criminologists, such as those discussed thus far, to substantiate his claim that there *is* a connection between personality disorders, criminality, and tattoos. Like Grumet, he adds the proviso that tattoos may indicate that a person *did* suffer a personality disorder that has since been "cured", but gives little indication of how such a process of "recovery" (normalization) might be possible, given the fact that the tattoo is also "a useful indicator of future deviancy" (524).

Unlike Lombroso, Post appears, on the one hand, to explicitly reject an essentialist account of deviancy, but, on the other hand, claims that deviancy is not socially constructed. In both his own words, and those of psychologist C. C. Rogers whom he cites, he says:

The individual's self-concept is going to determine the actions he will undertake in relation to his environment. "Behaviour is not directly influenced or determined by organic or cultural factors, but primarily (and perhaps only), by the perception of these elements". In other words it is the person's internal frame of reference, or how he perceives or views society that determines how he will act. If a person's internal perception of society is such that he feels he must embellish his body with signs, symbols, or figures to reflect his internalized self-perceptions, these markings should be taken as indicators of some type of personality disorder. Regardless of whether they are attempts to disguise homosexuality, inferiority feelings, defiance of authority, or any of the numerous forms of personality disorders, the mark was put there for a very definite reason by the person having such a mark. (523–24)

This passage raises a number of questions, not least of which is from whence does the subject's frame of reference or self-concept come, if not from biology, culture, or some combination of the two? Wouldn't it be true to say that we all, in varying ways, "embellish our bodies" with signs and symbols that reflect our perceptions of ourselves, the society to which we belong, and the relations between them, and for the most part, do so with something less than conscious intent? If, as Foucault puts it, power marks the body, forces it to emit signs, how could anybody, including Post himself, avoid this process and at the same time take up a position and be positioned by others as a social subject? Given this, to what degree can these signs and symbols be said to be indicative of an essential personality disorder? Is Post suggesting that internalized self-perceptions (at least if they are externalized) are phenomena that are "chosen" only by those who suffer from personality disorders? And if so, how do people not suffering from personality disorders engage with the world, given that behaviour is not influenced by organic or cultural factors, but by the perception of such elements in and through an internal frame of reference? Perhaps Post is suggesting that there are "healthy" frames of reference and "unhealthy" ones, but if this is this case it is unclear why and how individuals develop one as opposed to the other, and why tattoos indicate an unhealthy frame of reference (personality disorder), whereas wedding rings, for example, would supposedly signify a healthy one ("normal" heterosexuality).

Post's conflation of bodily signs and symbols, personality disorder, and attempts to "disguise homosexuality" is telling. According to the model he sets up here, the perception of oneself as homosexual, and the ensuing desire to disguise (or express) what one has perceived through the embellishment of the body with (perhaps "misleading") signs and symbols, suggests that the subject's perception is indeed influenced by cultural factors. If this were not the case, how would the subject understand, let alone fear, social responses to his or her impulses and desires? To even perceive these as sexual, or more particularly homosexual, the subject would have to be familiar with social codes and practices that constitute the body and bodily actions according to such categories. The only way this may not be the case would be if homosexuality were biologically determined, as were the feelings of fear, repugnance, and inferiority associated with it. If this is so, then Post's understanding of personality disorder is no less universalizing or rooted in a biologically determined notion of evolution than is that of Lombroso. Thus whilst Post's analysis of the subject in/of tattooing may appear less flagrantly prejudicial, at least in its prose style, than Lombroso's, theoretically it is no less problematic. Nor are the social and political implications of Post's work any less dangerous than those of his predecessors.

A large percentage of the criminological analyses of the subject in/of tattooing published since the 1970s focus on the association between tattooing, drug use or addiction, and other forms of "subcultural" behaviour and identity such as homosexuality, minority racial identity, and criminality[23]. These associative links are reaffirmed both explicitly and implicitly, as recently as 1993 in the work of Copes and Forsyth. Drawing on Eysenck and Eysenck's (1967) theory of extraversion and introversion as products of cortical arousal, the authors elaborate what they call a "Stimulation Theory" of tattoos that predicts that subjects with tattoos will be more likely to be extraverted than introverted, since the low level of cortical arousal characteristic of extraversion causes extraverts to seek increased external stimuli. Tattooing is one means of procuring this stimuli since not only does the process of being tattooed involve a high level of sensual experience, but moreover "by having tattoos, especially visible ones, the person draws attention to himself" (Copes and Forsyth, 1993, 87). Copes and Forsyth conclude that tattoos are not necessarily a sign of personality disorder or criminality, but rather are a sign of extraversion. However, group dependency, rebelliousness, extreme emotion, "dangerous" or exhibitionist behaviour, and delinquency are all also characteristic of what the authors define as extraversion. Given this, the validity of the claim that "[i]nstead of delinquency being caused by a personality disorder, it may be the result (as is the tattoo) of the extravert's [*sic*] low arousal level and their need for stimulation" (88) seems tenuous to say the least. Insofar as the extravert's need for stimulation is "excessive", it is tantamount to (potential) delinquency, and is therefore socially problematic and opposed to introversion, which is represented in their work in terms of normalcy. Since Copes and Forsyth make no mention of how and why extraversion, or more particularly low levels of cortical arousal, comes about or how it can be "cured", their analysis of the subject in/of tattooing fails, ultimately, to move beyond the thesis provided by Lombroso, except perhaps in terms of the discursive development of increasingly specialized medical discourses.

What I have attempted to demonstrate in this section is that criminological analyses of the subject in/of tattooing are no less problematic than the psychological theses discussed earlier. Indeed, it has been shown that both psychological and criminological accounts of tattooing inform, draw on, and reaffirm one another in a number of ways in relation to subjectivity, textuality, pleasure, and ethics. As a result, the basic premises underlying all of the works discussed have remained qualitatively unchanged despite the fact that the period in which they were published spans almost a century. This is not to suggest that nothing changes, but rather that criminological and psychological accounts of the subject in/of tattooing seem, for the most part, to be unaware of the reconfigurations of subjectivity and textuality, for example, that have taken place in other academic disciplines. In fact I would argue that this is generally true of contemporary "common-sense" perspectives on the subject in/of tattooing.

READING/WRITING THE MARKS OF DELINQUENCY

As I mentioned earlier, in *Discipline and Punish,* and also in the first two volumes of *The History of Sexuality,* Foucault provides a genealogical analysis of the ways in which systems of power/knowledge construct determinate types of bodies. Through processes of enculturation the body is discursively produced in and through procedures that mark. This inscription of bodies occurs via a plethora of social mechanisms and practices, that range from violent constraint to less obviously coercive means such as beautification, education, and the codification and partitioning of time, space, and movement. For Foucault, "the body" is neither a biological entity nor a pre-social *tabula rasa* upon which culture tortuously writes its repressive mandates, at least not in *Discipline and Punish.* Rather, as Elizabeth Grosz puts it:

The subject is marked as a series of (potential) messages from/of the (social) Other, and the symbolic order. Its flesh is transformed into a *body,* organised and hierarchized according to the requirements of a particular social and family nexus. The body becomes a text and is fictionalised and positioned within those myths that form a culture's social narratives and self-representations. (Grosz, 1990b, 65–66)

This notion of intextuation allows the possibility of moving beyond an understanding of the tattooed body as a text that simply externalizes the interior (truth of the) subject, and provides us with a means of critically analyzing the ways in which bodies are both agents and effects of power/knowledge, invested with meanings in accordance with socially specific variables such as gender, ethnicity, class, and so on. Foucault describes the relation between the "political anatomy", the "mechanics of power", and the construction of the liberal subject as follows:

Discipline increases the forces of the body (in economic terms of utility) and diminishes these same forces (in political terms of obedience). In short, it dissociates power from the body; on the one hand, it turns it into "aptitude", a "capacity", which it seeks to increase; on the other hand, it reverses the course of the energy, the power that might result from it, and turns it into a relation of . . . subjection. . . . Disciplinary coercion establishes in the body the constricting link between an increased aptitude and an increased domination. (Foucault, 1979, 138)

Thus the subject, according to Foucault, is not "merely placed in a relation to an external power that attempts to dominate and repress it, but, instead, becomes a form of the operation of power, the point where the dividing line between acceptable and unacceptable, normal and abnormal behaviour operates and is policed" (Feury and Mansfield, 1997, 175). Or to put it more simply, the body-subject is constituted as both an agent and effect of systems of power/knowledge. The discursive production of subjectivity and its relation to the (symbolic) law, and to bodily inscription, will perhaps become clearer if we turn to Tim Robbins' 1995 film *Dead Man Walking*. The film tells the story of Matthew Poncelet (Sean Penn), a prisoner on death row who is facing execution for his part in the brutal rape and murder of two middle-class southern teenagers. Poncelet, the sneering, swaggering, sexist, racist, chain-smoking, drug-taking, quintessential "bad guy", in a seemingly uncharacteristic move, requests the company, and possible legal and spiritual assistance, of nun-cum-social-worker, Sister Helen Prejean (Susan Sarandon). The story turns on three events, which, when read together, tell of the ways in which the body, and thus the subjectivity of the "criminal" is read and written (inscribed). Given this, it is plausible to view *Dead Man Walking* as providing a critical response to the analyses of the subject in/of tattooing posited by the criminologists and psychologists discussed earlier.

The first of these events is the attempt to reprieve the death sentence, and raises the question of reading and writing (the truth of) subjectivity. Here Poncelet's legal representative, recently procured by Sister Helen, endeavours to convince both the jury and the viewer that Poncelet's crime, and thus his current predicament, is less the result of an essentially debauched nature than the product of various social and legal processes that construct the subject, and his or her position in the order of things, in inequitable ways. He says:

You're not gonna find any rich people on death row. Matthew Poncelet's here today because he's poor. He didn't have any money for representation so he had to take what the state gave him and the state gave him a tax lawyer who never tried a capital case before. An amateur, . . . If Matthew had himself some money, well he could have hired a team of crackerjack lawyers and they would have hired a top-notch investigator, a ballistics expert, a psychologist to compile profiles of desirable jurors and you can be sure Matthew Poncelet wouldn't be sitting here today, before you, asking for his *life*. (Robbins, 1995)

Prior to this scene, the viewer is provided with a number of signs that suggest that Poncelet is representative of what might colloquially be called "white trash", scum. His bodily appearance, actions, and movements "emit signs", as Foucault puts it, of impropriety. We discover that in his familial environment he was no stranger to violence and alcoholism, that at school his truancy, increasing lack of interest, and disrespect for social norms led to eventual expulsion, that he has served time in juvenile homes; and that he is involved in the seedy underworld of drugs and violence. In supplying us with information as to Poncelet's "working-class" upbringing, to the ways in which he is marked in and through processes of socialization, the film does not simply present us with a sob story, but rather allows the possibility of critically analysing the ways in which the corporeal substance is rendered significant and functional. As is apparent from the above quotation, Poncelet's (working-class) subjectivity has been, for the most part, constructed as a threat—or at least as other—to the political anatomy and to the systems and values it promotes. Consequently, the range of alternatives open to him to rewrite or reread both his crime and his subjectivity are severely limited. His only access to the discursive expertise of psychologists and ballistics experts is as other. Thus, he is not so much excluded from the social order, as included in an increasingly insidious process of othering.

It is important to note that the argument posited by Poncelet's legal representative does not attempt to justify his crime and thus reaffirm his subjectivity as (inadvertent) criminal, or suggest that in truth Poncelet is, as his mother would have us believe, a victim of oppressive social regimes, a "good boy" who, for reasons beyond his control, has had a "bad" life. Rather, the statement gestures toward the ways in which (Poncelet's) "delinquent" subjectivity is constructed or manufactured, read and written, in and through corporeal relations with others and with a world in such a way that he, like all delinquent subjects, is both an object of judicial systems of power/knowledge, *and* an accomplice[24]. As Alphonso Lingis puts it:

[D]elinquents do not constitute a multitude of individuals upon whom the technology of the disciplinary archipelago has proven ineffective, and who are at large conducting a guerilla [*sic*] war on its institutions. . . . In multiple penitentiary enclosures—foster homes, public assistance institutions, residential apprenticeships, juvenile homes, disciplinary regiments in the army and the marines, prisons, hospitals, asylums, [schools]—delinquents are being progressively manufactured. Delinquents are not outlaws, nomads prowling about the confines of the docile and frightened citizenry; delinquency is not constituted through successive exclusions from the social order, but through successive inclusions under ever more insistent surveillance. . . . [Delinquents] are an identified, documented group, maintained under surveillance outside and used by the forces of order to maintain under surveillance the whole network of their contacts and their milieux. They are recruited and put to use. (Lingis, 1994b, 62)

In other words, delinquency or criminality is socially constructed rather than innate, and confirms and reinforces the disciplinary archipelago insofar as the delinquent body is inscribed with the civil code and signs of its transgression[25]. Or to quote Foucault again,

[i]n a disciplinary regime individualization is "descending": as power becomes more anonymous and more functional, those on whom it is exercised tend to be more strongly individualized; it exercises by surveillance . . . by observation . . . by comparative measures that have the "norm" as reference. (Foucault, 1979, 193)

And as we have seen in our examination of psychological and criminological analyses of the subject in/of tattooing, the constitutive power of the normalizing gaze allows the registration of difference only in terms of degrees of difference from the norm that is the ideal.

The second event from the film that I want to discuss illustrates what Foucault describes as the "double system of protection that justice has set up between itself and the punishment it imposes" (10), and how such a phenomenon functions to (re)produce a distinction between those who punish and those who are punished or punishable, that is, respectable citizens and delinquents, the self and (the body of) the other. The aim of the argument put forward by Poncelet's legal representative in this scene is to convince the jury to revoke the death sentence on the grounds that not to do so would implicate them, and by association us the viewers, in killing. In a typically Foucauldian manner, he begins by describing the various forms the death penalty has taken over the past few centuries—from the gruesome public spectacle of hanging, drawing, and quartering, to the relatively private form of "humane killing" by lethal injection. In doing so he gestures toward the changing ways in which the corporeal substance has been made significant and functional. He describes the current relation between the political anatomy, the mechanics of power, and the body of the delinquent or criminal subject thus:

Now we have developed a device that is the most humane of all—lethal injection. We strap the guy up, we anaesthetise him with shot number one, then we give him shot number two and that implodes his lungs, and shot number three stops his heart. We put him to death just like an old horse. His face goes to sleep while inside his organs are going through Armageddon. The muscles of his face would twist and contort and pull, but, you see, shot number one relaxes all those muscles so that we don't have to see any horror show, we don't have to taste the blood of revenge on our lips. While this human being's organs twist, writhe, contort, we just sit there quietly, nod our heads, and say "justice has been done". (Robbins, 1995)

What interests me about this quotation is that it not only calls into question the (supposed) distinction between criminal and noncriminal, self and other, but at the same time offers a poignant critique of the ways in which particular notions of subjectivity and textuality work in conjunction to reaffirm one another via historically and culturally specific mechanisms of punishment. As Foucault tells it, the spectacle of public torture that took place in Europe up until the end of the eighteenth century involved various processes that made the crimes manifest on the body of the one who committed them. Thus the tongues of blasphemers were pierced, the bodies of arsonists burnt, the hands of thieves torn off, and so on. As Foucault describes it, the body of the criminal is inscribed in and through the processes of punishment that produce a body marked with the signs of the "truth" of the crime committed, and the "truth" of the one who has committed that crime (35). In effect then, the body of the malefactor functioned in this particular epoch to performatively reproduce through a process of inscription the crime committed on or against the sacrilized body of the sovereign. In this way the crime was made manifest and annulled. Today punishment is a less spectacular, and more insidious, process. The executioner has been replaced by an array of technicians: psychologists, criminologists, social workers, prison warders, and so on, and it is something other than public torture that marks the body of the delinquent. Punishment is hidden, but no less constitutive. As both Post's and Lombroso's theses demonstrate, systems of surveillance now read and write (inscribe) the criminal body in advance of any crime being committed, through a set of procedures that identify, classify, and evaluate individuals "by a degree of approximation to the norm" (Lingis, 1994b, 60). Moreover, the criminal body is read as expressing the truth of the criminal (rather than his or her crime), and thus the inscriptive processes of subject formation are veiled over and the truth status of institutional discourses is reaffirmed.

Capital punishment is no longer an explicitly spectacular public performance; it has entered what Foucault calls the realm of the abstract. As a result, systems of justice need no longer take responsibility for the violence integral to its practice (Foucault, 1979, 9). Just as Lombroso, and those like him, can disavow their complicity in the system of legal violence by reaffirming a supposedly absolute distinction between self and other, the criminal and the norm, so too can the judiciary, and by extension the public, distance themselves from (humane) killing through entrusting such a process to an anonymous machine that functions behind the walls of a concealed space. Indeed, one could say that the marks of violence inscribed on the body of the condemned are written with invisible ink so that we do not have to "see the horror show, taste the blood of revenge on our lips", or read the (inter)textuation of self-other relations. As Poncelet's legal representative tells us, the use of "physiological disconnectors" writes the condemned body in such a way that it finally conforms with popular notions of propriety. We can read the exterior body of the dying criminal as a sign of the truth: the truth of the criminal's redemption, of the success of the legal system's correctional function, of justice as humane, and of ourselves as upstanding ethical subjects. But as we have seen, disconnectors produce illusory effects by rendering possible the (mis)reading/writing of social fictions as "truths", and by disavowing the intersubjective element of systems of categorization that produce subjects in dichotomous terms.

Whilst on one level *Dead Man Walking* reproduces the affect of the disconnectors, by allowing the viewer to condone the killing of Poncelet as the lesser of two evils, on another level, the text performs something of an epiphany, when, in the penultimate scene before the execution, we are confronted for the first time with the heavily tattooed body of the malefactor. At the literal and metaphoric eleventh hour, Sister Helen in her role as spiritual adviser, returns to Poncelet's cell to find him no longer clad in the homogenous prison uniform of criminality, but in cut-off jeans and a short-sleeved T-shirt. Her response to his picturesque body is a fairly common one. She asks him why he got tattooed, what the tattoos mean, and whether the process was painful. Thus if we identify with the altruistic[26] figure of Sister Helen whose feelings for Poncelet are, like our own, ambivalent, we find ourselves positioned normatively in relation to the subject in/of tattooing, insofar as we reaffirm the focus on individuality, on meaning and intentionality. What breaks up this hermeneutic process is Poncelet's response. In an attempt to avoid being positioned as the object of the gaze, he says: "you see these tattoos, you're gonna think I'm a bad person". This statement may strike the viewer as somewhat ironic given Poncelet's "badboy" behaviour throughout the film, and the increasing evidence of his participation in the crime for which he stands accused. But what these words generate, for me at least, is a moment of revelation in which the processes of interpretation and evaluation in and through which one reads and writes the body of the other in accordance with the normative criteria one assumes become painfully apparent, as does the systematic violence that such practices at once make possible and disavow.

It is not only Poncelet's words but, more importantly, the materiality of his textual body, which up until this point has functioned less explicitly, that speaks to us, that affects us in a way that exceeds meaning. It is perhaps telling that the camera focuses only fleetingly on the individual tattoos, and thus seems to divert any attempt to scrutinize the symbols for meanings that may tell us the truth of Poncelet's being. We briefly glimpse a figure in chains, a spider in its web, swastikas, and a Maltese cross, amidst a myriad of colours clashing and blending in a swirling profusion of excess. Whilst in retrospect we may, like the theorists discussed earlier, read these as signs of Poncelet's entrapment in a web of his own making, of his barbarous inclinations, or his association of heroism with killing, this is only achievable through a sleight of hand that separates or "disconnects" affect and sign, self and other, a point I will discuss in more detail in Chapter Four. It is my contention that this scene constitutes a textual apotheosis inasmuch as it dramatizes, at the level of carnal materiality or affectivity, the interconnected character of subjectivity, the viewer's complicity in the constitution of the other *as other*, which the "rational" arguments of Poncelet's legal representative never quite manage to capture.

In foregrounding the process of reading and writing the body of the other that makes the corporeal substance significant and functional, this scene implicates us, not by communicating an identifiable truth, but rather by moving or marking us in ways that defy definitive explanation. I will go on to critically discuss both the notion of affectivity and that of communication as the expression and reception of a message between individuals in Chapters 3 and 4, but for the moment suffice it to say that this encounter with (Poncelet's) carnality, with the flesh—positioned as it is, as the film's denouement—"is not only indicative, [and] informative but also vocative and imperative" (Lingis, 1986, 227). As Lingis puts it in a discussion of Levinas' notion of the self's encounter with the Other, which poignantly describes the affect this scene invokes:

In his flesh I see . . . the demanding insistence of his being. Skin is not hide nor covering, camouflage, uniform, adornment. It is a surface of exposure, zone of susceptibility, of vulnerability, of pain and abuse. In the skin inscribed with its own wrinkles, one . . . read[s] . . . the vulnerability of what is other. One's eyes touch it lightly, affected by the susceptibility of youth, the fragility of age, the organic dead-ends of birthmarks, the languor of eyes that close. . . . In this exposedness the other does not affect me as another substance that solidifies under my hold, that sustains and supports. His face is not the surface of another being. It is flesh of no identifiable colour, that does not hold its shape. There is want of being in all flesh; what faces is not something whose identity I can grasp. The anonymity of fingers, legs, genitals is not that of implements utilizable by anyone but the unrepresentable importunity of a want, the inapprehendable movement of a contestation, the unmeasurable force of a question that badgers and disrupts. (Lingis, 1989, 138)

To put it more simply, "the carnal materiality of the other [in this case Poncelet] weighs on me" (Lingis, 1989, 137), questions me, contests me, disturbs my perspectives and the law that governs or gives life to them. On the one hand then, it may be, and in fact is, possible to read the body of the other as a canvas upon which psychologically relevant themes are portrayed (Grumet, 1983, 482), but at the same time what such practices presuppose, and what disallows closure, is the vocative and imperative force of the fleshly encounter, in and through which both self and other are continuously (re)constituted, are (re)read and (re)written, mark and are marked.

Thus in the execution scene that follows, I taste the indeterminable blood of revenge on my lips, I sense the horror show that exceeds my grasp, and my body is marked as surely as is Poncelet's by the Kafkaesque killing machine that inscribes the sentence against which one has no opportunity to defend oneself. Like the explorer in Kafka's *In the Penal Colony,* I cannot just sit there quietly, nod my head, and say "justice has been done", for in and through this exposure to carnal materiality, I have been "exposed to the Other as a skin is exposed to that which wounds it" (Levinas, 1978, 49). The words of the officer caress me, mark me: "it isn't easy to decipher the script with one's eyes; but our man deciphers it with his wounds" (Kafka, 1995, 31), or more precisely, he/I sense(s) it.

What I have attempted to demonstrate via this discussion of *Dead Man Walking* is that the body is neither simply a biological entity, nor a presocial *tabula rasa* upon which repressive social mandates are inscribed or an innate essence is expressed, as the criminological and psychological analyses of the tattooed body (as text) suggest. The problem with both of these models is that they render (the materiality of) the body immaterial. This tendency is also apparent in the work of Hegel, who, writing at the same time as the phrenologists Franz Joseph Gall and Johann Christoph Spurzheim, claims, in a section of *Phenomenology of Spirit* entitled "Observation of the Relation of Self-

Consciousness to Its Immediate Actuality: Physiognomy and Phrenology", that "since the individual is . . . only what he has done, his body is also an expression of himself, which he himself has *produced;* it is at the same time a sign, which has not remained an *immediate* fact, but something through which the individual only makes known what he really is, when he sets his original nature to work" (Hegel, 1977, 185–86). These words, which could equally well have come from the mouths of the psychologists and criminologists discussed throughout this chapter, evoke a depth model of the subject in which the exterior body is seen as the (textual) expression of an inner psyche or spirit. Hence, the role of the dermal diagnostician, like that of the phrenologist, the criminologist, or in some cases the philosopher, is characterised by a movement from surface to depth, from the material to the immaterial, from the fleshly to the conceptual. Thus the body comes to matter only insofar as its matter or materiality is veiled over in and through the extraction of abstract and essentially immaterial truths. In effect, then, the question of the tattooed body-subject is, upon investigation, "the question of the possibility and/or the impossibility of knowledge and self-knowledge" (Taylor, 1997, 13).

Since counter-cultural analyses of the subject in/of tattooing often set themselves up in opposition to what they see as the moral conservatism of criminological and psychological accounts of bodily inscription, I will now briefly examine a number of works that seem representative of what has come to be known as modern primitivism. My aim in doing so is to evaluate to what extent they make possible alternative understandings of the subject in/of tattooing, of textuality, subjectivity, ethics, and pleasure.

BODY PLAY: STATE OF GRACE OR SICKNESS?[27]

The term "modern primitivism" was supposedly coined in the 1970s by Fakir Musafar, a practitioner and teacher of ritual practices of body modification, who has since become known as "the father of the modern primitive movement" (Musafar, 1996, 325). In the early 1980s in response to the increasing (counter)cultural fascination with practices such as tattooing, piercing, scarification, branding, and body sculpting more generally, Musafar proposed the production of a book on body modification and body rites to Re/Search Publications of San Francisco (327). The book, published in 1989, entitled *Modern Primitives*, and edited by Andrea Juno and V. Vale, has now achieved something like a cult status, and for many represents the Holy Writ of a rapidly growing movement opposed to what are held to be "repressive" social conventions. In 1991 Musafar started a magazine called *Body Play & Modern Primitives Quarterly,* and this was soon followed by a proliferation of similar publications such as *International Piercing Fans Quarterly, Ritual Magazine, Body Art, Piercing World,* and *Tattoo Savage,* to name just a few. So what is it that is so appealing about modern primitivism then? If, as Favazza concedes in the revised edition of his analysis of self-mutilation, "a psychiatric diagnosis cannot be presumed in persons who engage in body piercing, branding, tattoos, and so forth" (Favazza, 1996, 287)[28], how can we conceive of these practices otherwise? Perhaps modern primitivism can provide us with some insights.

For Musafar and his followers, the interpretation of such practices as forms of self-mutilation, and the ensuing charge of psychiatric illness, is hugely problematic, and in this we are in agreement, as my analysis thus far illustrates. However, the understanding of body modification that Musafar offers tends to simply reverse this paradigm by reading these supposedly freely chosen practices[29] not as a sign of sickness, but rather as a "state of grace", an overcoming of the insidious sickness created by the oppressive social systems of the Western world. In other words, for Musafar and his followers, normativity is something like a sickness that needs to be healed or transcended.

In the introduction to *Modern Primitives*, Juno and Vale, drawing on the ideas of Montaigne, Rousseau, and Wordsworth, and citing the *Princeton Encyclopedia of Poetry and Poetics,* describe a primitivist as

a person who prefers a way of life which, when judged by one or more of the standards prevailing in his own society, would be considered less "advanced" or less "civilized". The primitivist finds the model for his preferred way of life in a culture that existed or is reputed to have existed at some time in the past; in the culture of the less sophisticated classes within his society; or of primitive peoples that exist elsewhere in the world; in the experiences of his childhood or youth; in a psychologically elemental (sub-rational or even subconscious) level of existence; or in some combination of these. (Juno and Vale, 1989, 4)

Whilst Juno and Vale state that "a cliché-ridden allusion to what is 'primitive' provides no solution to the *problem*" (4) of the stifling and life-thwarting emphasis on rational logic in Western "civilized" culture, they see *modern* primitivism as a positive attempt to "achieve an integration of the poetic and the scientific imagination in our lives" (4). According to Juno and Vale, "our minds are colonized by images" (5) that repress what they call "first person experience" or individuality, and as a result we feel powerless, unsure about our "basic identities". Modern primitivism, they claim, as one particular response to this situation, exemplifies the individuals' ability to produce change by "freeing up a creative part of themselves, of their essence" (5), by reclaiming the body as the one thing that the individual still has power over. Or as they put it, citing Roger Cardinal, "body modifications perform a vital function identical to art: they 'genuinely stimulate passion and spring directly from the original sources of emotion, and are not something tapped from the cultural reservoir'" (5). Similarly, they claim that sex has been "bastardized" by the "flood of alien [cultural] images", resulting in the "wholesale de-individualization of man and society" (5). Luckily for us, however, "complex eroticism has always been the one implacable enemy of death" and consequently it is necessary, according to these theorists, to discover repressed desires so that an untainted form of eroticism that embraces so-called oppositions such as pleasure and pain, and reason and delirium, may emerge, and give rise to improved forms of social relations (5). The question, then, is exactly *how* do practices such as tattooing, piercing, cutting, and so on function in the formation of this new liberatory eroticism?

In an interview with Juno and Vale, Fakir Musafar repeatedly refers to what he calls "primal energy", that is, the individual creative urge that is the essence of who one is, both in this life time and in past lives, and that is continually denied expression in Western societies. Ritual body modification in its various forms is a positive means by which this primal energy can be expressed for the benefit of the individual, and insofar as it generates the realization of "the individual magic latent within", counteracts the modern world's attempt to "wipe out difference" (Musafar, in Juno and Vale, 12). In other words, the free expression of a unique inner essence, if practised en masse, will constitute a reclaiming of the essential heterogeneity that life-thwarting social conventions have attempted to constrain in and through processes, beliefs, and lifestyles that homogenize being. Given this, it comes as no surprise that Musafar believes that modern primitives are "*born*, not made" (8). Musafar argues that one's life, identity, and the practices one participates in are nothing more than a repetition of inclinations from a previous life.

This makes way for the claim that tattoo designs (at least those of modern primitives) come "from inner visions", and that tattooing is a process of completion (8). In effect, then, Musafar shares the opinion of the criminologists and psychologists discussed earlier that the tattoo is an external expression of an (essential) inner self, albeit with opposite ethical consequences. However, he qualifies this statement with the claim that there is a difference between "real fetishism", which is a clear expression of primal energy, and a superficial "fake fetishism", which is nothing but "a tired copycat of the original" (24). How one discerns the difference between authenticity and inauthenticity, however, remains unclear. Elisabeth Ostermann makes a similar claim when she writes, in the introduction to Chris Wroblewski's photographic text *Modern Primitives* (1988), that body modification that constitutes "real fetishism" does not involve the subjection of the body "to the dictates of functionalism obeyed by office employees sweating out in a fitness studio". Real fetishistic body modificatory practices "demonstrate a lust for dramatic expression without any moral implications, a predilection for communication without words" (Ostermann, in Wroblewski, 1988, 7).

For Musafar the body functions as a vehicle for the expression of primal energy, or as Ostermann puts it, for "communication without words". For the most part, body modification in its various forms involves an element of sensuous experience or pain, and surrendering to this experience inaugurates a "transcendental spiritual event" (Musafar, in Juno and Vale, 1989, 8). The event is tantamount to what is commonly described as an "altered state", or an out-of-body experience. Musafar describes both the process and the philosophy of altered states as a separating of consciousness and body. Since the body is understood as the prison of the soul, then this process of separation is liberatory insofar as it frees consciousness or soul from its mortal confines.

What we have here then is something like an Orphic or Pythagorean[30] ascetics in which the state of grace from which civilized wo/man has fallen can be reclaimed via an attitude summed up in the Augustine formula *Credo ut intelligam* (I believe so that I may understand). Hence the task of consciousness or reason is to elucidate divine revelation, or to release the primal energy that is at the heart of being and that has been repressed, both in an individual sense, and in terms of an essential heterogeneity. Communication without words, then, is affected in and through the attainment of a disembodied state of completion or truth in relation to the multiplicitous whole of which "the individual" is a unique part. One of the many problems with Musafar's analysis of the subject in/of tattooing and the religious mysticism that informs it is that it reaffirms the mind/body split that is fundamental to the analyses developed by the criminologists and psychologists discussed earlier, and consequently implies a moral hierarchy of ways of being, rather than, as Ostermann claims, demonstrating a lust for dramatic expression without any moral implications. For as Musafar sees it, "to *not* have . . . holes in your body, to *not* have tattoos, may be debilitating . . . [People] may not be getting the most out of life because they *don't* do these things . . . [They] may be missing beautiful, rich experiences because of *cultural bias and conceit*" (Juno and Vale, 1989, 15).

Moreover, in both cases, the materiality of the body is ironically rendered null and void in the search for abstract and essentially immaterial truths, that is, the truth of subjectivity and of being, and the knowledge of that truth as a form of freedom. In other words, the model of subjectivity assumed by Juno and Vale, Musafar, and Ostermann remains firmly entrenched in liberal humanism and embraces a dichotomous hierarchical distinction between mind and body, inside and outside, nature and culture, self and other, truth and falsity, and so on. At the same time, pleasure functions, at least implicitly, to reaffirm the subject as subject, for as Musafar describes it, the aim of modern primitive practices is the uninhibited expression of "*pleasure with insight*" (Musafar, in Juno and Vale, 1989, 13). And "pleasure with insight" consists of the free expression of the primal energy that is the essence of the individual and of difference.

But perhaps as Favazza, in a discussion of performance artist Tim Cridland, known as "The Torture King", puts it, there are ways of explaining the significance of modern primitive practices "without recourse to supernatural explanations or mystical mumbo-jumbo" (Favazza, 1996, 285). This is not to suggest that I want simply to dismiss what are obviously very "real" beliefs and experiences for Musafar and those like him with a charge of illogicality or irrationality. My claim is not so much that modern primitive beliefs and experiences are somehow "false" or erroneous, but rather that they are symptomatic of the ways in which the body-subject is (inter)textually constituted "and is fictionalised and positioned within those myths which form a culture's social narratives and self-representations" (Grosz, 1990b, 65–66). Let us turn now to less "mystical" analyses of modern primitivism and examine whether or not this is still the case.

Like Juno and Vale, and to a lesser degree Musafar, David Curry claims that the basic motivation for tattooing is "the desire to decorate the public outside of our private inside" (Curry, 1993, 69), and that this process both beautifies and expresses a message of political dissent. For Curry, tattooing constitutes a positive form of "perverse behaviour" that he defines as "that which is consciously adopted even though it is known to be found undesirable by the dominant group, embraced as a statement of one's role in (or more often against) the group and involving a choice of and a commitment to that role" (77). Similarly, Daniel Wojcik, in his book entitled *Punk and Neo-Tribal Body Art* (1995), describes punk as an *intentional* form of counter-cultural resistance that provided a sense of identity, self-esteem, and community for the alienated youth of the 1970s, and punk body art as "an aesthetic response to the inability of the larger society to meet the needs of individuals" (Wojcik, 1995, 5); an expression of estrangement (Wojcik, 1995, 11). Whilst punk embraced, at least as Wojcik tells it, an apocalyptic ethic as exemplified by the lyrics of Iggy Pop's *Search and Destroy*, The Sex Pistols' *Anarchy in the UK*, and so on, the neo-tribalism that grew out of it "tends to emphasize the transformative rather than the destructive aspects of body-modification, often expressing a yearning for idealized ways of life imagined to be more fulfilling emotionally, spiritually, and sexually" (36).

Wojcik's analysis of neo-tribalism is based primarily on discussions with Perry Farrell[31], a self-proclaimed modern primitive, ex-punk, and lead singer of Porno for Pyros. For Farrell, his tattoos, piercings, scars, and dreadlocks are "signs of defiance [that] symbolize both his estrangement from mainstream society and a triumph over dominant values and lifestyles that he finds oppressive" (Farrell, in Wojcik, 1995, 33). Whilst, like Musafar, Farrell mentions the importance of the role of ritual pain in the process of self-(trans)formation generated by various forms of body modification, he tends to place much more emphasis on the necessity for an assertive, perhaps even aggressive, form of body politics. The experience of pain, he says, makes you realize that

you can do anything you want, and there's the proof. . . . [T]hese are my signs . . . [and] I'm going to do more of this type of thing as I get older and become more of an outsider. . . . My stance is just getting more and more like "God damn it, I'm getting madder and madder and I'm just looking weirder and weirder!" (Farrell, cited in Wojcik, 1995, 33)

Thus, for Farrell, modern primitive practices provide a conscious means of self-expression as they do for Musafar. However, the "self" that is supposedly expressed through these practices, at least as Farrell tells it, seems much more concerned with confrontation and resistance than with the kind of transcendence Musafar describes. In other words, Farrell's tattoos, piercings, and scars function as signs that seem to communicate a single message—"Fuck You"—and thus reaffirm his sense of self in opposition to what he sees as dominant culture. But there is something of a paradox at work here, since Farrell writes and reads his body, fictionalizes and positions him"self", squarely within the social narratives and (self)representations that inform the beliefs and practices of the criminologists and psychologists discussed earlier. Thus the reversal of dominant values and conventions that is apparent here not only fails to challenge them at a qualitative level, but more ironically still reaffirms them. To Lombroso, Post, and Yamamoto et al., Farrell would represent all that they find ethically repugnant and threatening to the health of the body politic and vice versa. Thus identity and difference remain firmly entrenched in an Economy of the Same, and the body continues to function as nothing more than the (immaterial) vehicle of a hermeneutics of truth. Despite claims to the contrary, difference both within and between "dominant cultural" discourses and "counter-cultural" discourses turns out to be what Irigaray might call *indifference.* Moreover, (transgressive) pleasure still functions to reaffirm the subject in and through a (counter)relation with normative conventions and values.

Insofar as modern primitive accounts of the subject in/of tattooing share many similarities with the criminological and psychological analyses discussed, particularly a liberal humanist understanding of the body-subject, both could be said to constitute a form of dermagraphism (a reading and writing [of] the body) that, as Didi-Huberman puts it, "produces . . . a kind of *thanatography,* a sentence which controls the destiny of the [other], and which incarnates the corporeal to corpse" (Didi-Huberman, 1984, 70). I will discuss the deathly effects of such an ontology in more detail in Chapter Three, but for the moment suffice it to say that this rendering of the body of/as other is affected in and through a theoretical turn of the knife that reads and writes the body "as a sign whose significance can be discerned by stripping away the surface to uncover the depths. . . . Only when the body is under-stood as being finally grounded in spirit does knowledge become secure" (Taylor, 1997, 18). The role performed by all of the theorists discussed so far is something like that of the forensic pathologist, who dissects the body in the service of truth and knowledge. But, as Taylor suggests,

[p]erhaps the most startling conclusion emerges when the detective story is subjected to investigation. As the detective story bends back on itself, it appears to undo itself in the

process of its telling. Through an unexpected reversal, the condition of the possibility of dis-guising turns out to be the condition of the impossibility of detection. (17)

Let us ponder this suggestion for a moment via what appears, at first glance, to be a startling and graphic image of dissection.

Open the . . . body and spread out all its surfaces: not only the skin with each of its folds, wrinkles, scars, . . . but open and spread . . . the *labia majora*, the *labia minora* . . . dilate the diaphragm of the anal sphincter, longitudinally cut and flatten out the black conduit of the rectum, then the colon . . . the caecum, . . . with your dressmaker's scissors opening the leg of an old pair of trousers, . . . bring to light the supposed inside of the small intestine, the jejunum, the ileon, the duodenum, or . . . undo the mouth at its corners, pull up the tongue to its distant root and split it, spread the bat's-wings of the palate and its damp basements, open the tracheia and make of it the skeleton of a boat under construction; armed with scalpels and . . . tweezers, dismantle and lay out the bundles and bodies of the encephalum; and then the whole network of veins and arteries . . . extract the great muscles, the great dorsal nets, spread them like smooth sleeping dolphins. (Lyotard, 1993, 1)

For Lyotard, who would probably see himself as performing the role of libidinal economist rather than forensic pathologist or dermal diagnostician, the purpose of this imaginary exercise is not to strip away the surface in order to discover the truth that lies buried in the deep. Rather, Lyotard develops the notion of the libidinal economy as a critique of what might be called a representational economy that assumes an indexical relation between representation and reality, and that disavows affectivity as a generative process that makes meaning possible and simultaneously exceeds or undermines it. For Lyotard the libidinal zone in the body is the skin and "the mucous orifices which prolong it inwards" (Lingis, 1983b, 27). The skin, as Lyotard sees it, is a surface with invaginations rather than holes. Consequently, were we to dissect the body, as the previously mentioned quotation suggested, what we would find is "a vast skin with crannies, where slits are not entries, wounds, gashes or breaches, but the same surface carrying on after a pocket-shaped detour, a front folded back almost against itself" (Lyotard, 1993, 21–22). What this suggests, then, is that the imaginary dissection proposed above is not a means to an end since insofar as what appears to be depth supporting surface turns out to be nothing more than another surface, and thus there can be no end point at which lies the pot of gold or truth. Indeed, if we are to avoid falling back on the model of subjectivity, textuality, and ethics to which both dermal diagnosticians and their counter-cultural antagonists succumb, we must explore more complex models of the entanglements that (trans)form the body-subject, of which Lyotard provides one such example.

In this chapter I have critically examined what could be called a representational economy of the body that informs various analyses of the subject in/of tattooing. An alternative to this model has been briefly gestured toward in Lyotard's notion of the libidinal economy, which will be discussed in more depth in Chapter Five. In the following chapter I will turn to the work of Foucault, who in *The History of Sexuality Volume One,* calls for a different economy of bodies and pleasures as a counter attack against what he calls a hermeneutics of desire, as this would seem to offer a self-conscious attempt to rethink the body-subject beyond the dichotomies of inside/outside, self/other, expression/reception, and so on. More importantly, in *The History of Sexuality Volume One,* in particular, Foucault formulates an analysis of the ways in which systems of power/knowledge inscribe the body-subject and force it to emit signs that are then read (normatively) as the truth of the subject, rather than as social fictions, or truth-effects of power/knowledge.

NOTES

1. The research undertaken by Yamomoto et al. is based on a study of male subjects, and makes no mention of gender. Thus whether "man" in this case is assumed to be generic is somewhat unclear, although I would suggest that this is the case.

2. This raises a problem for a generic analysis of the tattooed subject. Whilst it might be possible to suppose that the tattooed woman may also be immature and impulsive, psychopathic, and have a criminal record, the claim that the tattoo signifies a desire to be more "masculine" than one's fellows implies that tattooing and femininity are mutually exclusive since, in this analysis at least, tattoos are unquestioningly associated with strength, the ability to endure pain, violence, and so on, as "masculine" characteristics.

3. Youniss (1959) also subscribes to this idea, claiming that a single tattoo may be the result of an impulsive decision, possibly made under the influence of alcohol or peer-group pressure, whereas the repetition of such a decision, irrespective of the circumstances, is of diagnostic relevance since it signifies an unhealthy compulsion.

4. Parry (1933) draws on psychoanalytic theory in order to explain the sexual significance of tattooing. He argues that tattoos in women can be said to signify sexual experience ("nice girls" don't get tattooed!); that there is a striking similarity in the emotional reactions of young men and women to their first tattooing and their initial sexual experience; that the act of tattooing is sexually symbolic since the needle, like the penis, introduces fluid into a cavity, and that the tattooist is something of a sadistic aggressor, whilst the person tattooed is a passive masochistic recipient; that tattooing, when both parties involved are men, may easily take on a homosexual aspect; and that pederasts are more likely to be tattooed on their sexual organs for exhibitionist and auto-erotic reasons. Parry's "findings" are still commonly drawn on to substantiate similar theses. One example is Samuel Steward's *Bad Boys and Tough Tattoos* (1990) in which the author, gathering information for Kinsey, suggests that the most common motives for tattooing are sexual. Of the twenty-nine motives he identifies, twenty-four involve or are connected with what he sees as sexuality.

5. Whilst on one level I find this categorization of desire/motivation interesting, I would nevertheless argue that in fact categories 1, 2, 3, and 4 are all aspects of category 5. This is evident if we consider the definition of the establishment of identity used by Edgerton and Dingman as "those efforts that people make to define and appraise themselves. . . . It is inextricably bound to the judgements of others and the efforts, by the self, to affect the judgements of those others" (Edgerton and Dingman, 1963, 144).

6. The positing of a fourth category of tattoos (idiosyncratic) that have significance for the self alone is a telling example of the assumption embraced by the theorists discussed thus far that the tattoo, as a form of nonverbal communication contains a particular symbolic meaning that is ascertainable or decipherable by others. And further, that when this is seemingly not the case, it signifies severe antisocial tendencies. Thus the assumption is that texts are a reflection of their author's subjectivity, and that both text and subject/author are interpretable by, or transparent to, others. As this book develops I will demonstrate the limitation of such a model of identity, and of textuality. For the moment suffice it to say that one example of the disjunction between symbol and perceived meaning can be found in the increasing preponderance of "tribal" tattooing, which in the majority of cases bears little, or no, relation to the subject's cultural ancestry.

7. I would argue that such characteristics are in fact applicable to all people to varying degrees at different times in their lives, and in different social contexts.

8. At no point in the article do Edgerton and Dingman define what they mean by "mentally retarded".

9. This distinction between mildly and severely retarded seems to foreshadow a similar distinction made by Norman Goldstein (1979) in an article that outlines the findings of a study undertaken by the author in 1964. The distinction posited by Goldstein is between "mental illness" and "character disorder". The latter, to quote the American Psychiatric Association, "is manifested by a life-long pattern of action or behaviour rather than by mental or emotional symptoms" (Goldstein, 1979, 885). The behaviour discussed as symptomatic of such a disorder is rebelliousness, immaturity, criminal tendencies, and so on. In other words, the implication is that character disorder is somehow more threatening to the body politic than mental illness since it is less easily treatable, and seemingly less blameless.

10. For a critical analysis of the role of the researcher, see Elizabeth Seaton (1987); Valerie Walkerdine (1986); and Stuart Marshall (1990).

11. It is telling that of the many examples of psychiatric approaches to tattooing that I have come across in the course of my research, not one attempts to do this. At most there is a suggestion that such hypotheses may not be simply extendable to the general population. However, at the same time, many of the claims made in these works are unquestioningly accepted as "truths" by society at large.

12. This idea was expounded half a century earlier by Albert Parry in an article entitled "Tattooing among Prostitutes and Perverts" (1933), and also in the previously mentioned book by the same author, which focuses solely on the psycho-sexual significance of tattooing. It is unquestioningly reiterated by the majority of the authors discussed in this chapter.

13. See also Gittleson et al. (1966).

14. See also Hamburger (1966).

15.   There is no consideration here of the high cost of professional tattooing, which denies, or at least makes difficult, the procuration of such by those with low incomes. Moreover, since the legal age limit for being tattooed is eighteen, many young people tattoo themselves and each other with materials that are both cheap and easily accessible.

16.   For example, the chronological mapping of a shift from "aggressive" to "transcendent" themes (e.g., butterflies, winged unicorns, and so on) is coextensive with, or indicative of, a "characterological shift from a combative lifestyle to one of escapism and drug abuse" (Grumet, 1983, 490).

17.   The model of identity and difference that Grumet's work (as an example of medical discourse) relies on allows Grumet to unquestioningly pathologize the other, and further to assume the role of the objective scientist, and thus to ignore the ways in which his position as interpreter functions to reaffirm a sense of himself based on his own normative criteria.

18.   See Foucault (1980b).

19.   For a discussion of masculine status and initiation rites in contemporary American culture, see Samuel M. Steward (1990, 57–59).

20.   The generic use of the term "men" in this quote nicely illustrates Diprose's claim, particularly if we consider the assumed association between masculinity and tattooing discussed earlier.

21.   For an extended and insightful discussion of Lombroso's work and his position in relation to other schools of criminology, see David G. Horn (1995, 109–28).

22.   See Gina Lombroso-Ferrero (1972).

23.   See for example, David A. Bennahum (1971); M. Baden (1973); Theodore Davidson (1974); Joseph Agris (1977); and Joan Moore (1978). For an interesting deconstructive reading of the racism and classism inherent in humanist accounts of the "deviant" tattooed body, see B. V. Olguín (1997).

24.   Dick Hebdige (1997) develops a similar thesis regarding the link between the construction of delinquency and the construction of "modern youth" as a category of juridical concern.

25.   For a more indepth analysis of this claim, see also "Illegalities and Delinquency" in Michel Foucault (1979, 257–92).

26.   Altruism is generally thought of as a concern for others that is opposed to selfishness. In this sense, altruism is constructed and praised as something of a virtue. But as Nietzsche claims in *The Gay Science*, altruism is far from selfless. Indeed, altruism functions to reaffirm the subject qua subject, or as Nietzsche puts it "the *motives* of this morality stands opposed to its *principle*" (1974, 94). The principle embraced by a common-sense notion of altruism is that the ethical individual should be prepared to sacrifice him or herself for the benefit of the greater good. But what motivates this principle is the promise of moral gratification that the subject will experience in and through self-sacrificial action. Moreover, it is assumed that "one can enter into another's feelings so that, from the outset, the Other is another myself whose interests can be reduced to my own: the starting point of my affect is my ego" (Wyschogrod, 1990, 239). In other words, altruism, in this sense, functions to reaffirm the subject's sense of self rather than simply "sacrificing" it, and at the same time reduces the other to an Economy of the Same—a problem that is discussed further in Chapter 3. For an extended analysis

of what might be called humanist and poststructuralist approaches to the question of altruism, see Wyschogrod (1990).

27.   This is the title of the epilogue to the second (revised) edition of Favazza's *Bodies Under Siege: Self-mutilation and Body Modification in Culture and Psychiatry*, written by Fakir Musafar.

28.   It is interesting to note that whilst Favazza questions the assumed association between body modification and personality disorder, he nevertheless adds the qualification that "as a group such persons [practitioners of body modification] *probably* have increased levels of psychopathology" (Favazza, 1996, 287).

29.   For a critique of what she calls "the rhetoric of choice" and the role this plays in contemporary metaphors of inscription that overlook the material conditions and limits of self-determination, and thus tend to reiterate the problem of universalism and dichotomous logic, see Pippa Brush (1998).

30.   Orphism was an ancient Greek form of religion that influenced the writings of Pythagoras, Empedocles, and Plato. In both *Gorgias* and *Cratylus* Plato describes the wise "who hold that the body is a tomb" as Orphics. Pythagoras, a Greek philosopher, mathematician, and mystic, and the supposed founder of a religious sect, promoted various practices of ritual purity that were adopted by his followers, the Pythagorists, or Akousmatics.

31.   Farrell changed his name to Perry Farrell, which is a play on the word "peripheral", in his punk-identified period, in order to signify his sense of social marginality and his fascination with cultural boundaries. At the same time the name evokes, according to Wojcik, the primitive, the feral, with which Farrell later came to associate. In other words, Farrell's "consciously chosen" name is read as the expression of his true self.

Chapter Two

(Re)Writing Subjectivity: A Different Economy of Bodies and Pleasures?

The *body* of what is strange must not disappear, but its force must be conquered and returned to the master. Both the appropriate and the inappropriate must exist: the clean, hence the dirty; the rich, hence the poor. (Cixous, 1975, 70)

In the previous chapter, I argued that the majority of psychological and criminological attempts to theorize the tattooed body share with the (supposedly) opposed accounts of modern primitivism a number of unquestioned and problematic related assumptions. These include a depth model of the subject that assumes a distinction, and at the same time a causal connection, between interiority and exteriority; a mimetic theory of textuality that embraces a distinction between reality and representation; and an expression-reception model of communication as the intentional expression of a sign designating the thought of an innate I, and the subsequent reception and deciphering of this sign (truth) by the other. Given that these assumptions are apparent to varying degrees in the vast majority of works on tattooing, the question of where to look for alternatives seems daunting to say the least. How can we begin to think (of) the subject in/of tattooing otherwise?

Given the limitations of a representational economy of the body-subject as outlined in the previous chapter, this chapter draws on the work of Michel Foucault in order to begin to elaborate an understanding of the subject as an agent and effect of processes of enculturation, rather than as the *causa sui*, an in-itself, whose relations with others are secondary. I begin with *The History of Sexuality Volume One,* since it is here that Foucault calls for a different economy of bodies and pleasures not founded on a hermeneutical model of the

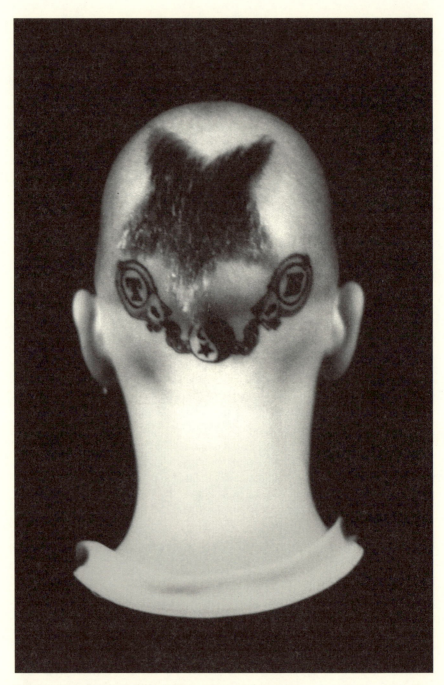

Billy-Joe, 1998. Photo copyright © Amanda James Photography

subject, and provides an analysis of the ways in which the subject is constituted in and through its relations with others, and with what he calls systems of power/knowledge. In *The Use of Pleasure* and *The Care of the Self* (volumes two and three respectively of *The History of Sexuality)*, and in various interviews and articles on sadomasochism, Foucault explores the possibility of the practice of pleasures as a strategic practice of self-(trans)formation that is again not tied to a hermeneutical project. Moreover, he conceptualizes such practices in terms of *ethics* and claims that ethics constitutes a mode of being, a way of relating to the self, and, in turn, to others:

Care for self is ethical in itself, but implies complex relations with others, in the measure where this *ethos* of freedom is also a way of caring for others. . . . *Ethos* implies . . . a relation with others to the extent that care for the self renders one competent to occupy a place in the city, in the community or in interindividual relationships. (Foucault, cited in Smart, 1998, 84)

In effect, then, Foucault provides an alternative configuration of the relation between subjectivity, ethics, and pleasure to that assumed by the theorists discussed in Chapter One. Thus he could be said to potentiate the possibility of moving beyond the limitations of an analysis of the subject in/of tattooing that relies on a representational economy of the body-subject—what Foucault calls a hermeneutics of desire. But perhaps I should state at the outset, that whilst Foucault's analysis of power/knowledge articulates an understanding of subjectivity as constituted in and through relations with others and with a world, the notion of an ethics of self-(trans)formation is problematic when applied to the subject in/of tattooing, as I shall demonstrate. Consequently, Foucault's texts will function here not so much as exegetical truths, but rather as "little toolboxes . . . in order to short-circuit or disqualify systems of power, including . . . the ones [his own] books come out of" (Foucault, cited in Halperin, 1995, 52).

THE SUBJECT IN/OF ETHICS

As is well known, the focus of Foucault's work in *The History of Sexuality,* particularly volume one, is sexuality, and whilst sexuality *per se* is not of primary concern to me in this book, Foucault's analysis, despite its focus, nevertheless provides a useful model of subjectivity, and this is one reason for engaging with it here. In the first volume of *The History of Sexuality*, Foucault describes Western culture since the eighteenth century as increasingly "sex-centric", and illustrates how, through a proliferation of discourses and discursive practices, a "*scientia sexualis*", sexuality, becomes the site of a "hermeneutics of desire". I will further explicate this claim in due course, but for the moment suffice it to say that Foucault is critical of the way in which the notion of sexuality becomes "naturalized", and further, of the assumption that sexuality as the externalization of desire is expressive of the subject's essential self. This shares resonances with my criticism of the tendency—apparent in the theses of the theorists discussed in the previous chapter—to read the bodies, gestures, and actions of the tattooed subject as the external expression of an innate interiority. Subsequently, in volumes two and three of *The History of Sexuality,* Foucault turns his attention to ancient Greek and Greco-Roman culture in order to again consider the conditions and ways in which "human beings 'problematize' what they are, what they do, and the world in which they live" (Foucault, 1987, 10). But here he discovers that rather than being tied to a hermeneutics of desire, the problematization of sexuality, or perhaps more appropriately *aphrodisia,* constituted as a moral domain, is linked to a group of ethical practices that Foucault refers to as "arts of existence". The ancient Greek notions of the ethical subject as an active and creative agent, and the practice of pleasure as a mode of self-(trans)formation, are seemingly identified by Foucault in his later works as attractive alternatives to a hermeneutics of desire. Consequently, there is a sense in which the ethical world of ancient Greece is held to provide important insights for contemporary ethics. This is not to suggest, however, that Foucault's intention is to naively posit the ancient Greek world as a superior past to which we could or should return, or as something that is simply translatable in any wholesale way to the present. But before going on to critically examine these texts in more depth, let me first turn to the work of Rosalyn Diprose in order to foreshadow the Foucauldian understanding of the social construction of subjectivity, the role that ethics plays in the constitution of self-other relations, and the possible structural limitations of self-(trans)formation.

In her book *The Bodies of Women: Ethics, Embodiment, and Sexual Difference*[1], Rosalyn Diprose writes that whilst the concern of ethics is most often thought to be moral principles and judgments, it is nevertheless also to do with location, position, and place. To use her words, "it is about being positioned by, and taking a position in relation to others" (Diprose, 1994, 18). It seems that ethics then concerns one's "dwelling", in the sense of one's habitat or positionality, and one's habitual way of life, which is constituted in relation to the habitat one occupies. Diprose concludes this discussion with the claim that "ethics can be defined as the study and practice of that which constitutes one's [dwelling] or as the problematic of the constitution of one's embodied place in the world" (19). What interests me in the work of Diprose is the sense in which one's ethos is conceptualized both as an *active* mode of maintaining oneself *in relation* to a world (one's habitat), and at the same time as a dramatization of a self that problematizes the material conditions of subjective experience. The implication, then, is that the subject is not a natural given, nor is it autonomous; it does not exist outside of, apart from, or prior to its relation with others, and systems of power/knowledge, but rather is (trans)formed in and through them. Like Foucault, Diprose argues for the necessary rejection of an *a priori* theory of the subject and a universalizing notion of ethics in order for a critical analysis of the relations that currently exist between "different forms of the subject and games of truth, practices of power and so forth" (Foucault, cited in Smart, 1998, 83) to be possible. In emphasising the performative (rather than the essential) character of self-(trans)formation, Diprose could be said to provide us with a critical ontology of the liberal subject and the possibility of moving beyond the limits of a hermeneutics of desire. Drawing on her insights, and the work of Foucault, the aim of this chapter is to develop what the latter calls a "critical ontology" of the subject in/of tattooing.

A critical ontology of ourselves has to be considered not, certainly, as . . . a doctrine, nor even as a permanent body of knowledge that is accumulating; it has to be conceived as an *attitude*, an *ethos*, a philosophical life in which the critique of what we are is at one and the same time the historical analysis of the limits that are imposed on us and an experiment with the possibility of going beyond them. (Foucault, 1991b, 50, my emphasis)

Given this, the work of Foucault and Diprose will be drawn upon to illustrate the ways in which the analyses of the subject in/of tattooing discussed in the previous chapter function in accordance with systems of power/knowledge, and at the same time, to provide a justification for the inclusion of this problematic under the term "ethics".

My fascination with tattooed bodies, my experience(s) of being a tattooed subject and a feminist cultural critic, and my subsequent dissatisfaction with the assumed truth status of the explanations of the tattooed body posited by the theorists discussed in Chapter One are just a few of the more obvious factors that motivate this attempt to rethink the subject in/of tattooing. But whilst it seems a relatively easy task to deconstruct the liberal humanist model of subjectivity, given the veritable stockpile of texts that perform just such a function, the attempt to reconsider the phenomenon of tattooing is considerably less straightforward. As I said, Foucault's call for a different economy of bodies and pleasures not founded on a hermeneutic model of the subject seems to me to offer a potentially fertile starting point for such an endeavour. However, since Foucault gives the reader very few clues as to how such a task could possibly be approached and what it could or would entail, the suggestion remains somewhat enigmatic. Turning to various theorists who have drawn on this particular aspect of Foucault's work in their different projects, it appears, as already stated, that it has most often been associated with the notion of an "aesthetics of self" as discussed in *The Use of Pleasure*, with the polymorphous perversity of the hermaphroditic body, and with comments made by Foucault in various interviews on sadomasochism (particularly in its relation to "queer" praxis) as a strategy for creating pleasure (Halperin, 1995, 86).

In the subsequent sections of this chapter I will outline what I see as being of value to feminist and critical theory in *The History of Sexuality Volume One,* ponder Foucault's readings of the lives of Jouy and Herculine Barbin, consider the notion of an "aesthetics of self" as outlined in *The Use of Pleasure,* and address the comments made by Foucault on sadomasochism, and the ways in which both these aspects of his work have been taken up by others working in the field. The aim of such a task is to evaluate how and to what degree the ethical practices of self-(trans)formation that Foucault elaborates may be useful to an attempt to rework notions of embodied identity, ethics, and pleasure; to strategically reformulate a different economy of bodies and pleasures; and thus, in turn, to rethink the subject in/of tattooing.

THE SUBJECT IN/OF POWER/KNOWLEDGE

It has been claimed that Foucault's *The History of Sexuality Volume One* is one of the most influential texts of cultural criticism to be published in the last twenty years. David Halperin, for example, describes it as "the single most important intellectual source of political inspiration for contemporary AIDS activists" (Halperin, 1995, 15). Let us turn then to the text itself in order to explicate some of the radical insights that have prompted such endorsements.

The History of Sexuality Volume One is not a history in the conventional sense of the word, rather it is a genealogy, a search for "instances of discursive production, . . . of the production of power . . . of the propagation of knowledge" (Foucault, 1980b, 12), which makes possible a "history of the present". Refuting what he calls the "repressive hypothesis", in which sex, as an instinctual drive or force, is believed to have been repressed by oppressive social institutions, Foucault instead claims that in Western culture the deployment of a proliferation of discourses and practices surrounding sex enabled something termed "sexuality" to incarnate the supposed truth of sex and the pleasures associated with it (68). Moreover, he argues that theories of sexual liberation, such as those expounded by Reich, Marcuse, and others, function to reinforce the systems of power that they aim to undermine.

Central to Foucault's critique of the repressive hypothesis is his formulation of power as a multiplicity of force relations that do not emanate from a single source, but rather are "produced from one moment to the next, at every point, or . . . in relation from one point to another" (92–93). Power is not a thing that is identifiable and locatable in a particular time and space, but rather it is a complex strategical situation that is everywhere.

To put it more simply, power is not something that is possessed and exercised by an elite minority to the detriment of those who are denied it. If, as Foucault claims, power is relational, then it is not merely negative or prohibitive (although in particular situations this may be the case), nor does it exist in opposition to freedom. Rather, according to Foucault's thesis, power is also positive and productive. Let us consider for a moment the analyses of the tattooed body posited in Chapter One in light of this claim. It could be argued that those who interpret the tattooed body as a sign of a defective personality oppress the other through a process of objectification that reduces the multiplicity of the other's being to a monodimensional stereotype. Likewise, the model of the tattooed body suggested by counter-cultural theorists, as a signifier of anti-authoritarian disdain for social conventions, could be understood as a reactive process of self-determination, an apocalyptic attempt to assert power over the enemy, the dominant culture. What emerges in both cases is a disturbing vision of the social milieu as battleground, in which the only option is to exercise power to the detriment of others, or become victim of it, to kill or be killed. Whilst I do not wish to overlook the fact that such interpretations delimit the other's freedom, what I want to suggest is that they do not simply function to *repress* the essential heterogeneity of the other, as Juno and Vale and Musafar would have it, but rather they constitute both self and other in culturally and historically specific ways.

As has been said, for Foucault, sexuality is a particularly privileged locus of the operations of power. In *The History of Sexuality Volume One* Foucault claims that toward the beginning of the eighteenth century there emerged a political, economic, and technical incitement to discuss sex. He goes on to illustrate how the belief that domination functions through prohibition and that truth, and therefore liberation, are external to power has aided and abetted techniques of self-formation that operate in conjunction with disciplinary power. One of the strengths of *The History of Sexuality Volume One,* for me at least, lies in Foucault's rigorous analysis of the proliferation of systems of classification of sex-desire that produces individuals, what he calls a *scientia sexualis*. In the chapter of the same name he outlines various ways in which rituals of confession and self-examination come to be constituted in scientific terms. These include a clinical codification of the inducement to speak; the belief that sex is the cause of anything and everything and that since it is intrinsically latent it must be extracted, if necessary, by force; and the necessity, for the confession to reach completion, of an authority who deciphers in order to "judge, punish, forgive, console and reconcile". The combination of such discourses and practices define sex as an extremely pathological field and confession as therapeutic (65–67). Foucault is of the opinion that the technologies of confession and self-decipherment are aspects of a particular form of self-formation that he calls a hermeneutics of desire. He describes how, through the process of self-examination as "an infinite extracting from the depths of oneself" (59), it is supposed that one comes to know the truth of oneself. The subject who knows him- or herself is at the same time able, or, perhaps more importantly, obliged, to make pronouncements concerning him- or herself, and this is what Foucault has in mind when he speaks of confession as being "at the heart of the procedures of individualization" (59). Moreover, according to Foucault, the obligation to confess has been embodied or normalized to such an extent that we no longer see it as an effect of a power that circumscribes us. In fact, the opposite is the case. Insofar as we experience subjectivity as autonomous and internal we presume that self-expression has been repressed by oppressive social systems and that self-confession is therefore liberatory (60). Confession then, Foucault argues, is a truth-effect of power, rather than a therapeutic practice of freedom, and thus it is a normalizing mode of self-formation in which individual bodies are constituted as both objects and instruments of power.

Perhaps even more importantly, Foucault's analysis demonstrates that such technologies create a disjunction between self-knowledge and the interpretation of that knowledge by others, since the processes of self-examination, confession, and interpretation take place within a network of power relations that function to identify, classify, and evaluate individuals in accordance with normative criteria. The confession, as Foucault describes it, is a structurally assymetrical ritual that presupposes the presence or virtual presence of an authority figure who interprets and evaluates in order to "judge, punish, forgive, console, and reconcile" (61–62).

This claim is exemplified by the disjunction between the understanding of the tattooed body posited by those who promote such practices and those who interpret them as signifiers of an essential personality disorder or an innate tendency toward crime. As we saw in the previous chapter, the letters H-A-T-E tattooed on the fingers *could* signify an aggressive attitude toward others, or they *could* indicate that the tattooed subject believes in or wishes to experience "happiness all through eternity". Either way, the tattoo is read as a (virtual) confession by the authority who requires the confession. As Foucault says, the body is made to "emit signs", and the subjectivity of the person bearing these marks is judged in accordance with the normative criteria that the one who interprets them assumes. This is not to suggest that one interpretation is correct and the other erroneous, or that one discourse is subservient to power whilst the other somehow escapes it. Rather, it demonstrates that insofar as identity and social values are (re)produced through a differentiation between the self and the other, subjectivity is always already inter-relational. Through a process of interpretation and evaluation, the one who is seen to "confess" (whether literally or virtually) is constituted through being positioned and taking a position in relation to others, and is validated or invalidated, rewarded or condemned, in accordance with normative values or "universal truths". Thus whilst the production of (self)knowledge is not liberating, it nevertheless (trans)forms the body. Likewise, as Rosalyn Diprose's work on ethics and embodiment shows, the agent "of interpretation reaffirms him- or herself against the discourse of the other . . . by re-constituting the body of the other according to normative criteria assumed by the self" (Diprose, 1987, 96), a point that she claims Foucault does not make explicit, and that I will return to in the following section. Meanwhile, suffice it to say that what my reading of Foucault's analysis of the techniques of self-decipherment, confession, and interpretation illustrates is that the meaning and value of identity and difference is constituted within, and as an effect of, the field of social relations and systems of power-knowledge.

Foucault's analytics of bio-power demonstrates the inadequacy of a repressive hypothesis founded on a theory of juridico-discursive power by bringing to light the ways in which the notion of liberation through the supposedly unencumbered expression of the truth of oneself is a product of the systems of power that it is formulated to attack. It is not, he argues, that knowledge, truth, identity, desire, and pleasure are outside of, prior to, controlled, or repressed by systems of power, but rather that they are truth-effects of power. Consequently, Foucault concludes that all attempts to liberate desire are politically bankrupt since "the law is what constitutes . . . desire . . . [w]here there is desire the power relation is already present" (Foucault, 1980b, 81). If we cast our minds back for a moment to the notion of the subject assumed by those who associate themselves with modern primitivism (as discussed in Chapter One), we find that not only do these theorists embrace a notion of power as repressive, but in doing so they reinforce the truth-effects of power by promoting a form of liberation through the expression of an essential self and/or desire. According to Juno and Vale, modern primitivism is evidence of the fact that individuals *are* changing the world by changing the one thing that they do have power over, namely, their own bodies. These ritual changes generate the expression of (previously unknown) latent desires and obsessions and free up the "creative essence". Juno and Vale conclude, then, that modern primitive practices, which are exemplificatory of sensual experience more generally, free us from social restraints by awakening what has, through repression, been rendered dormant. And this "free" expression of the unfettered imagination is what finally makes possible the creation of "complete" human beings who are no longer inhibited by the pervasive malaise of Western modernity.

What we witness in Juno and Vale's vision of normative contemporary culture is an image of life as mortal combat in which the warrior-like individual must continuously struggle for survival in an alien and alienating world that is understood as existing in complete and threatening opposition to the individual. This focus on freedom, on an essential or pre-social self, and on the "unfettered imagination" and the political importance of its expression, relies on uncritical assumptions about the self that do not scrutinize its origins or relation to a context.

So, if as Foucault demonstrates, attempts to liberate a true and essential self are theoretically and politically misguided, what form could political praxis possibly take? Foucault suggests that "the rallying point for the counter-attack against the deployment of sexuality ought not to be sex-desire, but bodies and pleasures" (Foucault, 1980b, 157), a claim I will examine in more depth in due course. But, as Foucault himself poignantly observes, the West has been fostering for several centuries a "pleasure of analysis":

a pleasure in the truth of pleasure, a pleasure of knowing that truth, of discovering and exposing it, the fascination of seeing it and telling it, of captivating and capturing others by it, of confiding it in secret, or luring it out in the open—the specific pleasure of the true discourse on pleasure. (71)

This being the case, how then can one begin to imagine a different economy of bodies and pleasures, and simultaneously resist recourse to the pleasurable truth-effects of the truth of pleasure?

RESISTANCE

Insofar as Foucault's analysis of subjectivity undermines traditional distinctions between self and other, power and powerlessness, nature and culture, truth and ideology, mind and body, and so on, resistance cannot simply consist, as for example Juno and Vale would have it, of expressing or freeing up an essential self that those in power have attempted to repress. For those for whom political praxis consists of consciousness raising or the overthrowing of patriarchy, the bourgeois, capitalism, and so on, Foucault's suggestion that power is immanent in every sort of social relation is seen as something like a monolithic determinism that courts despair. However, Foucault consistently argues that where there is power there is resistance since resistance is never external to power. Indeed, the "relational character of power relationships . . . *depends* on a multiplicity of points of resistance: these play the role of adversary, target, support, or handle in power relations" (Foucault, 1980b, 95, my emphasis). Consequently a Foucauldian model of political praxis would be characterized by a notion of resistance rather than liberation since, first, there is no "outside" of power, and, second, the notion of pure and/or universal truths is a truth-effect of systems of power/knowledge.

In his explication of resistance, Foucault argues that since it is in and through discourse that power and knowledge are conjoined, it is crucial not to conceive of a division between accepted and excluded discourses, those subservient to power and those at war against it. Rather, discourses generally are understood as "both an instrument and an effect of power, but also a hindrance, a stumbling block, a point of resistance and a starting point for an opposing strategy" (101). Thus it seems that resistance, employed as a tool with which to short-circuit systems of power, should not, or at least need not, consist of the affirmation or repudiation of truth. Alternatively, resistance should consist of a strategic analysis of discourses and discursive practices since it is the "tactical polyvalence" of discourses that makes possible the formation of what Foucault calls "reverse discourse". This consists of a tactical (re)creation of normalizing discourses from a position interior to them. To resist then is, as David Halperin points out, not simply a negation, but also a creative process (Halperin, 1995, 61).

The History of Sexuality Volume One, as an analytics of the discourses and discursive practices informing sexuality, exemplifies Foucault's notion of resistance insofar as it enables the denaturalization, problematizion, and politicization of sexuality, subjectivity, truth, and power/knowledge, and thereby opens up possibilities for intervention and social change. My aim in this book, then, is Foucauldian in the sense that it is concerned with analysing the ways in which the experiences, or marking and being marked, are inextricably bound up with one's ethos, with one's position, location, and place in relation to the social apparatuses of power/knowledge that constitute identity and difference. Consequently, this project, unlike those undertaken by the theorists discussed in Chapter One, will neither attempt to celebrate as liberatory, or denigrate as aberrant, the subject in/of tattooing.

Whilst I am decidedly aware of what my project does *not* involve, namely, a quest to discover the truth of the subject in/of tattooing and pleasure, I nevertheless feel a sense of foreboding at being faced with the enigmatic task proposed by Foucault of imagining a different economy of bodies and pleasures. First, what puzzles me is the distinction Foucault makes between pleasure and desire as exemplified in the following quote from a somewhat disquieting interview in a 1981 edition of *Mec* magazine.

I [Foucault] am advancing this term [pleasure] because it seems to me that it escapes the medical and naturalistic connotations inherent in the notion of desire. That term has been used as a tool . . . a calibration in terms of normality. Tell me what your desire is and I will tell you who you are, whether you are normal or not, and then I can qualify or disqualify your desire. The term pleasure on the other hand is virgin territory, almost devoid of meaning. There is no pathology of pleasure, no "abnormal" pleasure. It is an event "outside of the subject" or on the edge of the subject, within something that is neither body nor soul, which is neither inside nor outside, in short a notion which is neither ascribed nor ascribable. (Foucault, cited in Macey, 1994, 365)

Whilst I agree with Foucault's claim that the notion of desire has by and large, through the clinical apparatuses of power/knowledge, been understood to be the expression of individual identity or interiority, I nevertheless remain unconvinced that pleasure is a "virgin territory, almost devoid of meaning". The appearance of sociological and psychological texts such as, for example, Walsh and Rosen's *Self-Mutilation: Theory, Research and Treatment* (1988), would suggest that what counts as (the practice of) pleasure for some individuals will always already have been interpreted as a sign of social or psychophysical aberration by others. And as Foucault's work on confession demonstrates, interpretation takes place within a network of power relations that functions to identify, classify, and evaluate individuals in accordance with normative criteria.

Thus the disjunction between, for example, an individual's experiences of tattooing and the unquestioned interpretation of such practices by others as self-mutilation will transform the lived body and the potential for pleasures and pains of both parties. As anyone who has ever explicitly marked his or her body will know only too well, simply displaying wounds, scars, or tattoos can, and will, be grounds for interpretation by others[2]. Thus the potential for pleasures and pain will always be relative to one's embodied ethos. Perhaps the all important question here then, is how—considering that the pleasurable truth-effects of the truth of pleasure function to reaffirm the one who interprets by reconstituting his or her lived body in accordance with the normative criteria he or she assumes—can this "master of truth" be persuaded to think difference differently?

If one concedes, along with Foucault, that there is no "outside" of systems of power/knowledge and that the pleasure of interpretation consists in the reaffirmation of identity and difference, then it is hard to imagine how pleasure could remain unascribed or unascribable, if in fact this ever was the case. Since the above example of marking/self-mutilation suggests otherwise, I would argue that Foucault's statement that "the law is what constitutes . . . desire. . . . Where there is desire the power relation is already present" (Foucault, 1980b, 81) could just as logically read "the law is what constitutes pleasures. Where there is pleasure the power relation is already present". And if so, wouldn't the distinction that Foucault makes between pleasure and desire turn out to be no distinction at all? And so I find myself faced with something of a conundrum. Is Foucault implying that it may be possible to conceptualize or experience pleasure without recourse to systems of power/knowledge or universalizing truths? I would think not, for to do so would surely be to imply that bodies and pleasures exist somehow prior to, or outside of, deployments of power, which would inevitably lead us back to a repressive hypothesis with the attendant call for liberation.

I want to suggest that if we look more closely at *The History of Sexuality Volume One* we may find that there is something of a contradiction at work in Foucault's thesis. On the one hand, Foucault's critique of the repressive hypothesis and his analysis of the ways in which "deployments of power are directly connected to the body—to bodies, functions, physiological processes, sensations and pleasures" (151–52) suggests that the relation between power, identity, sexuality, pleasures, and so on is never ontologically distinct. On the other hand, in a perhaps telling change of genre, Foucault dons the cap of raconteur and tells the tragic tale of Jouy, a "simple-minded" nineteenth-century labourer whose illicit pleasures resulted in his lifelong incarceration in the sanatorium at Mareville.

What is of interest to me here is not so much the record of Jouy's "undoing", but the didactic mode of Foucault's fable with its consequent (implied) moral. What is significant about this story for Foucault is the fact that "these inconsequential bucolic pleasures" became, at a particular historical moment, not only the subject of scorn, but more particularly the object of legal action, clinical inquiry, and intervention, and "an entire theoretical elaboration" (31). With a flourish of pathos Foucault concludes his tale thus: "So it was that our society—and it was doubtless the first in history to take such measures— assembled around these timeless *gestures*, these barely *furtive pleasures* between simple minded adults and alert children, a whole machinery for speechifying, analyzing and investigating" (32, my emphasis).

The significance, it seems to me, of Foucault's telling of Jouy's story is that it provides a poignant opportunity to read Foucault against himself. Whilst it may be appropriate to claim that this particular point in history marks the beginnings of a proliferation of medical and/or psychiatric normalizing discourses and procedures, I want to suggest that implicit in this tale of woe is a lamenting of the loss of "bucolic" and/or innocent pleasures that supposedly exist(ed) prior to the imposition of regulative strategies[3]. The implied distinction between nature and culture embraced here is interesting, and not something one would expect to stumble upon in the work of Foucault. Let me refer back for a moment to the works of Lombroso and Loos (as discussed in Chapter One), and their use of such a distinction, in order to demonstrate its potential dangers. As I said earlier, the tattooed body is often read as a sign of (at least potential) criminality. In his anthropometrical study of criminals, Lombroso argues that in his or her body and conduct the criminal is an atavism—a re-emergence of the historical and evolutionary past in the present. Tattoos are just one example amongst many that Lombroso gives of signs of less evolved forms of life. In other words, the tattooed subject and the criminal (and the terms are interchangeable) are structurally linked to the savage, to nature, to that which is opposed to, and thus threatens, civilized culture. Similarly, Loos proposes a connection between tattooing (as a form of ornamentation), atavistic "nature", and crime when he states that "[t]he modern man who tattoos himself is a criminal or a degenerate. There are prisons where eighty percent of the inmates bear tattoos. Those who are tattooed but are not imprisoned are latent criminals or degenerate aristocrats" (Loos, 1908, 100). Loos concludes his argument with the claim that "the evolution of culture is synonymous with the removal of ornament from objects of daily use" (100). In effect, then, nature functions in both these texts as a degenerate or uncivilized state that is not only opposed to culture, but posits an inherent threat to it, and thus must be, at all times, kept at bay. Given this, it seems that "bucolic pleasures" are anything but "inconsequential". Further, as Foucault himself has demonstrated throughout his writings, such binary oppositions are truth-effects of power/knowledge.

This somewhat disturbing uncritical romanticization of rustic pleasures between "simple minded adults and alert children", combined with other such examples, has led to accusations of an "unacknowledged emancipatory ideal" and an "implicit pastoral impulse" in Foucault's work by Judith Butler and Leo

Bersani respectively (Butler, 1990, 94; Bersani, 1995b, 255). However, since such claims are made in connection with other aspects of Foucault's work, namely, his analysis of the journals of Herculine Barbin and his discussion of sadomasochism as a form of queer praxis, I will return to them in due course.

The questions and criticisms that have arisen in this section, and that I would like to keep in mind as this chapter progresses, are as follows: How valid is Foucault's distinction between desire as constituted by the law and pleasure as virgin territory, a notion that is neither ascribed nor ascribable? What does such a distinction imply, and what purpose does it serve? Does such a distinction and its ensuing implications fit comfortably with Foucault's analysis of power/knowledge, his critique of the repressive hypothesis, and his understanding of self-examination, confession, and evaluation as outlined in my reading of *The History of Sexuality Volume One*? Does this distinction provide us with a means of moving beyond the limitations of the analyses of the subject in/of tattooing outlined thus far or does it tend to reiterate them?

FOUCAULT'S BARBIN: CRITICAL ONTOLOGY OR ROMANTIC EULOGY?

In this section I want to examine Foucault's introduction to the journal of the nineteenth-century French hermaphrodite Herculine Barbin in order to explore the accusation made by Butler and others that Foucault assumes the existence of a pre-inscriptive body, and implies a notion of pleasure as precultural[4]. My aim in doing so is to examine in more depth some of the problems with Foucault's work identified earlier, and also to make way for those that will become apparent in my consideration of Foucault's account of an aesthetics of existence.

Since in *Gender Trouble,* Butler provides a more than adequate analysis of *Herculine Barbin, Being the Recently Discovered Memoirs of a Nineteenth Century French Hermaphrodite*, which includes Herculine's own journals, an introduction by Foucault, and medical documentation concerning her hermaphroditic designation, it seems unnecessary for me to reiterate such a task here. Butler begins her analysis by articulating her dis-ease with Foucault's description of Barbin's "world of pleasures" as the "happy limbo of a non identity" (Foucault, 1980a, xiii), a world in which the categories of sex and identity no longer seem constitutive or delimiting. As Butler points out, and as my explication of the themes of *The History of Sexuality Volume One* shows, such a world can only be the figment of an optimistic (and culturally and historically specific) imagination. For if sexuality and subjectivity are truth-effects of systems of power/knowledge, and there is no pure "outside" of these systems, then although identity may be fluid or ambiguous, nonidentity is nevertheless an impossible—albeit culturally desirable—state. Butler suggests, and I agree, that perhaps the reason for this puzzling contradiction on Foucault's behalf can be found in his (problematic) understanding of sexuality as an inevitably regulatory category, the abolition of which will result in a proliferation of bodies and pleasures not founded on relations of cause and effect. This explanation seems credible given Foucault's claim in *Le Gai Savoir* that

there is an entire biologism of sexuality and therefore an entire hold over it by doctors and psychologists—in short, by the agencies of normalization . . . It is not enough to liberate sexuality; we also have to liberate ourselves . . . from the very notion of sexuality. (Foucault, 1988, 31)

The call Foucault makes is for a notion of the subject of sex and pleasures that is no longer understood in terms of the hermeneutical project. Rather, "one"[5] will exist in a world in which, to quote Foucault, "grins hung [*sic*] about without the cat" (Foucault, 1980a, xiii).

However, as Butler's reading of Herculine's journals demonstrates, her life, prior to her suicide, was far from the happy limbo Foucault may have imagined it to be. In fact, Butler translates Herculine's condition as a "metaphysical homelessness" (Butler, 1990, 97). This is an interesting description, and one that I think may be worth dwelling on for a moment. Earlier on in this chapter, I made the claim, following Diprose, that one's *dwelling* or *ethos* is an active mode of maintaining oneself in relation to others and to a world, and that moreover, the potential for pleasures and pains will always be relative to one's embodied ethos. This being the case, what Butler's description seems to suggest is that whilst Herculine was a product of his/her particular historical and social environment, she/he nevertheless experienced profound feelings of alienation in relation to herself/himself, to others, and to the various habitats which she/he occupied. Far from existing then, in a happy limbo outside of or beyond systems of categorization, her/his identity is at once constructed and condemned by these systems, in much the same way as is the tattooed subject in/of criminological and psychological discourses. The material effects of her/his ambiguous embodiment were not, as Foucault may have imagined, simply the occasion for an uncontaminated proliferation of multitudinous pleasures. Again it seems we are compelled to ask whether Foucault posits, at least implicitly, a multiplicity of pleasures that is before or beyond the law. Butler's reply would be to the affirmative, and whilst I agree with her, I will let the question of why Foucault makes such a problematic distinction unfold as this chapter progresses.

The point I want to stress here is that even though Herculine's sex(uality) and identity do not easily conform to a female/male, heterosexual/homosexual dichotomy, they are nevertheless not simply outside or beyond the law, but rather are a concrete example of the ambivalent production of the law. As Butler puts it,

Herculine is "outside" the law, but the law maintains this outside within itself. In effect, s/he embodies the law, not as an entitled subject, but as an enacted testimony of the law's uncanny capacity to produce only those rebellions that it can guarantee will . . . defeat themselves and those subjects who, utterly subjected, have no choice but to reiterate the law of their genesis. (106)

Such a claim is concomitant with my analysis of the construction of the delinquent as both an object of judicial discourses and discursive practices, and as a necessary accomplice whose being justifies the law's existence.

What this discussion of both Foucault's and Butler's examinations of the figure of Barbin illustrates is the inevitable limitations on the free play of categories of sex, identity, and hence pleasures, and it again brings to the fore the question of how one is to begin to imagine a new economy of bodies and pleasures. It seems Foucault's analysis of Barbin offers us no alternative framework with which to begin such a task since the implications of his analysis are that his text functions as something closer to a romantic eulogy than a critical ontology. What I have identified as a problematic tendency in Foucault's discussions of both Jouy and Herculine—his positing some kind of disembodied pleasure prior to, outside of, or beyond the law—also has repercussions for his notion of an aesthetics of existence. The following section of this chapter will consider Foucault's analysis of the relation of the self to itself and the subsequent practices of self-(trans)formation in light of the problems raised thus far.

ETHICAL SELF-(TRANS)FORMATION

As many other commentators have noted, it is possible to map numerous shifts of focus in Foucault's work, from *Madness and Civilization* (1961) through to his final works on technologies of the self prior to his death in 1984[6]. Whilst the responses to these transitions are varied, they nevertheless all seem to agree that *The Use of Pleasure* marks a profound shift in emphasis, and at the same time involves a reworking of many of the major themes found in Foucault's earlier texts. For Clare O'Farrell, for example, this shift is a positive one, a "return to the limits", and a departure from the sombre views of *The History of Sexuality Volume One*, which she describes as "the increasingly sterile *huis clos* of a frozen and predetermined confrontation between power, and its mirror underside, resistance" (O'Farrell, 1989, 118–19). Rainer Rochlitz, on the other hand, is less impressed by this transition, and suggests that Foucault's unconvincing explanation of his change in subject may in fact be indicative of an inherent contradiction or dilemma in his thinking. Like Rochlitz, who notes that "the theory of bio-power disappears [in *The Use of Pleasure* and *The Care of the Self*] in favour of the exemplary management of one's personal existence" (Rochlitz, 1992, 251), Rosalyn Diprose argues that "what is of value to feminism in . . . *The History of Sexuality Volume One* is obscured by Foucault's account of Greek sexual ethics in *The Use of Pleasure*" (Diprose, 1987, 102). I will return to these comments in due course, but for the time being, suffice it to say, there is obviously some contention amongst critics as to the political or ethical exigency of Foucault's later works.

Earlier in this chapter, I outlined, borrowing from Diprose, a tripartite model of ethics. Whilst these component aspects are inextricably bound up with one another, it may be useful, for heuristic purposes, to list them separately here. They are, first, the study and practice of that which constitutes one's dwelling; second, the problematization of one's embodied ethos; and third, the creation of alternative possibilities for being. The important point to remember is that all three aspects of ethics function in relation to others and to a world. For example, one's habitual way of life is constituted on a molecular level through the formation of what Merleau-Ponty[7] calls a "corporeal schema". The corporeal schema is a set of habits, gestures, and conducts formed over time and in relation to others, through a process of mimesis. According to this model, the body is not so much an appendage to the self, or a vehicle directed by consciousness, but rather is the very fabric of the self, the locus of one's (embodied) ethos. Likewise, since the body is only a body insofar as it is in situation, the calling into question of one's embodied ethos, and the creation of alternative possibilities for being, is always contextual. As the discussion of Barbin demonstrated, the fact that one's identity and one's capacities are always relative to one's embodied ethos places inevitable limitations on the potential for being otherwise. This is not to revert to some sort of determinism that allows for no possibility of change. Rather, it is to emphasise that if ethics is to have political import it must engage critically not only with the systems that (in)form it, but perhaps, more importantly, with the fruits of its own labour if it is not to fall into the trap of reinforcing that which it is intended to displace.

Foucault's aim in *The Use of Pleasure* is to illustrate how, in classical antiquity, sexual behaviours and sexual pleasures were problematized through transformative practices of the self. These practices, pleasures, and the ways in which they were problematized are referred to as an aesthetics of existence. Both the problematization of *aphrodisia* and the technologies of self-(trans)formation were undertaken, Foucault goes on to show, in relation to morality. But morality, in the sense Foucault uses it, is never simply strict adherence to a unified and all encompassing, prescriptive moral code. Morality also refers to the various modes of behaviour of individuals (practices of self-(trans)formation) in relation to the ethos of the social body of which they are both agents and effects. This latter description could be said to be synonymous with my understanding of ethics as posited throughout this chapter. However, the above-mentioned definitions of morality are by no means mutually exclusive. Inasmuch as one's dwelling as an active mode of self-maintenance/(trans)formation always takes place in relation to others and to a world, one's conduct is always relative to moral codes, whether these codes take the form of explicit juridical rules, the contravening of which results in punishment or incarceration and so on, or are relatively heterogeneous and rudimentary. Interestingly, Foucault is drawn to what he calls "ethic-oriented" moralities rather than "code-oriented" moralities, and as a result, the emphasis of *The Use of Pleasure* is "on the forms of relations with the self, on the methods and techniques by which [the individual] works them out, on the exercises by which he [*sic*] makes of himself an object to be known, and on the practices that enable him to transform his own mode of being" (30).

Foucault begins by identifying what he sees as four aspects of an aesthetics of existence. These include, first, *the determination of the ethical substance*, or that aspect of the self presumed appropriate as prime material for ethical practice, such as desires, emotions and so on; second, *the mode of subjection*, or manner in which the individual establishes his or her relation to codes and mores, whether through a sense of obligation or a commitment to a particular group and the ideals it represents; third, the *elaboration of ethical work* that one performs on oneself in order to (trans)form oneself as an ethical subject in relation to one's habitat; and fourth, the *telos*, or the aims and accomplishments toward which one's actions tend.

Foucault's fascination with ancient Greek culture seems to stem from his dissatisfaction with two factors of subjectivity, as constituted by the Christian West. The first of these is the hermeneutics of the self, whereby one's desires and actions are thought to be the external manifestation of one's integral interiority. Second, and related to the first point, is the universalising tendency that Foucault argues is inherent in the notion of morality stressed by the Christian church and pastoral ministry. Consequently, Foucault attempts to demonstrate that in ancient Greek culture, the problematization of *aphrodisia*, and thus of identity, was not founded on an authoritarian, universalizing, moral system. This is not to suggest that Foucault explicitly sets up a dichotomy of good and bad, or right and wrong, ways of being. Rather, he claims that the aim of juxtaposing the ways in which the problematization of *aphrodisia* and sexuality is constituted as a moral domain in different cultural contexts is to bring to light the dangers inherent in ethical systems, and simultaneously to open up new possibilities for ethical being. In other words, Foucault's aim is to provide a critical ontology of the ways in which subjectivity is (historically) constructed, and experiment with the possibility of moving beyond the limitations inherent in such constructions. The question is, how successful is Foucault's project? Can his work on the use of pleasure as an ethical practice of self-(trans)formation be said to provide a starting point from which to begin to imagine a new economy of bodies and pleasures not founded on a (hermeneutical) theorization of sex-desire? What would it mean to conceive of tattooing as an ethical practice of self-(trans)formation and not simply the expression of an inner self?

Foucault suggests that rather than seeing Christian morality as being pre-formed in antiquity, it is perhaps more pertinent to imagine instead that early on in moral thought "a quadri-thematics formed around and apropos of the life of the body, the institution of marriage, relations between men and the existence of wisdom" (23), and that despite numerous and varied permutations, this thematics maintained some kind of constancy over time. What this quadri-thematics makes apparent is the socially constructed character of identity, namely, that identity is embodied, that it is relative to others, that the sexed bodies of these others are also relative, and that identity is inextricably bound to the social body one inhabits. In this section, I will critically explore the consequent material conditions of this cultural ethos whose understanding of identity was (supposedly) neither a hermeneutical nor a universalizing one, but was nevertheless, I would argue, no less inequitable or exclusory. I shall begin with a quote from Foucault that I find both puzzling and disturbing, perhaps even telling. In setting out the differences between what he sees as code-oriented moralities of Christianity and ethic-oriented moralities of ancient Greek culture—a distinction that has resonances with that posited between desire and pleasure as discussed earlier—Foucault makes the following statement in favour of the latter: "[t]his is doubtless one of the most remarkable aspects of [ancient Greek] moral reflection: it did not try to define a field of conduct and a domain of valid rules . . . for the two sexes in common" (22).

Thus Foucault happily concludes that the Greek system was not a universalizing moral system[8]. But if we continue on with his description of the ancient Greek ethical system what becomes apparent is a problem to which Foucault is either oblivious or about which he is not largely concerned.

[I]t was an elaboration of masculine conduct carried out from the viewpoint of men in order to give form to their behaviour. . . . It spoke to them concerning precisely those conducts in which they were called upon to exercise their *rights, their power, their authority, and their liberty* in the practice of pleasures that were not frowned upon, in a marital life where no rule or custom prevented the husband from having extramarital relations, in relationships with boys . . . which were even prized. These themes of sexual austerity should be understood, *not* as an expression of, or commentary on, *deep and essential prohibitions*, but as the elaboration and stylization of an activity in the *exercise of its power*, and the *practice of its liberty*. (23, my emphasis)

What astounds me is Foucault's suggestion that these themes of sexual austerity should *not* be understood as an expression of, or commentary on, deep and essential prohibitions. Only by identifying them as a subject of rights, power, authority, and liberty could one possibly (mis)read this situation in the way Foucault proposes. As I shall go on to show, and as Foucault himself does concede, if somewhat fleetingly, women and other "others" were not only not accorded these "privileges", but moreover figured only as objects in "an ethics for men" (22). What Foucault fails to recognize is that in being constituted as other, woman (or non-man) is not simply omitted from the position of ethical subject. Rather, her body functions as the foundation upon which the subject maintains himself *as* subject, and thus her position as excluded other is the *necessary* condition of his access to the exercise of power and the practice of freedom and of pleasure. In a rigorous analysis of the connections between sexual imaginaries and social imaginaries, in particular a political imaginary that posits an anthropomorphic representation of the body politic (or artificial man) as unified and autonomous, Moira Gatens makes a similar point:

The metaphor of the "artificial man" has been important in . . . political narratives. It has allowed the sphere of political relations to be constructed as a sphere of relations between certain types of male body. This construction had, and continues to have, political and ethical consequences for those whose bodily specificity bars them from this representation. . . . [This being the case] fighting to have women included in the . . . body politic will be counterproductive unless it is accompanied by some analysis of the exclusions of women's corporeality that . . . define the body politic. (Gatens, 1996, 97, 50)

It seems we are compelled to ask then, whether the ethical practice of self-(trans)formation is possible for women and other "others", at least in the model developed by the Greeks and outlined by Foucault. In order to respond to this question I will provide a brief synopsis of what Foucault defines as four aspects of the constitution of *aphrodisia* as a domain of moral concern. These aspects will then function as a framework through which to consider the "quadri-thematics" mentioned earlier, and the types of stylization of sexual conduct associated with them.

THE ETHICAL PROBLEMATIZATION OF PLEASURE

Foucault defines *aphrodisia* as "the acts, gestures and contacts that produce a certain form of pleasure" (Foucault, 1987, 40). What was of concern to the ancient Greeks, according to Foucault, was not the form these acts assumed, but the *dynamics* they manifested, which produced a circular rather than a linear movement from desire, to action, to pleasure, back to desire, and so on. For the ethical subject the problematization of the ethical substance (the dynamic) consisted of two important considerations. The first of these is quantitative and is concerned with the intensity of the dynamic. What differentiates individuals according to this particular ethos is not object choice or the preferred mode of sexual practice, but rather the division between moderation and excess, or restraint and indulgence. Foucault quotes from numerous texts by Plato, Aristotle, and others to illustrate the culpability of excess or lack of self-restraint.

The second variable considered by Foucault concerns the role played in and through the use of pleasure. What is significant here is the distinction between *aphrodisiazein* as the active function of penetration and *aphrodisiathenai* as the passive role of the penetrated object. Unsurprisingly the first of these is associated with the role of men (the active subjects of pleasure, and thus of ethics), and the second with women, children, and slaves (the passive objects of another's pleasure). Inasmuch as these roles were assumed to be natural, the two main forms of immorality (for men) in the practice of pleasures and the ethical (trans)formation of the self as an ethical subject were excess and passivity. Interestingly, the criminological and psychological analyses of the tattooed body in Chapter One seem to reify these terms of evaluation insofar as tattooing is read as proof of a lack of moderation and self-control. Further, the tattooed body as that which is excessive and thus not deserving of the status and rights of the subject could be said to be rendered passive in these texts, at least inasmuch as it is denied an agenic "voice".

Since for the Greeks morality was not a question of adherence to a god-given code, the ethical task was to define a style for the use of pleasures (*chresis aphrodision*). Thus *chresis,* identified by Foucault as the second aspect of the constitution of *aphrodisia* as a domain of ethical concern, is associated with the mode of subjection, or manner in which the ethical subject establishes his relation to the social codes. As Foucualt tells it, *chresis* was problematized on the basis of three different considerations, namely, the strategies of need, of timeliness, and of status. The first of these is concerned with the maintenance of pleasure through the art of moderation, and moderation in this sense is defined as "a practice of pleasures that was capable of self-limitation through the 'use' of those pleasures that were based on need" (57). The strategy of timeliness consisted of determining the opportune time (*kairos*) for making use of pleasure. *Kairos* was considered according to the scale of one's life, of the year, of the day, and of the moment, and thus was also associated with the art of self-regulation. Perhaps most interesting is the strategy of status, the belief that the art of making use of pleasure must always be considered and practiced in relation to one's social status. Inasmuch as there developed an emphasis on virility and moderation in one's "private" life, these qualities were held to be essential if one was to be worthy of social esteem. As Foucault makes clear, if one desired to procure a position of power and authority in the public world, then it was essential that one be seen to adopt and maintain rigorous standards of sexual behaviour (60).

What interests me about this form of ethical conduct is the fact that the individual (trans)forms himself by means of attitudes and actions that not only individualize him, but in setting him apart from others, position him above them. Inasmuch as there is a necessary connection between what were believed to be masculine or ethical traits, namely, virility and self-restraint, access to "the elaboration and stylization of an activity in the exercise of its power and the practice of its liberty", and social position and status, women and other "others" were structurally barred from access to all three except in (negative) relation to the subject of ethics. Such debarment has inevitable material effects on the manner in which the bodies of women and other "others" (their ethos) are constituted not only in the present, but, perhaps more importantly, in the future. Thus I would suggest that whilst this model may to some degree embrace a plurality of ways of being, in the end it is no less universalizing than the Christianity of which Foucault is critical, since differences are reduced to one valued term and its antithesis. What becomes obvious—albeit unstated—in Foucault's discussion of *chresis* as the manner in which the subject establishes his relation to the social codes, and thus his sense of self (his ethos), is that the establishment of such a relation is not simply achieved by an individual in and through intentional activities. Rather, his activities are always already (in)formed by social values and mores, and are interpreted by others accordingly. If the subject does not already occupy a position of "privilege" then it is unlikely that his actions will be read as ethical, at least by those who see themselves as ethical subjects.

This conundrum is apparent in the case of the subject in/of tattooing. Insofar as the research undertaken by the criminologists and psychologists discussed in Chapter One is limited to an analysis of inmates of prisons and psychiatric institutions, then it is already assumed that these people are "unethical". Consequently they function merely as objects of another's ethics rather than as ethical subjects. Alternatively, proponents of subcultural praxis explain the practices of pleasure in which they engage, in terms of a reactive ethics that challenges the normative (and erroneous) ethics of the moral majority. Either way, the subject in/of tattooing illustrates my claim that Foucault's analysis of the ethical subject's establishing of his relation to social codes does not go far enough. Whilst Foucault recognizes that one's ethos and thus one's subjectivity is never simply self-determined, but is constantly (re)negotiated in relation to others and to a world, the structural necessity of the construction of the other *as other* remains relatively unproblematized.

The elaboration of ethical work, or the attitude necessary to the ethics of pleasures, and the manifestation of this ethos in practice is what are meant by the term *enkrateia*. According to Foucault, *enkrateia* is characterized by an active form of self-mastery, whereby one is able to resist and/or control one's desires and pleasures (64). Foucault describes this as a "heautocratic structure of the subject in the ethical practice of pleasures" (70), and differentiates it from the Christian belief in a constant conscious struggle to overcome man's fallen state through hermeneutic practices such as self-examination and confession. According to the ancient Greek model, virtue or moderation is conceived as a relationship with the self, of domination and mastery; it is a practice of freedom. Moreover, as Foucault points out, self-mastery and the mastery of others were considered to be structurally synonymous, and emblematic of a virtuous life and of the practice of freedom (75–77).

Sophrosyne, as the goal toward which the ethical subject strives, is characterized as a freedom, or a certain form of relationship of the self with itself (self-mastery), and a power that the subject exercises over others. In other words, "mastery as active freedom, was the 'virile character of moderation'" (82). Foucault again reinforces the necessary connection between the practice of pleasures, hierarchized and dichotomous notions of identity and (sexual) difference, and the ways in which individuals are positioned, and take up a position, in relation to others and to a world when he explains that mastery of the self and of others was regarded as the enactment of qualities proper to the ethical subject. For example, the rules or propriety, held that only men, and not women, children, or slaves, should exercise power, that men should direct the latter, who were considered to be incapable of self-direction, and should impose principles of reason on those who lacked the capacity to reason for themselves. In short, the subject in/of ethics (man) was expected to perform the characteristics of activity in relation to those who were believed to be naturally passive (82–83).

As Foucault goes on to demonstrate, it was impossible for one to constitute oneself as an ethical subject in the use of pleasure without simultaneously establishing oneself as a subject of knowledge (86). It is interesting that Foucault offers no critical commentary on such a connection between pleasure and knowledge, particularly given his rigorous analysis of the pleasurable truth-effects of the truth of pleasure in *The History of Sexuality Volume One*. Inasmuch as there exists, on the Greek model, an inextricable link between pleasure and knowledge, one's potential for pleasures is relative to one's access to, or position in relation to, knowledge and truth. And this access is determined by and determines one's positionality or ethos. Thus the pleasurable truth-effects of the truth of pleasure render the particular aesthetic practices espoused by the Greeks pleasurable, insofar as they function in accordance with—or at least in relation to—the dominant ethos.

Let us return for a moment to the subject in/of tattooing and ponder whether or not such a practice could possibly have been considered by the ancient Greeks as an ethical practice of pleasure and thus of self-(trans)formation. C. P. Jones argues that the ancient Greeks and Romans "associated decorative tattooing with lesser breeds of barbarians and never adopted it [themselves]" (Jones, 1987, 155). The tattooing and branding of slaves, however, particularly runaways, is frequently mentioned in Attic comedy. For example, in Petronius' *Satyrica* we witness the tattooing of two citizens as a means of disguise and escape from a difficult situation. Their servant Giton marks their "faces with an elaborate inscription to give the impression that [they] have been punished with a mark. That way the same letters will both allay the suspicions of [their] pursuers and hide [their] faces with the appearance of punishment" (cited in Jones, 1987, 139). The impression we get from this and other texts of the time is that tattooing and other forms of body marking were signifiers of stigmatization, inscribed on the body of the other. Thus we could say that the body of the other was (trans)formed in and through its relation to what it was not: namely, the subject in/of ethics. Consequently, it is highly unlikely that tattooing could have been considered by the ancient Greeks as a practice of pleasure, since a practice can only be experienced as ethically pleasurable insofar as it functions in accordance with the dominant ethos with which one identifies, and which reinforces one's sense of self in relation to the other.

We can conclude from this discussion of the four aspects of the problematization of *aphrodisia* in ancient Greek culture that identity and (sexual) difference were inscribed within an hierarchical structure of power/knowledge. Whilst this system may not have been prescriptive or prohibitive in a juridical sense, and may not have been universalizing in the sense of a homogeneous god-given code applicable to all people alike, it nevertheless remains intrinsically problematic for women and other "others" for numerous reasons. First, since the ethical practice of self-(trans)formation, at least as it is outlined in *The Use of Pleasure,* is isomorphic with the construction of a particular kind of male body and ethos, it is necessarily exclusory. Second, since identity cannot be separated from the relation to others (difference), the valorization of a particular form of ethical subjectivity cannot be divorced from the negative positioning of the other as an object of pleasure, power, knowledge, and ethics. To put it another way, ancient Greek ethics is founded on a dichotomous, hierarchical logic that still prevails today despite the differences in practices and the understanding of the relation of the self to itself and to social codes as outlined by Foucault in his discussion of both ethic-oriented moralities and code-oriented moralities. As I have argued, ancient Greek ethics embraces a system of evaluation that identifies and classifies individuals in accordance with normative criteria, and thus produces very real material effects and limitations on the possibility of being otherwise. Given this, it is not possible to consider the constitution of the self as an ethical subject of pleasure as free from social, political, and economic structures.

I will now examine two of the four themes discussed by Foucault in his analysis of the quadri-thematics of sexual austerity and outline in more detail some of the implications of the problematization of *aphrodisia* and the ensuing practices of ethical self-(trans)formation for women and other "others". The two themes I want to explore are economics, which is concerned with the institution of marriage, and erotics, which focuses on relations between males.

As Foucault tells it, the institution of marriage in ancient Greek culture designates the stylization of a necessary dissymmetry. Whilst polygamy was prohibited for both parties, the question of monogamy functioned differently for men and women. According to Foucault, women were not only denied the right to partake in sexual activities outside the conjugal relationship, but moreover they were punished severely if they committed adultery. Men, on the other hand, were accorded access to a range of sexual relations and pleasures outside of marriage. Nevertheless, they were obliged to abstain from sexual involvement with married women because to do so would be tantamount to an infraction of another man's property. Therefore, for a man, marriage consisted of having and exercising authority and power over one's family, and, in doing so, actively demonstrating his freedom and his right to a position of social status. Integral to these isomorphic so-called "public" and "private" ways of being is the virile characteristic of moderation that an aesthetics of existence demands. And as I have argued, women were necessarily excluded from the position of ethical subject, were constituted as other in relation to men, and could therefore expect ethical treatment only insofar as they were appendages to men: that is, as wives, daughters, mothers, and so on.

Similarly, the use of pleasure in relations between males demanded a special stylistics. Inasmuch as there existed an evaluative hierarchy between virility and passivity, mastery and subjugation, and a principle of isomorphism between sexual relations and social relations, a boy's potential position as an ethical subject was precarious. Whilst no law prohibited an adolescent boy from being recognized as the sexual partner or object of pleasure of an older man, paradoxically, the boy could not recognize himself as such. The relationship he was expected to establish with himself if he were to become an ethical subject, a free man, and a master of himself and others was incumbent on his rejection of the role or position of passive object or other. Insofar as identity is constituted in and through relations with others and with a world, rejection of such a position could not consist of a simple denial of the interpretation possibly posited by ethical subjects (and the ensuing material consequences of such interpretations). Rather, it must necessarily take the form of an active demonstration of those characteristics deemed to be an essential aspect of ethical subjectivity. This would inevitably involve continuous self-examination, through the monitoring and moderation of behaviour that may be thought to be excessive or passive. This being the case, to what extent is this relation of the self to itself qualitatively different from the practices of self-examination or self-policing criticised by Foucault in *The History of Sexuality Volume One* and *Discipline and Punish,* respectively?

What this discussion of relations between men and women and men and men demonstrates is that inasmuch as particular bodies and particular pleasures function in accordance with an aesthetics of existence, embodied identity and the potential for pleasures are always already constituted in relation to other bodies and to the social body. Foucault appears to recognize this when he says that

the way[s] in which the subject constitutes himself in an active fashion, by the practices of the self [is] . . . not something the individual invents by himself. They are the patterns that he finds in his culture and which are proposed, suggested, and imposed upon him by his culture, his society and his social group. (Foucault, 1994, 11)

Nevertheless, his failure to critically explicate the connection between the relation of the self to itself, and the relation of the self to others and to a world, results in the legitimation of a particular form of ethical being that necessarily functions to the exclusion of "others". Whilst those accorded access to the position of ethical subject are expected to excel in the practice of pleasures, and the coextensive exercise of power and liberty, the other is granted no such opportunity. And as I have argued, this does not consist of a simple omission of the other. Rather, through an essential prohibition, a categorization of the other as an object of ethics and of pleasure, the other's identity (his or her ethos) is constituted in a wholly negative relation to the subject, whereas the subject, in exercising his freedom, disavows the fact that his identity is maintained by an oppositional sleight of hand that reduces the other to object. Or as Barry Smart puts it,

Foucault's . . . references to cultural practices which are proposed, suggested, and imposed draw attention to, but neglect to analyse, the social context(s) in which forms of subjectivity are constituted and subjects participate, along with others, in processes of mutual self-development. (Smart, 1998, 82)

If, as I have suggested, systems of power/knowledge constitute the very morphologies and potentialities of bodies, why and how can Foucault claim that bodies and pleasures are a potential source of subversion whereas sex and desire are not? It seems that an adequate answer is not to be found in Foucault's interpretation of the ancient Greek ethical system. However, in an interview with Paul Rabinow and Herbert Dreyfus, Foucault does concede the necessary dissymmetry of the ancient Greek ethical system and states that whilst he is by no means positing classical Greece as an exemplary Golden Age, he nevertheless sees it as "an example of an ethical experience which implied a very strong connection between pleasure and desire" (Foucault, 1991a, 347). In comparison, the focus of modern philosophy, and of psychoanalysis in particular, has been, according to Foucault, solely on desire, leaving pleasure virtually untouched. Nevertheless, this does not adequately answer my question. Even if we accept Foucault's claim that his intention is not to posit the ancient Greek model as an alternative way of being that is translatable to the present, it could be argued that what Foucault does do in *The Use of Pleasure* is to offer an example of a different economy of bodies and pleasures: a heautocratic rather than a hermeneutic model. However, whilst the former may be quantitatively different from the latter, it nevertheless fails for numerous reasons to function as a counterattack against systems of power/knowledge that constitute identity and difference in dichotomous, hierarchized terms. Indeed, I would argue that just as practices of confession, interpretation, and categorization function largely in accordance with phallocentric systems of power/knowledge, so too do the practices of pleasures employed by the Greeks. It seems that both in the present day and in classical antiquity, the construction of identity, difference, and hence pleasures is most often founded on an unquestioned understanding of (ethical) being or becoming as adversarial, asymmetrical, anthropomorphic, and hierarchical. The problem that I have identified here, then, is that such an ontology fails to provide a starting point from which to begin to imagine a different economy of bodies and pleasures since it is unable to offer an adequate account of difference and to acknowledge that different forms of embodiment are themselves historical and open to change.

In the same interview mentioned above, Foucault articulates an interesting question and one that will reverberate throughout my examination of the subject in/of tattooing. He asks:

Are we able to have an ethics of acts and their pleasures which would be able to take into account the pleasure of the other? Is the pleasure of the other something which can be *integrated* in our pleasure, without reference either to law, to marriage, to I don't know what? (346, my emphasis)

This is an interesting choice of terminology, and one that, as I will go on to argue in the next section of this chapter, signifies a fundamental problem with Foucault's implicit ontology. For the moment, suffice it to say that the notion of the "integration" of the other's pleasure into our own exemplifies a model of ethics in which self-(trans)formation takes moral and political precedence over interpersonal relations[9].

SADOMASOCHISTIC PLEASURES: A CONTEMPORARY ETHICS OF SELF-(TRANS)FORMATION?

Throughout this chapter my concern has been primarily with Foucault's *interpretations* of the events of Jouy's life, the ambiguities of Barbin's identity, and the ancient Greek arts of existence rather than with the objects of his analysis *per se*. Similarly, this section will consider comments made by Foucault in various articles and interviews on sadomasochistic practices as possible forms of resistance, or as the elaboration of new possibilities of pleasure and of being. I will also consider the ways in which these comments have been taken up by others, in particular David Halperin. Again, my aim is to explore the (unacknowledged) underpinnings of the claim that sadomasochism is a potential strategy for creating a different economy of bodies and pleasures, and thus to evaluate the political and ethical exigency of such claims.

First, I should acknowledge that it was Halperin who brought to my attention the possible connections between the significance Foucault attributes to the Greek practice of ethical self-fashioning and the elaboration of "queer" styles of being. In particular, my interest was aroused by Halperin's claim that such connections attest to the fact that the practice of pleasure as an aspect of self-(trans)formation need no longer be restricted to a social élite as it seems to have been in the ancient Greek world. A second point of significance is Halperin's inclusion of practices such as tattooing in his discussion of sadomasochism. Such a connection is also made by Sheila Jeffreys, although for very different ends. I will return to this point in due course, but for the moment suffice it to say that the practices that are of interest to me in this book have been linked to sadomasochism, and to the creation of pleasures and pains with completely opposing consequences. This is demonstrated in Chapter One in the discussion of the work of Favazza, who argues that there are parallels between body modification and pathological self-injurious behaviour, and Fakir Musafar, who claims that such practices are not a sign of sickness, but rather exemplify a "state of grace".

Like Foucault, who, as I have said, claims that the ancient Greek ethical practice of pleasure should not be understood as an expression of, or commentary on, deep and essential prohibitions (Foucault, 1987, 23), Halperin argues that the Greek principles of ethical conduct did not function "as standards by which to normalize populations but as elements in a procedure that a few people might adopt with the aim of living what they consider a beautiful and praiseworthy life" (Halperin, 1995, 69). The premise from which these conclusions are drawn is that in the case of antiquity self-(trans)formation was not a hermeneutical introspective preoccupation, but rather consisted of a broad range of freely chosen occupations. However, as I argued in the previous section, a heautocratic structure of the self is not necessarily, in the end, any less normalizing, universalizing, or prohibitive than a hermeneutic one, since it seemingly fails, at least as Foucault represents it, to account for difference except in terms of complementarity or opposition of one valued term and its antithesis.

Keeping in mind the fact that for Foucault the self that is (trans)formed through practices of ethical self-fashioning is not so much an innate essence or personal identity, but rather something that could be described as a "strategic possibility"[10], it is perhaps not surprising that Foucault states that "to be gay is to be in a state of becoming . . . it is to make a sexual choice into the impetus for a change of existence" (Foucault, cited in Halperin, 1995, 77–78). One's "sexual" practices are understood here as practices of self-(trans)formation rather than as the expression of an innate identity. As one would expect, Foucault nowhere provides a blueprint for resistance as it is implied in the aforementioned quotation. Nevertheless, he does make some rather sketchy comments on his understanding of the way (gay male) sadomasochistic practices function as potential sites for the creation of a new economy of bodies and pleasures, and it is these that I will now turn to.

Earlier in this chapter I mentioned a question raised by Foucault in an interview with Paul Rabinow: is it possible to articulate "an ethics of acts and their pleasures which would be able to take into account the pleasure of the other?" (Foucault, 1991, 346). Put another way this question might read: are we able to conceive of or experience erotic relations and the practice of pleasure as something other than a form of domination and subjugation that functions in accordance with systems of power/knowledge (or that functions to reduce the other to an object of pleasure)? The following quotation from a 1984 interview originally published in *The Advocate*[11] suggests that Foucault's response would be that sadomasochism provides just such an opportunity:

What strikes me with regard to SM is how it differs from social power. What characterizes power is the fact that it is a strategic relation that has been stabilized through institutions. So the mobility in power relations is limited . . . the strategic relations of people are made rigid. On this point the SM game is a very interesting one because it is a strategic relation, but it is always fluid. Of course, there are roles, but everyone knows very well that these roles can be reversed. . . . Or, even when the roles are stabilized, you know very well that it is always a game. . . . This strategic game as a source of bodily pleasure is very interesting. But I wouldn't say that it is a reproduction . . . of the structure of power. It is an acting out of power structures by a strategic game that is able to give sexual pleasure or bodily pleasure. [SM is] a process of invention . . . it's the real creation of new possibilities of pleasure, which people had no idea about previously. The idea that SM is related to a deep violence . . . is stupid. We know very well what all those people are doing is not aggressive, they are inventing new possibilities of pleasure with strange parts of their body—through the eroticization of the body. I think it is a kind of . . . creative enterprise, which has as one of its main features what I call the *desexualization* of pleasure. The idea that all bodily pleasure should always come from sexual pleasure, and the idea that sexual pleasure is the root of all our possible pleasure—I think *that's* something quite wrong. These practices are insisting that we can produce pleasure with very odd things, very strange parts of our bodies, in very unusual situations, and so on. (Foucault, 1997, 165–69)

There are two propositions being made here that need to be addressed. The first is the notion of the "desexualization" of pleasures, and the second is the question of the relation between pleasure, the exercise of power, and the constitution of identity and difference, or of one's ethos.

Drawing on the French word *sexe* meaning sexual organ, Halperin suggests that the term *degenitalization* may be a more appropriate translation since what Foucault is implying is not that sadomasochistic pleasure is somehow distinct from sexual pleasure, but rather that the emphasis is on producing new forms of pleasure with "very strange parts of our bodies". To put it another way, the genitals are no longer *the* privileged zones of pleasure, and thus bodily pleasure is not simply reducible to what is conventionally understood as sexual pleasure. So, what exactly are these strange parts of our bodies to which Foucault enigmatically refers, the eroticization of which supposedly disrupts the "erotic monopoly traditionally held by the genitals" (Halperin, 1995, 88)? Halperin compiles a list of possibilities that includes "the nipples, the anus, the skin and the entire surface of the body" $(88)^{12}$. And whilst Foucault is not as forthcoming, he does provide an example when, in a discussion of gay male machismo, he claims that "physical practices of the fist-fucking sort are practices that one can call devirilized, that is desexed" (Foucault, 1988, 34). In the same article, Foucault goes on to suggest that the performance of gay male machismo "does not at all coincide with a revalorization of the male *as* male", but rather functions as a strategic possibility to

invent oneself, to make one's body into the site of production of extraordinary polymorphous pleasures, pleasures that at the same time are detached from the valorization of the genitals and especially the male genitals. . . . [T]he point is to detach oneself from this virile form of obligatory pleasure—namely orgasm . . . in the ejaculatory . . . masculine sense of the term. (34)

Again I find Foucault's statement somewhat cryptic. What exactly does gay male machismo as a stylization of being involve? Why single out fist-fucking as a potentially creative or transformative practice of pleasure? And what are the implications of the notion of desexualization for thinking about the links between the practice of pleasure, the exercise of power, and the social construction of identity and difference? In order to address these questions in light of the claims made by Foucault, I will turn to the work of David Halperin, who claims that queer praxis can be said to be a contemporary version of the ancient Greek aesthetics of the self.

Halperin argues that fist-fucking differs from sexual intercourse, at least as it is normatively understood, in several important ways. First, "it is less an end-driven teleological action . . . than a gradual lengthy process; an art" (Halperin, 1995, 91). Second, drawing on the research of Edgar Gregson and Gayle Rubin, Halperin claims that fist-fucking is an exemplification of the "creation of new possibilities of pleasure, which people had no idea about previously" (Foucault, 1997, 165) since, to use his words, "it was the only such practice invented in the twentieth century until the fin-de-siècle discoveries of phone sex and fax sex" (Halperin, 1995, 92). And third, again echoing Rubin, he posits the emergence of such practices as the basis of community formation, of "an entire subculture complete with its own clubs and organizations, its own urban spaces, its own artwork and insignia, and even its own public, communal events" (92). In effect, then, Halperin is suggesting that such a practice is comparable to an ethics of self-(trans)formation inasmuch as it consists of an ascetic creation of the body-subject in and through the use of pleasure, which makes possible the elaboration of a social body (or community).

Moreover, in deference to the Foucauldian distinction between a heautocratic structure of the subject and a hermeneutic model, Halperin claims that the pleasures produced by practices such as fisting, anonymous sex, and recreational drug taking function to "shatter identity, and dissolve the subject" $(95)^{13}$, rather than to reaffirm it. This is also in keeping with Foucault's discussion of sexuality as it functions in gay bathhouse culture. For Foucault, "these places [bathhouses] afford an exceptional possibility of desubjectivization . . . [Anonymity is important] because of the intensity of the pleasure that follows from it. It's not the affirmation of identity that's important, it's the affirmation of non-identity" (Foucault, cited in Halperin, 1995, 94). What puzzles me about this is first, the unquestioned reduction of anonymity to non-identity, which I would suggest is reminiscent of Foucault's problematic representation of ambiguity as non-identity in the case of Barbin discussed earlier. And second, there is no indication of what a seemingly utopian dissolution of the subject would entail or what purpose it serves. Perhaps Halperin's claim that modern versions of ascesis (such as the above) and the ancient Greek practice of pleasures can be thought of as "structurally isomorphic" (104) is a key to unravelling what is actually going on here.

Earlier I argued that Foucault's interest in the ancient Greek art of existence stems from his dissatisfaction with a hermeneutical model of the self and with the universalizing tendency of code-oriented moral systems. The notion and practice of ethical self-fashioning, at least as Foucault understands it, seemingly avoids a reaffirmation of the self as an innate essence, and at the same time is non-universalizing inasmuch as it does not consist of adherence to a god-given code applicable to all people. Thus it appears that for Foucault there is something like a natural progression from the use of pleasure, to desubjectivization, to the (trans)formation of individual bodies and social bodies, and so on in a circular motion. I have a number of objections to both Foucault's thesis and the way in which it is taken up and extended by Halperin, and these are perhaps best expressed by way of a consideration of the relation between the practice of pleasure and the exercise of power.

In the aforementioned quotation from *The Advocate,* Foucault describes sadomasochism *not* as a reproduction of structures of power, but rather as "an acting out of power structures by a strategic game that is able to give sexual pleasure or bodily pleasure" (Foucault, 1997, 166). Similarly, Pat Califia states that "in an SM context, the uniforms and roles and dialogue become a parody of authority, a challenge to it " (Califia, 1983, 135). Moreover, since for Foucault, the strategic relation of the SM game is always fluid, role reversal is possible in a way that it may not be in the wider context of power relations, or to quote Califia again, sadomasochism is "power unconnected to privilege" (135). In other words, to offer just one rather basic example, in an SM scene a woman may exert psycho-physical authority over a man in ways, and to degrees, that may not be acceptable, or even possible, in other social contexts. The question that needs to be raised here, is to what extent can sadomasochistic power play be disassociated from the exercise of power in general, and in particular from the pleasurable effects of normative discourses and discursive practices? As the quotations from Foucault and Califia demonstrate, proponents of sadomasochism do not posit an absolute distinction between the two since they see sadomasochistic practices as a parody or tactical (re)creation of systems of power. However, it seems to me that what is most often overlooked or left unexplored in such discussions is the *structural* connection between power and pleasure[14].

Inasmuch as a "parodic repetition of the 'original' . . . reveals the original to be nothing other than a parody of the *idea* of the natural and the original" (Butler, 1990, 31), sadomasochistic practices could be said to denaturalize and problematize normative associations between, for example, women and passivity, and men and virility. But this is not necessarily coextensive with an analysis of, or challenge to, the ways in which the meaning and value of identity and difference is constituted within, and as an effect of the field of social relations. To put it another way, whilst the use of parody may call into question essentialist notions of difference, it cannot be assumed that it therefore supplies an account of identity and difference in which differences are not reducible to one valued term and its antithesis.

In order to elaborate on this point I will turn briefly to some comments made by Foucault and Robert Hopcke respectively. In a discussion of sexual relations between men that echoes those contained in *The Use of Pleasure*, Foucault argues that "SM has actually helped to alleviate [the feeling that] being the passive partner in a love relationship is in some way demeaning" (cited in Bersani, 1995a, 14). Similarly, although perhaps more melodramatically, Hopcke writes:

[I]n SM and the powerful initiation into archetypal masculinity that it represents, gay men have found a way to reclaim their primal connection to the rawness and power of the Masculine, to give a patriarchal, heterosexist society a stinging slap in the face by calling upon the masculine power of men's connection to men to break the boxes of immaturity and effeminacy into which gay men have been put. (Hopcke, 1983, 71)

Whilst the statement made by Foucault may appear less overtly problematic than Hopcke's, the two nevertheless contain some common assumptions. For example, if one were to ask *how* it is that sadomasochism has helped to alleviate feelings of degradation associated with being passive or penetrated, a number of possible responses spring to mind. First is the suggestion that the "bottom" in a sadomasochistic scene is always in control inasmuch as she or he can call a halt to proceedings at will; second, is the assumption that those who choose to be "shattered" do so freely, and with the intent to transcend the limitations of the flesh; third, practices such as fist-fucking are believed to function as "a strategic possibility to invent oneself"; and fourth, since sadomasochism is just a game in which roles are reversible, then the role of "bottom" is in no way a signifier of an essential tendency toward subjugation. The emphasis in all four examples is on autonomy, agency, intentionality, and "the elaboration and stylization of an activity in the exercise of its power and the practice of its liberty" (Foucault, 1987, 23). Thus one sidesteps, rather than critically examines, the normative structural association between passivity, femininity, objectivity, immaturity, and inferiority.

What these examples suggest is that whilst sadomasochism (at least as it is represented by many of its proponents) may be said to provide an opportunity for individuals to inhabit positions of "privilege" from which they are in other contexts excluded, it nevertheless does little, if anything, to challenge the hierarchical, dichotomous system of evaluation on which normative notions of identity and difference are founded. The same could be said of tattoo scenes in which members gain status and respect in regard to the number, size, location, and design of their tattoos. The privilege accorded in such circles, however, is not necessarily concomitant with the interpretation of such bodies when they step outside of such an ethos, as we have seen. In other words, whilst it is possible, within certain cultural enclaves or subcultures, to experience shared pleasures in and through such practices, this ultimately does little to challenge normative systems of evaluation. Leo Bersani supports this claim when, in response to Califia's statement that sadomasochism is "power unconnected to privilege", he states that "this doesn't mean that 'privilege' is contested; rather you get to enjoy its prerogatives even if you're not one of the privileged" (Bersani, 1995a, 18). Indeed, as Nick Mansfield demonstrates in a compelling critique of modern and postmodern representations of masochism and the insights they provide regarding the relationship between aesthetics, power, and subjectivity,

the dispersal of the subject [in and through masochistic practices] does not preclude its centering. . . . The subject maintains a consistency of agency and intention that preserves a centred authoritarian subject at the same time . . . [that it disperses itself]. It constantly initiates its own destruction with the reassertion of itself as goal, remaining consistently present throughout, at least as its throbbing narrative core. (Mansfield, 1997, 19)

This being the case, it seems valid to conclude that Foucault's claim that gay male machismo does not at all coincide with a revalorization of the male *as* male is questionable to say the least, since many of the discourses proponents of sadomasochism draw on inadvertently constitute a revalorization of characteristics conventionally associated with the masculine (as the autonomous and active subject of [ethical] pleasure whose identity is self-defined).

Again I find myself wondering to what degree such discourses and discursive practices rely on an unacknowledged acceptance of binaries, and in so doing inadvertently reinforce normative understandings of difference as oppositional or complementary. To quote Bersani again, in sadomasochism "everyone gets a chance to put his or her boot in someone else's face—but why not question the value of putting on boots for that purpose in the first place?" (Bersani, 1995a,

18). What I am suggesting here is that representations of sadomasochistic practices of pleasure, such as those posited by Foucault, Halperin, and others, remain firmly entrenched within a pro/anti (dualist) framework as a result of their failure to analyze the structural or necessary connection between systems of power/knowledge and the production of bodies and pleasures. In an interesting, and somewhat shocking comparison between sadomasochism and Nazism, Bersani convincingly argues that sadomasochism confirms the eroticism or the pleasurable effects of the master/slave configuration on which the construction of identity and difference as it is normatively understood is founded. Rather than reiterate his argument here, I will explore this claim by considering two opposing representations of sadomasochistic practices proposed by David Halperin and Sheila Jeffreys.

As stated earlier, Halperin argues that sadomasochistic practices can be seen as a modern form of an aesthetics of existence inasmuch as they consist of an ascetic process—an art. They create the possibility of new forms of pleasure, and make possible the elaboration of a "marginalized" community or subculture. Sheila Jeffreys, on the other hand, categorically states that "sadomasochism . . . has no place in a feminist aesthetic" (Jeffreys, 1994, 19). Included in her vehement attack on sadomasochistic practices are forms of "self-mutilation" such as tattooing, piercing, and scarification. She writes:

Some of the enthusiasm for piercing in lesbians, gay men, and heterosexual women arises from the experience of child sexual abuse. Self-mutilation in the form of stubbing out cigarettes on the body, arm slashing and even garrotting are forms of self-injury that abuse non-survivors do sometimes employ. . . . Sadomasochism and the current fashionability of piercing and tattooing provide an apparently acceptable form for such attacks on the abused body. Young women and men are walking about showing us the effects of the abuse that they have tried to turn into a badge of pride, a savage embrace of the most grave attacks they can make on their bodies. (21)

For Jeffreys, the Foucauldian distinction between pleasure and desire is no distinction at all. Jeffreys interprets such marks on the body as "stigmata of body abuse" (21), as a corporeal confession, an external expression of the subject's integral interiority. Any pleasure that may be experienced in such practices is reduced to a signifier of false consciousness, and of the internalization of abuse. Far from providing a strategic possibility for (re)creating the individual body and the social body, such practices are read by Jeffreys as a perpetuation of the innate violence of oppressive social relations and structures.

As has been said, central to Foucault's critique of the repressive hypothesis in *The History of Sexuality Volume One* is his analysis of the technologies of confession, self-examination, interpretation, and evaluation, as aspects of a particular form of self-formation that he calls a hermeneutics of desire. He describes how, through the process of self-examination, it is supposed that one not only comes to know the truth of oneself, but that, moreover, one is obliged to confess this truth. Perhaps even more importantly, Foucault's analysis implies that such technologies create a disjunction between self-knowledge and the interpretation of that knowledge by others, since the processes of self-examination, confession, and interpretation take place within a network of power relations that function to identify, classify, and evaluate individuals in accordance with normative criteria.

In effect, then, as Foucault demonstrates, identity can never be autonomous or open-ended. Rather, through a process of interpretation and evaluation (or reading and writing), the one who confesses—whether literally or virtually—is constituted through being positioned and taking up a position in relation to others, and is validated or invalidated, rewarded or condemned, in accordance with normative values or "universal truths". What Foucault's analysis of the techniques of self-examination, confession, and interpretation attests to is that the meaning and value of identity and difference is constituted within, and as an effect of, the field of social relations and systems of power/knowledge. And insofar as normative understandings of identity and difference are founded on dichotomous logic, differences are reduced to one valued term and its antithesis. Jeffreys' statement is a quintessential confirmation of Foucault's analysis of the role of interpretation in the construction of identity and difference. Jeffreys interprets tattoos, piercings, and scars as an external expression of the subject's integral interiority and evaluates and positions the marked other by a degree of approximation to what she sees as the norm.

As I said earlier, elsewhere in *The History of Sexuality Volume One,* Foucault claims that for several centuries the West has been fostering a "pleasure of analysis: a pleasure in the truth of pleasure, a pleasure of knowing that truth, of discovering and exposing it" (Foucault, 1980b, 71). The implication here is that the pleasurable truth effects of the truth of pleasure consist of a reaffirmation of the self against the discourse of the other, by reconstituting the body of the other according to normative criteria assumed by the self. Or, perhaps to put it more simply, pleasure, including the pleasure of interpreting the other as other, is experienced as pleasure insofar as it functions to reaffirm the ego. This being the case, in constructing the tattooed, scarified, pierced individual in accordance with the normative criteria she assumes, Jeffreys reaffirms herself in opposition to the "self-abusive victim" and perpetrator of patriarchal oppression as the Valkyrian subject of feminism. Consequently, following Foucault, I would argue that the unquestioned assumptions on which Jeffreys' thesis is founded function to reinforce that which it is intended to challenge. For example, she implies that power is oppressive and exists in opposition to freedom; that ideology is a tool of systems of power whereas truth is liberatory; and that difference is reducible to either complementarity or opposition. To put it simply, Jeffreys' "repressive hypothesis" inadvertently reaffirms the binarisms that, as many contemporary critics have demonstrated, are an integral aspect of Western systems of power/knowledge.

Whilst it may be relatively easy, and common, to dismiss Jeffreys' work as a spurious example of political correctness or sexual conservatism, this was not the reason for its inclusion in this chapter. Rather, I want to suggest that a more productive approach to her work would be to view it as providing an opportunity to read Foucault against himself. Insofar as Jeffreys can, and does, interpret sadomasochistic pleasure in its various forms, as a politically devastating redeployment of what is essentially (self)abuse, Foucault's claim that pleasure is "virgin territory" and that there is no pathology of pleasure, is seriously challenged. Jeffreys' statements illustrate the fact that one does not have to literally confess in order for one's pleasures, actions, or appearance to be interpreted by others as expressions of one's individual identity, or interiority. And since pleasure can be "read" hermeneutically, that is, as tantamount to desire, the Foucauldian task of inventing new possibilities of pleasure and of being is significantly limited. In confirming—albeit inadvertently—Foucault's analysis of the role of interpretation in the construction of identity and difference, Jeffreys' work demonstrates that the potential for pleasure, and for self-(trans)formation, will always be relative to one's embodied ethos.

Insofar as Foucault's interpretation of sadomasochistic practices overlooks the inevitable limitations of the free play of categories of pleasure and (non)identity, his model of ethical self-(trans)formation through the use of pleasure comprises an individualistic attempt "to resist or even to escape one's social and psychological determinations" (Halperin, 1995, 76)[15]. Consequently, whilst Foucault's understanding of sadomasochism may appear on one level to be antithetical to that of Jeffreys, it nevertheless runs the same risk of reinforcing the ways in which the meaning and value of identity and difference is normatively constituted.

The central problem with Foucault's elaboration of the use of pleasure as an ethical practice of self-(trans)formation in various cultural contexts is that it fails to provide an alternative model of identity and difference that is irreducible to complementarity and opposition. In overlooking the situated and intersubjective character of identity and of pleasure, Foucault's work on sadomasochism not only limits the possibility of being otherwise, but more importantly—and in spite of itself—argues "for the continuity between political structures of oppression and the body's erotic economy" (Bersani, 1995a, 19). His uncritical acceptance of the ways in which the meaning and value of identity and difference are constituted within and as an effect of the field of social relations, perpetuates an hierarchical binary system that, as many before me have argued, is politically devastating for both women and for other "others".

This chapter began by suggesting that Foucault's call for a different economy of bodies and pleasures may well prove to be a fruitful starting point from which to rethink the subject in/of tattooing. His critique of confession, interpretation, and evaluation, and the role such processes play in the constitution of identity and difference, were drawn on in order to critique the "hermeneutic" approach taken by Jeffreys and also by the critics discussed in Chapter One, and simultaneously, to experiment with the possibility of moving beyond such theoretically limiting positions. But whilst Foucault's work could be said to provide a convincing critique of the liberal humanist notion of the subject, I have argued, following commentators such as Diprose and Smart, that Foucault's notion of ethical self-(trans)formation through the practice of pleasure implies "an unclarified sense of an auto-biographicalizing, albeit de-centred subject" (Smart, 1998, 83). In a sense then, Foucault's understanding of ethics is no less universalizing than the code-oriented moralities of which he is critical since, as Rochlitz points out, Foucault's later works contain something like a moral imperative for the subject to create him or herself as a work of art. Further, such ethical practices, rooted as they are in individualism, are as detrimental to others as the essentializing form of individualism that they are intended to replace.

In an article entitled "Beyond Life and Death: On Foucault's Post-Auschwitz Ethic", James Bernauer suggests that the aesthetics of self, at least as Foucault represents it, is an "intellectual ethics": "an ethic of responsibility for the truth one speaks, for the political strategies into which these truths enter, and for those ways of relating to ourselves that make us either conformists or resisters to those relations" (Bernauer, 1994, 271). The problem Bernauer identifies as implicit in Foucault's notion of an aesthetics of self is the emphasis on rational intentionality and self-mastery or management. What seems to be missing from the equation is the notion of ethics as an active mode of maintaining oneself in relation to others and to a world, which does not refer back to, or presuppose, an auto-biographicalizing subject who administers such a phenomenon.

Through an analysis of Foucault's work on Herculine Barbin, the ancient Greek ethics of self-(trans)formation, and contemporary sadomasochistic practices, I have demonstrated that ultimately these accounts fail to provide a substantial starting point from which to begin to imagine a different economy of bodies and pleasures. The limitations discussed in each of these examples stem, I believe, from an inadequate model of self-other relations. Consequently, the following chapter will draw on the work of Sigmund Freud and Emmanuel Levinas in an attempt to develop an alternative account of self-other relations, and of ethics, which in turn, may allow for the 'possible development of a different economy of bodies and pleasures.

NOTES

1. I am indebted to the work of Rosalyn Diprose (1994) for an understanding of the term "ethics" as it is used throughout this book.

2. For example, West and Farrington (1977) include being tattooed and/or scarred in a list of antisocial characteristics that they associate with delinquency. Thus it seems that one does not have to literally confess in order for one's pleasures (in this case the list also

includes smoking, drinking, drug use, and sexual activity) to be interpreted as indicative of one's "essential" self.

3. In the original French text, "these inconsequential bucolic pleasures" reads *"ces infines délectations buissonniere"*. Since *buissonniere* translates as "to play truant" the implication is that these infinitely small pleasures are outside of the institution; they are something closer to the pleasures of the field, of nature—a picture of life that shares uncomfortable resonances with that outlined by Juno and Vale.

4. For a critical analysis of Foucault's supposed tendency to posit a pre-inscriptive body and the implications of this for metaphors of inscription at least as they are applied to the phenomenon of cosmetic surgery, see Pippa Brush (1998).

5. The use of the term "one" here may be misleading insofar as Foucault is suggesting the possibility of a world in which actions will not be read as the external expression of an innate and autonomous "I".

6. See for example, Rochlitz (1992); O'Farrell (1989); Crossley (1994); Diprose (1987; 1994); Smart (1991; 1998); and Dews (1992).

7. See for example, Merleau-Ponty (1962); Rosalyn Diprose (forthcoming).

8. I would argue that in fact Christianity, whilst it may be universalizing in one sense, has rarely, if ever, defined a field of conduct common to both sexes. One example of this is the role traditionally accorded to men as priests and ministers, from which women have, until fairly recently, been excluded.

9. For an extended and convincing discussion of this claim, see Smart (1998).

10. In "The Genealogy of Ethics", for example, Foucault states that "the self is not given to us . . . [and] . . . there is only one practical consequence: we have to create ourselves as a work of art" (Foucault, 1991a, 351).

11. Reprinted in Rabinow (1997).

12. Freud has argued in a number of his works that these areas of the body constitute erotogenic zones.

13. For an indepth critical analysis of the current tendency of "masculine" power to operate by attempting to annihilate the difference between power and powerlessness, by continually disavowing itself and staging its own demise, see Nick Mansfield (1997).

14. I am particularly indebted to Leo Bersani (1995a) in regards to this claim.

15. Here Halperin takes the premise that the self is not a personal essence, but rather is a strategic possibility, or to use his words "nothing but the bare reflexive pronoun", and from this concludes that it is possible to practise a stylistics of the self that will allow one to transcend one's relations with others. It is the innately individualistic character of this claim that I believe is the fundamental problem in Foucault's later works, in Halperin's thesis, and in much of what has come to be known as "queer theory". Jean Grimshaw makes a similar criticism of Foucault's later work on ethics. See Grimshaw (1993, 51–72).

Chapter Three

Encountering the Other: Ontological (In)Difference and the Metaphysics of Alterity

In Chapter One I argued that criminological, psychological, and counter-cultural analyses of the subject in/of tattooing lack an appreciation of self-other relations in their own hermeneutics of desire, and in relation to an understanding of body marking itself. In Chapter Two I drew on Foucault's notion of subjectivity as the embodiment of discourses and discursive practices that are culturally and historically specific, and demonstrated that despite his call for a different economy of bodies and pleasures not founded on a hermeneutics of subjectivity, his elaboration of the use of pleasure as an ethical practice of self-(trans)formation is nevertheless problematic insofar as it fails to provide an adequate account of self-other relations. The aim of this chapter, then, is to develop a model of self-other relations that allows for the possible elaboration of a different economy of bodies and pleasures, and, perhaps more importantly, for a reconsideration of the subject in/of tattooing. At the same time, I will attempt to offer an understanding of ethics that can take into account the pleasure of the other without reducing either the experience or the subject to an object of knowledge: the consistent strategy of the analysts encountered in Chapter One. Such a rethinking necessitates a move beyond a binary understanding of self-other relations, as the previous chapter has illustrated.

My method in this chapter is to juxtapose two models of self-other relations—namely, those formulated by Sigmund Freud and Emmanuel Levinas. In a sense, the Freudian model of self-other relations is analogous to that assumed both by the theorists discussed in Chapter One and in Foucault's account of the ethical practice of self-(trans)formation, in that it conceives of the

Lucky Rich, 2000. Photo copyright © Amanda James Photography

other as a threat to the self, and thus implicitly recognizes the role of the other in the constitution of the self, but attempts to overcome, or at least veil over the mutually constitutive character of identity and difference. Another reason for engaging with Freud's work in this chapter is that in *Civilization and Its Discontents* the question of excess, or the "oceanic feeling", and its relation to self and other is raised and tellingly dealt with by Freud. Hence I invoke Romain Rolland's notion of the oceanic feeling as paradigmatic of the self-other relation and the way in which it is understood by each of the theorists discussed.

The purpose of such a juxtaposition is not to declare one wrong and the other right, but rather to draw out the fundamental assumptions on which each model is founded, and in so doing to consider the material repercussions of both. I will demonstrate that for Freud, who engages explicitly with the notion of the oceanic feeling, such a phenomenon represents the subject's contradictory desire for oneness with the universe, and simultaneously for absolute autonomy. Thus I will argue that for Freud, the oceanic feeling is both a product and paradigm of a self-other relation founded on complementarity or opposition. For Levinas, however, the self-other relation, as I will demonstrate, is founded in and through alterity, and thus the oceanic feeling could be said to *figure*—rather than re-present—that which precedes and exceeds existents and existence. In order to preempt the themes with which this chapter will concern itself, I would like to begin by looking at a novel by Michel Tournier entitled *Gemini* (1985), which outlines two very different fictional accounts of self-other relations that illustrate nicely the contrast between Freud and Levinas.

GEMINATE BEING: A DYADIC MODEL OF THE SELF-OTHER RELATION

In Tournier's *Gemini,* one of the narrators, Alexandre, tells of his youth spent at Thabor College, a Catholic boarding school for boys. Here, Alexandre becomes involved in a homosexual group, another member of which is Thomas Drycome. Thomas, who, Alexandre tells us, "brought to everything a breadth, a loftiness which was essentially religious" (Tournier, 1985, 36), had decorated the interior of his desk with holy pictures. "This triumphant iconography had, as it were, a kind of signature tucked away in the left hand corner . . . it was a crude portrayal of [Doubting] Thomas putting two fingers into the wounded side of the risen Christ" (34–35). A little later we are informed of an episode in which Alexandre inadvertently stumbles upon Drycome in the chapel crypt, lying prostrate beneath a life-size statue of the crucified Christ. Drycome, however, in a state of extreme rapture, is unaware of the presence of his friend, and so the scene comes to nothing, at least for the time being.

Time passes. The boys leave Thabor College and go their separate ways, knowing nothing about the life the other has chosen, and spending little or no time remembering the adolescent years they had shared. This state of affairs is brought to a halt, however, when Alexandre, by chance, meets up once again with Thomas Drycome, now a Catholic priest, and finds himself party to a theosophical exegesis on the dyadic nature of the self-other relation, and the possibility of moving beyond it. Drycome tells Alexandre of what he sees as his spiritual journey, which began as a young man obsessed with the wounded body of Christ. Identifying with the figure of Doubting Thomas, the young Drycome found he was no longer content with what he saw as a superficial relationship with Christ, but rather needed "the mystical experience of a bodily communion, a penetration of his own body into the body of the Beloved" (110). Haunted by the figure of his patron saint, who, in the gospel of St. John is known as Didymus (coming from the Greek *didumos,* meaning twin), Drycome, as he tells Alexandre, became increasingly convinced that in fact Doubting Thomas was the twin of Christ, his "alter-ego"; "the twin Absolute, whose like was to be sought nowhere but in God" (110). As this notion took hold of him, Drycome experienced a growing conviction that he must literally become Didymus. His physical appearance underwent a metamorphosis: he grew his hair and a beard; he became, as he puts it, almost ephemeral; and lastly, and perhaps most importantly, he manifested the signs of the sacred stigmata upon his body. In effect, what Drycome's story illustrates is a process of being marked in and through a relation or encounter with the other. We are told that everything about him "betrayed a blasphemous mimicry which, however, was very far from deliberate" (111). As a result, Drycome was sent into retreat at the monastery of the Paraclete.

It is here that Drycome is exposed to an alternative doctrine to which he becomes a lifelong disciple. According to this particular (and marginal) branch of Catholicism, Christianity is guilty of a form of Christocentrism or Christomonism, in that its primary focus on the wounded body of Christ renders it a religion of suffering, agony, and death. In keeping with this tendency, *the* Christian festival *par excellence* is held to be Easter, and especially Good Friday. Alternatively, the doctrine of the Paraclete proclaims that the festival "whose resounding splendour shall eclipse all others . . . is Pentecost" (112), since this is the day when the apostles were filled with the Holy Spirit and thus spoke in "other tongues", in "the divine logos whose words are the seeds of things" (115). Thus, according to this doctrine, the (mutilated) figure of Christ is superseded and the relationship between wo/man and God now functions "by and through the Holy Ghost" (113).

What intrigues me about this doctrine is the way in which the Holy Spirit is conceptualized, and the dyadic structure of the self-other relation is reconfigured. Drycome relates that in Hebrew the name given to the Holy Spirit is "Ruah", which has also been translated as wind, air, breath or life force, seed, word, as something vast, spacious, open, and again as "a light contact, a gentle caress, a sense of well-being in which one bathes" (Tournier, 1985, 113). Thus it seems that Ruah has something of an elemental constitution, one that precisely overflows all attempts at definitive representation. More importantly, Ruah seems to function as something like a structural possibility that precedes and exceeds the self-other relation. I will return to this point in due course.

What Drycome's description of his early relationship with Christ implies is that he, like his patron saint, desired, to put it somewhat crudely, to "poke" Christ, to penetrate and thus incorporate the other in order to (re)gain a state of symbiotic completion. Here we have a model of desire, identity, and the self-other relation that has resonances with that expounded by Freud, as I will demonstrate in the following section. But such a relationship has disastrous repercussions. As we are told, Drycome becomes "Christ-sick" (110) as a result of his assimilation of the suffering, the agony, the death, the body, of the other whom he assumes to be his alter-ego. As I will go on to argue, this phenomenon could be read then as an analogy of the detrimental character of a self-other relation in which the other is not present "in-itself", but rather is appresented, or revealed, by analogy. The point worth stressing here is that such a relation does not simply deface the other through a process of incorporation, but moreover is damaging to the self in as much as it significantly reduces the possibility of being otherwise, as will become apparent when we turn to Freud's *Civilization and Its Discontents*.

THE OCEANIC FEELING AND SELF-OTHER RELATIONS

In a letter of response to Freud's *The Future of an Illusion* (1970, originally published in 1927), Romain Rolland stated that whilst he agreed entirely with the former's judgment upon religion, he nevertheless felt that Freud "had not properly appreciated the true source of religious sentiments" (Rolland, cited in Freud, 1973, 1). This, Rolland claims, "consists in a peculiar feeling . . . a sensation of 'eternity', a feeling as of something limitless, unbounded . . . as it were 'oceanic'" (Rolland cited in Freud, 1973, 1). Rolland goes on to emphasize that this feeling is "not an article of faith; it brings with it no assurance of personal immortality, but it is the source of the religious energy which is seized upon by . . . religious systems, directed by them . . . and doubtless also exhausted by them" (1).

Freud's response is one of perplexity. He ponders why it is that others seem to experience such a feeling, and yet he cannot, as he tells the reader, find it within himself. Consequently, he begins his examination of the oceanic feeling by posing the following, somewhat leading, question: Can "this feeling of an indissoluble bond . . . with the external world as a whole" (2) in fact be understood as a form of consolation in the face of one's mortality, or more particularly, an attempt, on behalf of the subject, to dissipate the threats posed by the external world? He answers the question by stating that if in fact this were the case, one could conclude that the oceanic feeling seems to be "something rather in the nature of an intellectual perception (which is not, it is true, without an accompanying feeling tone)" (2). I will return to what I see as the motivating principle underlying this particular line of questioning in due course, but for the moment I would like to pose a few questions of my own.

First, why is it that Freud devotes only the first section of the text, a mere ten pages, to the oceanic feeling, before returning to the more comfortable question of what the ordinary person understands by his religion (11), and what the subject's behaviour demonstrates to be the *purpose* and *intention* of his or her life? Why is it that Freud categorically denies the existence of such a feeling in himself, and in the next breath states that it is difficult to deal scientifically with the intangibility of feelings (2)? Why does he attempt to establish a causal association between religious *needs* and the oceanic feeling? Perhaps there is something telling in Freud's rephrasing of Rolland's description. Rolland, unlike Freud, does not speak of the oceanic feeling as a "oneness with the universe" or as the source of religious needs, but rather as something limitless, unbounded, the source of religious *sentiments*.

At the close of the first section of *Civilization and Its Discontents,* Freud, after proposing that "a feeling can only be the source of energy if it is itself the expression of a need" (9), goes on to claim that the derivation of religious needs from infantile helplessness, and a constant longing for the protection offered by the father, seems indisputable. This then paves the way nicely for the dismissal of the oceanic feeling on the grounds that its ideational contents are symptomatic of an attempt to disavow the dangers of the external world that pose a threat to the ego. The oceanic feeling, then, is functionally equivalent to the various forms of religious consolation that Freud criticizes in *The Future of an Illusion* (9).

For Freud the oceanic feeling is nothing more than an illusory palliative measure, the expression of a need directed toward a divine Providence that the individual imagines in the form of "an enormously exalted father" (11), who watches over one and compensates in a future existence for the suffering experienced in this life. With typically Freudian contempt we are told that "[t]he whole thing is so patently infantile" (11). There are a number of assumptions at work in Freud's analysis of the oceanic feeling. As is apparent, Freud understands the subject as existing in an inevitable relation of danger and suffering. The other and/or the world is seen primarily as a potential threat to the self. And in accordance with a dyadic model of self-others relations, what motivates the self, at the most fundamental level, is need: the need to overcome, or at the very least compensate for, the (potential) suffering experienced at the hands of the other.

In short, the oceanic feeling is of relevance to Freud only insofar as it provides an opportunity for him to reaffirm the thesis posited in *The Future of an Illusion* that religion is an illusory palliative measure that is misdirected and self-defeating. What is of interest to me in Freud's analysis is the way in which the oceanic feeling seems to function as something like a paradigm of the self-other relation, that is, as an impossible and contradictory demand addressed to the other in an attempt to overcome the susceptibility to the threat posed to the self by the external world. Later in this chapter I will turn to the work of Emmanuel Levinas in order to elaborate an alternative model of both the oceanic feeling and self-other relations. For the moment, however, I would like to consider very briefly Freud's story of oedipalization in order to explore the assumption, central to Freud's work, at least as discussed here, that the relation between self and other is, from the outset, a threat to the subject.

It is supposed that the infantile substance—in its pre-oedipal state—is the locus of unbound intensities or excitations, or, to put it another way, the primary process libido is multiplicitous and in tangency with everything. At this stage the infant does not distinguish itself from the (m)other. Through the processes of subjective development the infantile substance comes to be a (supposedly) unified, discreet, intentional, teleological subject. For Freud, the emergence of an ego that unifies the disorganized and multiplicitous sensations of the infantile substance seems strangely undertheorized, and is possibly implied to be something like an "inevitable", "natural", or universal phenomenon. This being the case, I will turn for a moment to Lacan's notion of the Mirror Stage, which provides an explanation of the constitution of the ego as the ambiguous ground of being.

Lacan argues that during the Mirror Stage the identification that the child makes with the mirror image, or reflection of himself[1], is both affective and projective, and provides the child with a *gestalt;* an image of itself as a unified totality. The child's identification with its specular image impels it to nostalgically long for a (perhaps mythical)[2] past in which it was symbiotically complete, and at the same time to project itself into an ideal (but ironically impossible) future identity in the coherence of the totalized specular image. This recognition then, is for Lacan a form of *mis*recognition in that it is both visually accurate and at the same time delusory, since it prefigures a unity and mastery that the child lacks, and in fact will always lack. The child takes as its own an image that is both other and outside its control. In effect then, the subject recognizes itself at the very moment that it loses itself in/as the other. Perhaps more importantly, as Elizabeth Grosz has pointed out, "the subject's identity is based on a (false) recognition of an other as the same" (Grosz, 1990b, 41)[3]. Consequently, the other functions as the foundation of the subject's sense of self and simultaneously as that which threatens to disrupt or even annihilate the self. The basis of the ego then, at least as it is understood by Lacan, is a contradiction that is insurmountable.

The development of the subject, according to this model, is built upon a progressive renunciation of instinctual pleasure or instant gratification. The avoidance of pain acquires priority over the obtaining of pleasure, as Freud explains in his analysis of the modification of the pleasure principle by the reality principle. Indeed, the psychoanalytic story ultimately paints a disturbingly pessimistic picture of life insofar as it assumes that, at a fundamental level, self-other relations are antagonistic, and that therefore the *primum mobile* of the post-oedipal subject is the avoidance of suffering. Consequently, pleasure is understood solely in negative terms; that is, as a lack of, or at least an avoidance of, pain. Moreover, feelings such as those described by Rolland are read by Freud according to this paradigm of suffering: as the expression of a need that, as an intrinsic aspect of the subject's constitution, is ultimately unsatisfiable. The self will never overcome the threat posed by the other, and is thus prone to illusory palliative measures—of which the oceanic feeling is but one example.

If we return to *Civilization and Its Discontents,* this paradigm of suffering can be seen to be at work not just in terms of guiding Freud's analysis of the oceanic feeling as discussed, but also in the role of the modification of the pleasure principle by the reality principle in the constitution of civilization. Whilst Freud acknowledges that people pursue pleasure, he goes on to claim that despite this pleasure is less often experienced than pain and suffering. Pain, he claims, derives from three sources to which the subject is constantly exposed, namely, the body; the external world of nature; and his or her relations with others. Freud goes on to suggest that one possible way to evade the "primary mutual hostility" (Freud, 1973, 49) of the self-other relation is voluntary isolation. But, he adds that there is another preferable option, and this is to become a member of the human community (14), since civilization *(Kultur)* consists, in part, of the measures we take to protect ourselves. It is this aspect of Freud's notion of civilization (the regulation of social relations) that most interests me since it is here that we see evidence of a structural parallel between the aims and processes of social life and the libidinal development of the subject.

Just as the infantile substance is required to separate itself off from all that is tangential to it, and in doing so relinquish a state of instant gratification in the name of the reality principle (or in and through the process of socialization), so too the individual members of a community are required to sacrifice, or at best curtail, the possibility of personal satisfaction, to the greater good of all. Civilization, or social relations, therefore are founded on the sublimation of instinctual aims, as is the individuation of the subject. Whilst Freud seems at times to acknowledge what he calls the "similarities" between the constitution of the subject and that of civilization, he nevertheless describes them as two processes and at least implies that they are separate. For example, he claims that there is one feature that distinguishes between the two processes, namely, the program of the pleasure principle. He argues that individual development is an effect of the interaction of two urges: the egoistic urge toward individual or personal happiness, and the altruistic urge toward union with others. Whilst the dominant egoistic urge is experienced as a form of freedom, the other is often understood as the imposition of social restrictions. However, Freud claims that the development of civilization functions differently than the development of the individual in that the aim of creating harmony between individuals outweighs the aim of the attainment of individual happiness (77). He goes on to add that these two urges (toward personal happiness and union with others) are in competition with one another, that they stand in hostile opposition to one another, and that this struggle constitutes a dispute within the economics of the libido between ego and objects (78).

What I want to suggest is that whilst it may be useful for heuristic purposes to consider the "two processes" separately in order to examine possible quantitative differences in manifestation, it is nevertheless essential to recognize that the "two" are inextricably bound: mutually constitutive and simultaneously incommensurable. In failing to articulate this Freud implies that the separation of the ego from a world occurs somehow prior to the self's membership of a community, or at the very least, that the pleasure principle precedes the reality principle. This allows Freud to argue that suffering and aggression are somehow an intrinsic aspect of individual psychology, and that the central concern of civilization is the controlling of aggression and thus the minimalisation of suffering. However, I would argue that the processes of oedipalization or individuation are in fact themselves civilizing processes or processes of enculturation, and that the "two urges" of which Freud speaks are the seemingly paradoxical product of a particular model of being-in-the-world that simultaneously (mis)recognizes and disavows difference or intersubjectivity[4]. This problem of origins, of what comes first (the urges, the subject, or civilization), and its inevitable impact on any conception of self-other relations, will be taken up in a discussion of the work of Levinas later in this chapter, but for the moment let us examine one particular example Freud provides: of the response by civilization to the inevitable dangers faced by the individual.

Citing Plautus' words, "*Homo homini lupus*" (man is a wolf to man), Freud argues that the inclination to aggression that we can detect in ourselves, and by extension deduce to be present in others, poses a perpetual threat to both individual subjects and to civilization, and must therefore be regulated somehow. One such form of social regulation, according to Freud, is the incitement of individuals into love relationships that inhibit the egoistic urge and its aims (49), an example of which is the biblical commandment, "thou shalt love thy neighbour as thy self". Freud begins his discussion of this commandment by asking why it is that we should obey it, what good will it do us to do so, and perhaps more to the point, how will we manage to fulfil such a seemingly impossible task (46). His response is illuminating for a number of reasons that will be discussed in due course.

Freud describes love as something valuable that should not be given away without serious deliberation, something that imposes duties and demands sacrifices. Consequently, he concludes that the beloved must deserve to be loved. He says that the stranger only deserves to be loved if he is so like the self that "I can love myself in him" (46). Alternatively, one has an obligation to love those held dear by family members and friends, since the pain that one's friend or relative would experience if his/her loved one was harmed would also be felt by the self (46).

But where does this leave the stranger with whom one is not connected by marriage, blood, friendship, or shared characteristics? According to Freud, if the stranger does not attract me by an apparent worth of his own, or any significance that his being may have for me, then not only would it be hard for me to love him, but, more importantly, I would be wrong to do so. Freud substantiates this claim on the grounds that one's love is a form of value, a sign that one prefers, or makes commitments to, one person or group of people over another. Given this, it would constitute an injustice to one's loved ones if one were to also give one's love to strangers, since such action would devalue one's commitment to one's family and friends. Whilst this may seem like a logical common-sense position to take, what is interesting, and perhaps telling, is the way in which the stranger is characterized by Freud in the following statement:

Not merely is this stranger in general unworthy of my love; I must honestly confess that he has more claim to my hostility. . . . He seems not to have the least trace of love for me and shows me not the slightest consideration. If it does him good he has no hesitation in injuring me. . . . [T]he more secure he feels and the more helpless I am, the more certainly I can expect him to behave like this to me. . . . [I]f this grandiose commandment had run "Love thy neighbour as thy neighbour loves thee", I should not take exception to it. (46–47)

It seems that for Freud this commandment is at best naive, and at worst dangerously misdirected. So, why should we do it? Freud's response to the question is that this commandment seems to be the epitome of all that is counter-intuitive to what he holds to be the fundamental nature of human being(s) (49). What Freud is implying is that since aggression, rather than love, is an instinctual response, an attempt to limit human aggression and minimize personal suffering is necessary. But given that, as Freud continuously reiterates, "instinctual passions are stronger than reasonable interests" (49), how shall we fulfil such a commandment? Freud enumerates four possible ways of controlling aggression. The first two of these are manifestly social in as much as they explicitly involve social institutions.

As Freud's discussion demonstrates, aggression can be regulated—to some degree—by the formation of communal and libidinal bonds. However, the quotation also illustrates the limitations of such an approach. It seems that what accompanies the strengthening of communal feeling is the constitution of all others not included in this group (my family, my friends, my loved ones) as outsiders whose very status signifies a threat not only to myself, but also to my "community". Thus what we end up with is a conceptualization of the body politic as a macrocosmic version of both the oedipal subject, and the antagonistic self-other relation.

The second form of institutional control involves the abolition of private property, unequal wealth, nationhood, and other such exclusionary and oppressive sources of power. However, Freud chooses not to explore this possibility in any depth, and since it is not the focus of my interests, suffice it to say that for Freud such an approach is flawed for the same reason as the first—namely, that the psychological premise on which such an approach is based is "an untenable illusion" (50). In other words, Freud argues that the inclination to aggression is "an original, self-subsisting instinctual disposition in" (59) the subject that cannot be eliminated, or even radically controlled through purely social means. There are a number of problematic assumptions at work in Freud's critique. They include the distinction made between the subject and the social, the claim of a fundamental antagonism integral to the structure of the subject—what Diana Fuss describes in a critique of the work of Lacan as a "complicity with an unacknowledged humanism" (Fuss, 1989, 10), and following on from this, the assumption that power is something the subject possesses and/or intentionally employs. As we saw in Chapter Two, Foucault argues that power is not alien to the individual or an imposition upon it that acts to limit or restrict its nature, but rather power is productive, and the subject is both an agent and effect of systems of power/knowledge. Thus there can be no purely subjective or purely social.

The remaining possibilities suggested by Freud to curtail aggression are the replacement of instinct by intellect, and the formation of a cultural and/or individual super-ego that "sets up strict ideal demands, disobedience to which is visited with 'fear of conscience'" (79). The ideal demands of the super-ego are comprised, according to Freud, under the heading of ethics. Thus it could be said that the commandment to love one's neighbour as oneself exemplifies an ethical attempt to minimize aggression, and thus to render the world a safer place for the individual. But, if we agree with Freud's analysis, ethics, as an attempt to achieve something that to date has not been achieved, and is unlikely ever to be achieved, is not only internally contradictory, but moreover "has nothing to offer . . . except the narcissistic satisfaction of being able to think oneself better than others" (79–80).

In other words, ethics—as Freud understands it—fails to accomplish its goal, as does the commandment to love one's neighbour as oneself, since ethical commandments are both exterior and posterior to one's being, and a contractual proposal to be rationally considered in terms of the other's value, the cost of "self-sacrifice", and the likelihood of reciprocity or self gain. The ethical commandment consists of "receiving an order by first perceiving it and then subjecting oneself to it in a decision taken after having deliberated about it" (Levinas, 1987a, 112). Moreover, the other or the stranger is, it seems, far more likely to be a threat to the self than an ally. Either way the other is understood solely in terms of its relation to the self: she or he is either *with me* (like me), or *against me* (opposed to me). This understanding of both self-other relations and ethics differs radically from that elaborated by Levinas, as we shall come to see.

Despite the existence of social and libidinal imperatives to form interpersonal bonds, Freud's thesis reiterates repeatedly the belief that aggressiveness is what founds all relations of love and affection between people (50), and therefore must be one of the universal and transhistorical founding characteristics of civilization. Consequently, civilization, according to this model, is something of a paradox, since its purpose is to protect the self from the threat of destruction by others, while, at the same time, it requires the annihilation of difference (or of otherness) in the name of unity, or Sameness. Further, since the subject and civilization are inextricably bound, the inner economy of the subject (the ego) is also a contradiction that will never be overcome because if the self is to survive intact, it can only do so through the incorporation of the other. But as we have seen in the earlier discussion of the Mirror Stage, the incorporation and/or annihilation of otherness in any absolute way is impossible since, first, the other is by definition that which is outside my control. And, second, since the other functions as the foundation of the subject's sense of self, to kill the other would inevitably result in the annihilation of the self, at least as we know it. The subject it seems is doomed to a life of suffering. As Jonathan Dollimore puts it, "the dialectic is less a process than an energized fixation permanently haunted by loss" (Dollimore, 1991, 202).

What strikes me as most interesting about the psychoanalytic model of the development of the subject is the way in which freely mobile excitations become reduced to the mass of the individual body, and pleasure is transformed into a need addressed to the other, who, distinct from the self, represents both the promise of completeness and the threat of annihilation. According to this model, contact becomes contract[5]—a claim that can be clearly seen in Freud's response to the commandment to love one's neighbour as oneself.

What my reading of *Civilization and Its Discontents* demonstrates is that Freud's structurally isomorphic model of identity and social relations is based on an Hegelian master/slave dialectic that leaves little, or no, room for difference. Consequently, the oceanic feeling can be understood by Freud only as an illusory feeling that in actual fact is merely a sublimated expression of the desire to experience happiness or pleasure, or more particularly, to avoid suffering or unpleasure—a state of being that is always just beyond the subject's reach, at least in any sustainable way.

Whilst I do not wish to completely refute Freud's theorization of the antagonistic character of social relations, I nevertheless remain unconvinced that this model of self-other relations is an apodictic certainty integral to a universal and transhistorical form of being-in-the-world. In effect, what I am implying is that what Freud provides us with is a partial model of identity and social relations that is founded on a universal ontology. I also want to suggest, drawing on the work of Levinas, that perhaps there is another side to this story. This, I would argue, is in fact the claim being made by Nietzsche in an aphorism entitled "Two Kinds of Causes Which Are Confounded" (Nietzsche, 1974, #360).

This aphorism proposes that the way in which cause and effect have been traditionally conceptualized is not only erroneous, but is based on a confounding of *driving* forces and *directing* forces. Opposed to this is Nietzsche's claim that he has "learned to distinguish the cause of acting from the cause of acting in a particular way, in a particular direction, with a particular goal" (Nietzsche, 1974, 315). Using an analogy that seems apt in the context of this chapter, Nietzsche suggests that the helmsman and the steam are most often confused, the former being assumed to be the driving force when in fact it is merely the directing force. Is it not, he asks, that the helmsman, who is thought to represent the aim or mastery of his being-in-the-ocean(ic), is nothing but "an extenuating pretext, a self-blinding of conceit, who does not wish it to be said that the ship *follows* the current into which it has accidentally run, which it "wills" to go that way *because it—must?* (317). What this analogy illustrates is the (problematic, or in Nietzsche's view, erroneous) separation of the ship (the self) from the elements (the ocean, the wind, the world of others) in which it subsists, and the ensuing representation of the helmsman (the ego), as the one who drives or masters the ship (or being-in-the-world) through the implementation of aims and purposes. Nietzsche argues that what is in fact the directing force—in this case the helmsman or ego—presupposes a driving force, "a quantum of damned-up energy that is waiting to be used up somehow" (315). Moreover, he claims that "compared to this energy . . . [the directing force] is something quite insignificant, for the most part a little accident in accordance with which the quantum 'discharges' itself in one particular way—a match versus a ton of powder" (315).

Keeping my reading of the Nietzschean aphorism in mind, I want to pose the question of whether it is possible, whilst granting that libidinality is coded, channelled, and regulated in culturally, historically, and sex-specific ways, to suggest that there is at the same time an excess, something beyond being that the rational aims and intentions of the subject presupposes, something that is not simply disruptive, or the cause of suffering, but that rather, figures what Levinas would call the metaphysical (rather than the ontological) structure of self-other relations, something that Nietzsche calls the driving force, but that could perhaps also be thought of as the oceanic feeling as a paradigm of an alternative model of self-other relations?

In *The Gay Science*, Nietzsche claims that life is power, and will to power, productivity. In *The Anti-Christ*, he argues that will to power as a productive driving force is seized upon by religion, and inverted into a life-negating asceticism[6]—a suggestion reminiscent of that made by Rolland, who claims that the oceanic feeling is "seized upon by . . . religious systems, directed by them

. . . and doubtless also exhausted by them" (Freud, 1973, 1), but somehow sidestepped by Freud. So, just as Freud's conceptualization of the development of the libidinal subject as a *directing* force leaves unaddressed the notion of an excessive *driving* force, so too does Drycome's description of his early relationship with Christ illustrate the ways in which the oceanic feeling (or the driving force) is "inverted" by religious systems, although, as I will go on to argue, it is *never entirely exhausted by them.* It is only when Drycome is exposed to an alternative doctrine, or model, of self-other relations that he "senses" the oceanic feeling, at least as I want to configure it. What the doctrine of the Paraclete provides Drycome with is an alternative account of self-other relations in and through which he develops a relationship with the Other (God/Christ) that avoids a reduction of the Other to an Economy of the Same.

LEVINASIAN METAPHYSICS

Let me begin my discussion of Levinas' work by suggesting that despite its breadth of range, the Levinasian "phenomenology of sociality" (Levinas, 1987a, 109) seems informed by an endeavour to continuously (re)formulate an ethics of alterity: an understanding of self and other in which both are independent (separate), although not autonomous (individual), self-sufficient inasmuch as the self and its relation with others is not founded on a universal lack, and at the same time is always already in relation. Levinas' various attempts to rethink self-other relations whilst avoiding the hegemony of the Same raise the question of whether, and how, it is possible to philosophise about the Other[7] without reducing otherness to an epistemological object that the philosopher can know.

Since the previous section of this chapter contained references from Freud, Nietzsche, Rolland, and Drycome to the subject of God, let us pick up this thread again and begin with a reading of Levinas' allusion to the third of René Descartes' *Meditations* (1641). It is here that Descartes formulates the *cogito* as proof of the existence of the self, and also as a proof of the existence of God. According to Descartes the idea of God must have come from some external source, since it would be impossible for the imperfect Cartesian "I" to think the idea of a God whose perfection radically exceeds the capacities of the "I". Thus the "I" who "thinks" God can be certain of God's existence precisely because the idea of God that the "I" thinks overflows any idea that could have derived from the imperfection of the "I" (Chanter, 1995, 183).

Levinas is not so much concerned with the logical validity of Descartes' argument, nor with the *truth* of God *per se.* Rather, he claims that Descartes' thesis is illuminating, first, because in attempting to prove the existence of God, the Cartesian subject "finds itself" in and through a relation with that which transcends it. In other words, the bonds of this relation do not reduce self and Other to an Economy of the Same. Self and Other are not united into a whole, but rather are constituted in and through a relation that Levinas calls the "idea of infinity" (Levinas, 1969, 48).

In short, the subject's relation with God is paradigmatic of Levinas' understanding of the fundamental structure of the self-other relation. When Levinas claims that Descartes' concept of the idea of God (the infinite) denotes a relation with an Other that remains exterior to the "I" who thinks it (48), he is suggesting that the Other is transcendent to me, that it cannot be contained by any idea that I may have of the Other. In short, "[t]he absolutely other is the Other" (39). The implication here is that rather than being a subject that represents others as objects of consciousness and/or knowledge, the subject is founded in and through the encounter with the inalienable Other (infinity), as something beyond knowledge, beyond being or nothingness, and absolutely resistant to all attempts to relativise or assimilate it by representing it (Westphal, 1993, 492). As Levinas puts its, the infinity of God is not a theme of the finite *cogito* (1969, 211). This is because the infinite is radically Other, is transcendent, and therefore exceeds the idea that the "I" can think. "To think the infinite, the transcendent, the Stranger, is hence not to think an object" (49).

Second, and related to the first point, Levinas claims that Descartes outlines a relation with a radical alterity that is not reducible to interiority, but that nevertheless does not do violence to interiority (1969, 49). In effect then, Levinas reads, and in so doing rewrites, Descartes' insights in order to demonstrate that the encounter with the Other does not threaten the subject with annihilation, as Freud has suggested, but rather provides the very grounds of its possibility.

Unlike Freud whose work, it could be argued, exemplifies what Levinas refers to as the ontological imperialism of the West, insofar as it functions to reduce the Other to the Same, Levinas attempts to "conceptualize" the self-other relation, that is, the ethical relation (*l'ethique*) as founded in alterity or infinity rather than through analogical apperception. Thus rather than simply describing the self as the same as, or different from, the Other, Levinas offers us a model of the self as *separate from* the Other—and in doing so attempts to articulate a distinction between *singularity* and *individuality,* a point that will become clearer as this chapter progresses.

THE SUBJECT IN/OF ALTERITY

For Levinas the "I" is not a continuous essence (the selfsame), but is rather the being whose existing consists in identifying itself as 'self' in and through the myriad things that happen to it. The self "has the *ossature* of a subject, of the first person" (36, my emphasis). In other words, the self is the *site* where the Same identifies itself as such in and through "its" changes. However, despite, and at the same time because of, its separateness, Levinas' "I" differs from the humanist Transcendental Ego in such a way that the I is not produced tautologically: "I am I". Rather, it is "that in which the I is revealed precisely as preeminently the Same, is produced as a *sojourn* . . . in the world. . . . It finds in the world a site . . . and a home" (37). Thus, unlike Freud who (perhaps inadvertently) implies a distinction between being and in-the-world—and by extension, a distinction between self and other that turns out to be no distinction at all—Levinas offers an understanding of the "I" as separate (but not individual or autonomous); as an active identifying with itself that can only take place in and through its dwelling in-the-world. What Levinas describes as the "at home" (Le "*chez soi*") is a site where *I can*[8], where, in and through that which is other, "I am, despite this dependence or thanks to it, free" (37). The point Levinas is making is that the separateness of the self is only possible insofar as the Other also exists. Indeed, as Davis points out, alterity constitutes the grounds that make separation possible (Davis, 1996, 44). In other words, the self—as an Other for the Other—and the Other are both separate and singular inasmuch as neither is reducible to universal categories, and at the same time they exist in and through the encounter with alterity—an encounter that is not an event situated in time and space, but rather "a structural possibility that precedes and makes possible all subsequent experience" (45).

In the subsection of *Totality and Infinity* entitled "*Vivre de* . . . ",—*Living from* . . . —Levinas describes the things from which life lives "('good soup', air, light, spectacles, work, ideas, sleep etc)" (Levinas, 1969, 110) as delineating "the independence of enjoyment". The contents from which life lives are at once other to the self, that is, separate from the self, and yet simultaneously this encounter with the other (an encounter that is always already "past"), is described by Levinas as the transmutation of an energy that is other that becomes, in and through enjoyment, "my own energy, my strength, me" (111). He says, "[w]hat I do and what I am is at the same time that *from which* I live . . . Enjoyment [is] the very pulsation of the I" (113). In effect then, the self acquires its own identity in and through its dwelling in the other, separate from the other, but never in a relation of simple opposition to the other. Nourishment for Levinas is not the incorporation of the other into the Same, but a transmutational productivity in and through which separateness and relation are affected, or mutually constituted and yet incommensurable.

Living from . . . is also referred to by Levinas as to-be-in-the-element: as a process of involution and ipseity that "belongs to sensibility, which is the *mode* of enjoyment" (135). Sensibility, however, precedes and exceeds reason. Sensibility belongs to the order of sentiment rather than that of thought, to affectivity, in and through which the very pulsation of the "I" is made possible. "One does not know, one lives sensible qualities: the green of these leaves, the red of this sunset" (135). In other words, Levinas argues that "prior" to sensibility in the Heideggerian sense of taking hold of the world, there is sensuality—a sensuous contact with the elements, the contents from which life lives, which is reminiscent of Rolland's notion of the oceanic feeling. In

Otherwise Than Being or Beyond Essence, Levinas suggests that the space in which the sensuous material is laid out is always already extended by the sense of alterity[9]. Sensuality, then, is understood as an exposure to alterity; a sensuous contact with the carnal materiality of the other and the world.

Moreover, the *need* of the Levinasian self differs from its Freudian/Lacanian counterpart inasmuch as it is not understood as stemming from a fundamental lack at the heart of being. Indeed, Levinas' model of the self in/of enjoyment (*living from . . .*) moves beyond the dependence/mastery conundrum in which the subject of psychoanalysis appears eternally entrapped since it articulates a notion of "mastery in dependence". *Living from . . .* , says Levinas, "is the dependency that turns into sovereignty, into happiness—essentially egoist" (114). But this "ego" is not the solipsistic ego of transcendentalism. Whilst the "I" *is* enjoyment, this enjoyment (and thus the "I") is *of* something else, something other than itself. "Autochthonous, that is, enrooted in what it is not, it is nevertheless, within this enrootedness, independent and separated" (143).

What I have argued in this section is that contra to the claim implied in Freud's analysis of the relation between the individual and the social, the self is at once "enrooted", as Levinas puts it, in the other and the world, and, as a result of the infinitude of the self-other relation, it is separate, but not autonomous. Thus the world and the other are neither a threat to the self nor the locus of a lost unity from which the self has fallen, and, as a consequence, are driven by need or desire as lack to continuously but uselessly attempt to reconnect or disavow. As Levinas puts it, "the idea of creation *ex nihilo* expresses a multiplicity not united into a totality" (104). In other words, the self does depend on the other, but not as an aspect of the other from which it has been separated, or with which it can be united. Moreover, sensibility or dwelling, as an active mode of maintaining oneself in relation to a world, to the other, to the elements is not the intentional project of an already constituted "I", but rather is an affective encounter with the other and the world wherein the egoism of the "I"—the psychism—pulsates. One's ethos is affected in and through the relation with infinity as that which is exterior to the self and as that which constitutes the very egoism of the "I" as sentience—as the mode of possibility of (un)becoming. In the following section I will discuss Levinas' understanding of the self's encounter with the Other as that which disrupts the familiarity of the *living from. . . .*

THE FACE TO FACE AS ETHICAL RELATION

In *Totality and Infinity,* Levinas writes of the face to face as a relation whose terms do not form a totality, an originary and irreducible relation. The face (*visage*) that the "I" encounters is always the face of the Other. Yet it is never simply an object of the self's perceiving consciousness. Rather, the face of the Other is invocative and imperative "before" it is indicative or significant[10]. The face of the Other, says Levinas, calls consciousness into question rather than being reflected in it: "It resists it to the point that even its resistance is not converted into a content of consciousness. The visitation consists in overwhelming the very egoism of the I" (Levinas, 1986, 352–53).

To put it another way, the face of the Other overflows any idea "I" may have of the Other. The subject finds itself in and through an encounter with that which transcends it[11]. This encounter with the Other, as the discussion of Descartes' *Meditations* suggests, enables the subject to differentiate itself from the Other since it occasions the "discovery" of the irreducibility of the alien Other. At the same time, the Other's face(ing), as an encounter with alterity, calls into question the self's sovereign authority in the world of the other(s) that defines *living from.* . . . The Other's face(ing) is tantamount to the calling into question of the self's joyous possession of the world (Levinas, 1969, 75). Or as Andrew Tallon puts it:

This meeting is an event which by transcending the ego, calls forth from the self a response that exceeds and determines the ego—precisely by driving it out of the paradise of enjoyment as the centre of consciousness back to an anarchic "past" so remote as to arise from a nonintentional, nonconscious affectivity—and places it into question in such a way that one experiences it as answer-ability, respons-ibility. (Tallon, 1995, 113)

The question of responsibility will be returned to later in this chapter, but for now suffice it to say that this encounter with the Other, which both undermines and at the same time constitutes the egoism of the self, delineates the structure of a metaphysics that functions as the grounds for ontological possibility. For Levinas, this calling into question of the self's spontaneity in and through the face(ing) of the Other is what is meant by the term "ethics" (Levinas, 1969, 43). Indeed, the face to face is denotative of *l'ethique par excellence* insofar as it affects human relations at their most primordial or metaphysical level. This is the point at which the fundamental difference between the work of Freud and Levinas becomes strikingly evident. It could be argued, for example, that Freud's thesis, as discussed earlier, functions to thematize being since it "rests upon the assumption that all diachrony can be synchronized" (Taylor, 1987, 200). As I shall go on to explain in more depth, Levinas' work, on the other hand, could be said to constitute a "dethematizing" or destructuring of rational discourse insofar as it recalls the unassimilable remainder of the self-other relation (alterity or infinity).

In *Otherwise Than Being or Beyond Essence,* Levinas claims that in and through the encounter with the Other "there is inscribed or written the trace of the Infinite, the trace of a departure, . . . [the] trace of what is inordinate, does not enter into the present, and inverts the *arche*[12] into anarchy" (Levinas, 1978, 117). Hence the Other's face(ing) is seen by Levinas not as a phenomenal event that takes place in the present, but rather as a way the Other has of "manifesting

himself without manifesting himself" (66). Thus we see that just as the Other
exists in a relation of transcendence, rather than immanence, to the self, so too
the face to face relation and the response-ibility it evokes occur as a past that
cannot be re-presented: a past "more ancient than every representable origin, a
pre-original and anarchial *passed*" (9), "a past which was never present" (24).
Levinas' *anarchie*, then, connotes the trace of the Other; it indicates the
withdrawal of that which is indicated not a re-presentation that would "rejoin it"
(65). Insofar as the trace leaves a trace by effacing its traces, it moves beyond
the presence/absence dichotomy and in doing so implies that the Other's
face(ing), as an "event" always already "passed", radically resists recuperation
into an Economy of the Same. This "beyond"—presence/absence, self/other,
being/nothingness, dependence/mastery, and other such ontological categories
characteristic of Western philosophy—which Levinas gestures toward (rather
than represents) in relation to *anarchie*, is *otherwise than being or beyond
essence*. It implies an account of the genesis of the subject in *otherwise than*
chronological terms: the subject in/of alterity. As I will demonstrate in the
following chapter, Roland Barthes could be said to share Levinas' position in his
understanding of what he calls the "anachronic subject"[13].

In *Otherwise Than Being or Beyond Essence*, Levinas speaks of the face to
face relation in terms of *exposure*. He argues that the "I" enters language with
the utterance *"here I am"*, but this *"here I am"* is neither an act of self-
representation, nor a signifier of exposedness. Rather, the utterance *affects*
exposure. Indeed, it is not the case that "I" exists prior to its relations with
others, but that one's existing forms in the trope *the-one-for-the-other:* a mode of
existence that inscribes the very contours of bodily-being. For Levinas the self
exists through and for the Other; the self/psyche is engendered—or inspired, as
Levinas puts it—in and through alterity. He says, "[t]he psyche can signify this
alterity in the same . . . as being-in-one's-skin, having-the-other-in-one's-skin"
(114–15). As I suggested earlier, this encounter with, or exposure to, the Other
has always already taken place in a "pre-original" and anarchial *passed*, or as
Levinas explains it, "the relationship with the non-ego precedes any relationship
of the ego with itself" (118). Thus the "I" is not first in-itself and/or for-itself,
but rather is constituted in and through a process of inscription: the trace of the-
Other-in-me that "inverts the *arche* into *an-archie*" (117).

This can perhaps be further understood if we turn to Levinas'
conceptualization of the difference between the Saying (*le dire*) and the Said (*le
dit*), or to put it another way, the difference between exposure and representation
or thematization. For Levinas Saying is the (non)site where exposure "takes
place". Levinas concedes that Saying is communication, but only insofar as it
could be said to figure the condition for/of exposure as the grounds of possibility
for communication (48). As Taylor points out, "this exposure to the Other,
establishes a 'communication' that cannot be understood in terms of sending and
receiving messages" (Taylor, 1987, 202)[14]. Communication, says Levinas, is a

becoming open in and through which "one is exposed to the Other as a skin is exposed to that which wounds it" (Levinas, 1978, 49). Communication, then, is not a modality of cognition that serves to reaffirm the ego, but rather, is a vulnerability, a sensuous contact with alterity which is the grounds of possibility for the circulation of information[15]—an encounter in and through which self and Other mark and are marked.

Levinas goes on to further elaborate the difference between the Saying and the Said when he speaks of the Saying as a foreword preceding linguistic systems: as "the proximity of the one to the other, . . . the very signifyingness [*signifiance*][16] of signification" (5). The implication, then, is that the Said—as that with which systems of thought such as Western philosophy have traditionally been concerned—functions to reduce the unknown or unknowable (alterity) to object(s) of knowledge through a process that Levinas terms "designating identities" (41). To designate, as it is used here, is to make present, to re-present a past that was (supposedly) once present. The Said, then, as a phenomenological sleight of hand, is characteristic of a system in which knowledge "derives from the assembling of terms united in a system for a locuter who states an apophansis. . . . Here the subject is origin, initiative, freedom, present" (78). The point being made here is that representation (the Said as a totalizing system) presupposes the ego's intentional activity as that which founds meaning, and thus identity. Moreover, the ontology of the Said consists of "the reduction of the other [*Autre*] to the Same, synchrony as *being* in its egological gathering" (Levinas, 1987a, 99).

Communication, according to the representational model of which Levinas is critical, is understood as the intentional expression of a sign designating the thought of an innate I, and the ensuing reception and deciphering of this sign (truth) by an other. Such an understanding—as assumed by the theorists discussed in Chapter One—is founded on a model of the subject of knowledge as fully self-present, and further, one whose relations with others are secondary. At the same time the other's "otherness" is understood in terms of complementarity or opposition. The other either agrees with me or contests me, but either way the other is nothing more than an alter-ego whose being is re-presented through the exchange of ideas understood as a "gathering" or a "texture of presence" (Levinas, 1987a, 99–101). In other words, insofar as the Said is a systematic totality, in which all parts are integrated, the other is reduced to the Same through the process of designation (identity).

But, as Levinas suggests, one must ask if the discourse that is called interior (the "I think") and thus remains egological does not presuppose an an-archical metaphysical relation with the Other in which self and Other are simultaneously mutually constitutive and incommensurable (102). This question is explored via the notion of the Saying. According to Levinas, unlike the Said, Saying "signifies before *essence,* before identification" (45). Indeed, Levinas argues that the Said (as the birthplace of ontology) presupposes the Saying, which is pre-original, not in any chronological sense, but inasmuch as the I is constituted by, and as, exposure to the Other that Saying affects. This then is in keeping with the claim made by Levinas in *Totality and Infinity,* that "ontology presupposes metaphysics" (Levinas, 1969, 48).

As I hope I have made clear, the Saying and the Said are not considered by Levinas to be distinct or disparate modes of communication. Rather, they are inextricably bound to one another and yet irreducible to one another, in much the same way as are the self and the Other. As Levinas demonstrates, the Saying can only take place in and through the Said, and yet the former is not completely absorbed by the latter in and through this manifestation.

[The Said] imprints the *trace* on the thematization itself, which hesitates between, on the one hand, structuration, . . . and on the other hand, the order of a non-nominalized apophansis of the other, in which the [S]aid remains a *proposition* . . . made to a neighbour. . . . But the apophansis is still a modality of [S]aying. The predicative statement . . . stands on the frontier of a *dethematization* of the [S]aid, and can be understood as a modality of approach and contact. Over and beyond the thematization and the content exposed in it . . . the apophansis signifies as a modality of the approach to another. It refers to a [S]aying on the hither side of the amphibology of being and entities. This [S]aying, in the form of responsibility for another, is bound to an irrecuperable, unrepresentable, past. (Levinas, 1978, 46–47, my emphasis)

What this quotation highlights nicely is the parallels between the Saying and the Said, and my reading of Levinas' understanding of the self-Other relation, as discussed throughout this chapter. In both cases we see how the alterity of the Other, and of Saying, is reduced to an Economy of the Same through thematization—a phenomenon that Levinas' work continuously struggles against. However, it has also been argued, contra to Rolland's claim regarding the oceanic feeling, that infinity, alterity, the Other, and Saying, are not exhausted in this manifestation. This is because, in and through Saying as exposure, there is inscribed the trace of infinity, of what does not enter into the present, and inverts the *arche* into anarchy.

Thus whilst, on the one hand it has been shown that Saying is impossible apart from the Said (or in the case of the self-Other relation, separation is impossible apart from relation), on the other hand, the Said (thematization) presupposes something "beyond essence", something it cannot incorporate, namely, Saying. Consequently, a dethematization of the Said "takes place", or perhaps more precisely, has always already "taken place", through the Said (insofar as it presupposes Saying). Or to use the words of Taylor, "Saying undoes the [S]aid by repeating the eternal return of a before that is never a now" (Taylor, 1987, 201). *Significance* then could be said to be that which makes signification possible, and simultaneously that which undermines it.

The connection between the Saying and the Said and the self-other relation becomes clearer still if we focus for a moment on a reading of Levinas' notion of responsibility. Responsibility, says Lingis, "is coextensive with our sensibility; in our sensibility we are exposed to . . . [exteriority], to the world's being in such a way that we are bound to answer for it" (Lingis, 1986, 226). In short, responsibility, like sensibility, is affected in and through the exposure to alterity that Levinas calls the face to face. As has been said, the Other's face(ing) is vocative and imperative "before" it is indicative and informative. It invokes a response and an "I", the "I" of response-*a*bility[17]. This is not to suggest that the encounter with the Other functions in terms of cause and effect, or consists of two successive phenomenal stages. Rather, in facing the Other singularizes my existence, calls forth an "I", and this becoming "I" *is* response-ibility. Indeed, responsibility is not "exercised in a will to be that affirms and assumes itself", but "is discovered in expropriation and exposure" (Lingis, 1979, 157). The Other's claim on me, then, is—contra to Freud's understanding of the biblical commandment to "love thy neighbour as thyself"—unconditional in the sense that it both precedes and exceeds any conscious decision on my part to accept or reject it on the grounds of the Other's merit. Even if I choose to turn away from the Other, the Other has nevertheless always already singled me out, singularized my existence, called forth an "I" (Lingis, 1979, 157). Thus my singularity is never independent of the Other, but rather the "I" as separate, as an active identifying with itself, is affected by and through exposure to the Other, or alterity. This leads me back to the claim made earlier in my discussion of *living from* . . . , that the space in which the sensuous material is laid out is always already extended by the sense of alterity. What I argued, and what I hope my discussion of responsibility has clarified, is that it is before the face of the Other that my enjoyment becomes my own, my own to give. The Other's face(ing) calls upon me vocatively and imperatively to give of my own sustenance, my own sentient becoming-in-the-world.

Perhaps I should briefly reiterate here what I see as the crucial difference between the Levinasian understanding of the self-other relation founded in and through responsibility and alterity and the Freudian notion of self-other relations that informs his discussion of the commandment to "love thy neighbour as thyself". I have argued that for Levinas, in and through the exposure to alterity, a sensuous contact with the others and with a world, I am called forth as a singular "I", and called to answer for all being. The face to face relation, since it is founded in alterity, avoids reducing the Other to the Same insofar as it delineates a model of self-other relations in which the "I" is singular and at the same time exists in and through relation to the Other. For Freud, on the other hand, the notion of responsibility evoked by the aforesaid commandment, is exterior and posterior to the "I" (rather than constitutive of it), and is a contractual proposal to be intentionally negotiated by the "I" who thinks and knows. In other words, the other is understood by Freud solely in terms of opposition and/or complementarity. The other is secondary to the subject's sense of self, and has no significance in-itself. Thus the other is reduced to the Same. He or she is either incorporated by the self through the economic bonds of love or constituted as against me. Either way the other is understood as a potential threat to the subject's sense of self, a threat that must be overcome, and yet one that paradoxically can never be entirely annihilated as Levinas' discussion of the commandment "thou shalt not kill"—as the responsibility affected in and through the Other's face(ing)—demonstrates (Levinas, 1987a, 105–10).

I will now return briefly to Tournier's *Gemini* in order to offer an alternative analysis, informed by my reading of Levinas, of the oceanic feeling.

THE IDEA OF THE INFINITE

As you may remember, Thomas Drycome, prior to his exposure to the doctrine of the Paraclete, described himself as being in an "unpaired state", "suffering as from an amputation" (Tournier, 1985, 116), or—as Freud might interpret it—castration. Thus, as we saw, Drycome attempts in various ways to become Didymus, the twin of Jesus/God: "the Twin Absolute, whose like was to be sought . . . in God" (110). Drycome's desire to penetrate and/or incorporate the mutilated body of Christ (the Other) as a metaphor of the phallus could be said to be paradigmatic of the subject's futile attempts at omnipotence through the paradoxical negation and/or incorporation of the Other—both of which, in effect, function to reduce the Other to the Same. Moreover, one could argue, following Levinas, that this attempted negation of alterity, this de-facing that pronounces a death sentence on the Other, is symptomatic of the ontological and sociopolitical status of the body in/of Western culture, as Freudian logic poignantly demonstrates. Drycome's stigmata, then, could be read as a sign(ifier) of the symbolic (and the corporeal) stigmatization of the other and the inevitably concurrent wounding of the self. I will return to this point in the final section of this chapter.

During what might be called the second stage of his spiritual experience, Drycome is exposed to (the notion of) the spirit (Ruah), or what he describes as "the flaming wind of the Paraclete" (116). In and through this exposure Drycome comes to speak of the Pentecost as the "inauguration of Parousia" (112). This term from the Greek *ousia* (substance) suggests, at least in Aristotle's *Categories,* the idea of subjectivity as presence[18]. But I want to argue, following Levinas, that there is another way to understand *being here* that is beyond presence and absence, and thus is not reliant on a notion of essence. As I stated earlier, what extends space is the exposure to, and contact with, the Other, who withdraws in the midst of this contact. As Lingis points out, exposure (contact) does not reveal the essence of the Other to the observing "I". Rather, contact inaugurates the *here* insofar as it reveals (without reducing) the proximity of the Other, and at the same time determines the one contacted as here (Lingis, 1986, 228–29). To be here is to be exposed to the Other, or, to phrase it in terms used earlier, the utterance *Here I am* both affects, and is an affect of, exposure. Thus the *here* is responsibility, the existence of the "I" through the Other and for the Other. What I want to suggest, then, is that it is in and through this exposure to the sensuosity of the elements (Ruah) that Drycome finds himself *here* in the face to face relation with the Other/God. But insofar as this *being here* is founded in and through an exposure to alterity, the Other overflows an Economy of the Same. Drycome no longer describes himself as a severed aspect of the Absolute, but *is* in the *here I am,* the exposedness to the Other and to the elements. Or to put it another way, Drycome could be said to figure existence as an inter-subjective process of (un)becoming, rather than to re-present being as static, universal, and knowable, since, as my reading of Levinas has demonstrated, it is both in and through the Other that the "I" is affected as separate and in relation[19].

What then becomes of the oceanic feeling with which this chapter opened? The framework employed by Freud predisposes him to theorize the oceanic feeling as a product of lack and an attempt on behalf of the individual to overcome this lack that is central to being. Thus his universalizing, or totalizing, theory of being functions to de-face the Other, since it assumes the possibility of knowing the Other through the interpretation of his or her actions as the manifestation of an intentional ego that is transparent[20] to others or knowable through a process of analogical apperception. My reading of Levinas, however, has provided an alternative way of attempting to "understand" the oceanic feeling without reducing it to an epistemological phenomenon. In short, the Levinasian framework offers me a means of sensing the oceanic without reducing it to an ideal object that I can know[21]. Like the infamous Canute, I cannot arrest the flux of the ocean(ic), nor can I call it forth in its entirety, circumscribe it, or idealize it. My relation with the Other, as Levinas argues, is one of infinitude, alterity—it is oceanic.

The movement of (un)becoming then is not simply, as Freud would have it, a dialectic from plenitude to lack, but a *being here,* an "otherwise than being" beyond plenitude and lack, beyond presence and absence, beyond essence. This is not to suggest that the metaphysical desire toward the absolutely Other is not directed and/or manifested in culturally and historically specific ways that are symptomatic of the ontological and sociopolitical status of being-in-the-world, but rather that there is at the same time something that precedes and exceeds all attempts to relativize, to economize, to thematize, to universalize what Levinas calls the ethical relation. And this "something else" is perhaps what Rolland means by the oceanic feeling, what Levinas calls alterity or infinity, and what Nietzsche terms "driving forces".

(DE)THEMATIZING THE MARKED BODY

The question that begs to be asked at this point is how the work of Levinas could prove useful in an attempt to develop a different economy of bodies and pleasures. It is my contention that the Levinasian model of self-other relations allows for a reconsideration of the marked body that overcomes the limitations of the Foucauldian project of self-overcoming through the practice of pleasure, since it acknowledges the power of interpretation to create life on an ontological level, and at the same time demonstrates that there is something that exceeds and destabilizes—makes possible and impossible—such a process. This "something"—namely, alterity, infinity, the Saying—is not a utopian possibility toward which the politically enlightened subject can strive, but rather is something like a process of (un)becoming that has always already "past", and that inaugurates change in terms beyond intentionality and individuality. Perhaps these claims will become clearer if we return briefly to some of the theorists discussed in Chapter One.

As I argued earlier, the works of Yamamoto et al., Edgerton and Dingman, Grumet, and Jeffreys are founded on a particular model of the subject, as is that of their counter-cultural antagonists. This model embraces a number of assumptions that include a distinction between mind and body, with the attendant location of individual identity in consciousness; an understanding of communication as a relatively straightforward process of the intentional giving out of signs by an ego, and a reception and deciphering of these signs by another ego; and a distinction between subject and object, self and other. I will critically address each of these assumptions and in doing so offer alternatives informed by my reading of the work of Levinas.

For those theorists discussed in Chapter One, identity is uncritically assumed to be located in consciousness. Further, the body is seen as secondary, as an object that the subject owns and/or inhabits. It can be intentionally manipulated or modified by the actions of the subject who owns/inhabits it for erotic, aesthetic, magico-religious, and/or communicative purposes. Indeed, the article authored by Yamamoto et al. is a particularly poignant example of a practice driven by such preconceptions. The article opens with the question, "who is the tattooed man? (Yamamoto et al., 1963, 365), and it is this desire to know the other, and the assumption that such knowledge is attainable, that precipitates the research. The work of these theorists relies on and reinforces all of the above-mentioned dichotomies. For example, the starting point of their thesis are the assumptions that the individual identity of the "tattooed man" is interior—that is, it is located in consciousness—and that the (tattooed) body can be read as an exterior expression of this interiority. "Objective information" regarding the identity of the "tattooed man" can be obtained, the authors believe, via a number of rational scientific methods. This archaeological process of unearthing the identity of the tattooed other as a suitable object of scientific knowledge is assumed to have no bearing on the identity of the researchers themselves, since the relation of the other to the self is secondary. Yamamoto et al. conclude their article with the following statement:

This investigation revealed that the tattooed man . . . shows definite personality deviations from his contemporaries. These deviations are in terms of a greater tendency to "act out" in both military and civilian life . . . [the investigation revealed that] that the tattooed man is more impulsive, and much more likely to have difficulties in heterosexual adjustment, despite . . . aspiration[s] to be more "masculine" than his fellows. (367)

This list of scientifically produced "revelations" is reiterated again and again throughout psychiatric and criminological discourses on the tattooed body. But as this quotation makes clear, despite the fact that the tattooed man's identity is understood in terms of an autonomous integral interiority, it is at the same time also defined in relation to "his fellows"—those who are not tattooed—who, it must be said, include the researchers themselves even if they are unaware of this. In other words, the pathologizing of the tattooed man relies on dichotomies such as normal/abnormal, moral/immoral, and so on. Such a process of categorization is never purely descriptive. It does not simply slot individuals into the essential categories to which they belong. Rather, categorization—or thematization as Levinas puts it—affects a (re)constitution of both the "subject" and "object" of interpretation according to the normative criteria assumed by the subject who interprets the bodily-being of the other. Insofar as the tattooed other is revealed through a process of analogical apperception, the alterity of the other is denied. Rather than finding itself in and through an encounter with the Other that transcends it (as Levinas would claim), the subject (in this case Yamamoto et al.) reaffirms his sense of self through the reduction of the other to the Same. The ethical relation is covered over through a denial of the self's interdependence on the Other.

As I suggested in Chapter One, tattooing is most often understood as a form of nonverbal communication. This is apparent in the work of all the theorists discussed, despite their polarised positions, but perhaps is most explicit in the article by Grumet. Grumet's model of "dermal diagnosis" is again founded on a distinction between mind and body, inside and outside, subject and object. As the subject of rational research, of knowledge, Grumet reaffirms these dichotomies through an increasingly complex process of interpretation and evaluation of the tattooed other. His reading of the tattooed body as a diagrammatic representation of integral interiority is given impetus by an understanding of communication as a process of expression and reception that takes place between two autonomous egos. But as I have argued via my reading of Levinas' understanding of the Saying and the Said, communication, as the supposed exchange of ideas that produces a "texture of presence", "an account naming or displaying a knowledge" (Levinas, 1987, 101), is only possible through a disavowal of that which it presupposes. Again, what motivates Grumet's analysis is the search for meaning, the desire to know. The tattooed other as the exotic object of knowledge whose sole purpose is to reaffirm the subject *qua subject*, is de-faced in and through a process of intellectual striptease—or is it more aptly a strip search? The other is once again reduced to nothing more than a pawn in the game of self-aggrandizement that the self plays according to the rules he or she sets. Or as Monique Wittig puts it in a rather scathing critique of Lacanian methodology, "there is no doubt that the [dermal diagnostician] found in the [other] the structures he said he found there, since he had previously put them there" (Wittig, 1992, 23).

As I argued earlier, Levinas' work is driven by an attempt to move beyond the ontological imperialism of the West—of which the works of Yamamoto et al. and Grumet are but two examples—which functions to reduce the Other to an Economy of the Same. For Levinas, the "I" is not an autonomous essence, but rather is affected in and through sensibility, or exposure to the Other. Unlike Yamamoto et al. and Grumet, who conceptualize identity as innate, autonomous, and located in consciousness, Levinas argues that identity is "sensible" (corporeal), and inter-subjective, and *is* in a continuous process of (un)becoming. Thus a Levinasian approach to the tattooed body would inevitably begin with an acknowledgment that any such encounter with the Other would always already affect a (re)constitution of the self, the Other, and the world. Moreover, the Levinasian model of self-other relations refutes the assumption held by Yamamoto et al. and Grumet that the other is an object of knowledge. Levinas argues that the Other is transcendent to me and therefore cannot be contained by any idea that I may have of him- or her. Rather than being a subject designating objects (as is the case in Yamamoto et al. and Grumet), the self is produced in and through an encounter with that which resists all attempts to assimilate it by representing it. The Other of Levinasian metaphysics is not simply a threat that must be contained by the self through a process of interpretation and categorization[22], but rather is its very condition of possibility. The self, according to this model, is not an autonomous essence, but the "site" of affective and inter-subjective processes; the "I" exists through and for the Other. This is not, however, to suggest that the "I" is alienated from itself in and through the relation with that which is not the self as Freud claims. Rather, both self and Other mark and are marked in and through this encounter; each could be said to have the other-in-one's-skin.

Thus not only is the distinction between mind and body, self and other, undermined by Levinas, but the very question of what the tattooed body of the other means, or whom the tattooed wo/man is, is rendered redundant. Where, then, would a Levinasian approach to the marked body begin, if not with the assumption that meaning/identity is reducible to an essence present in the textual body of the other, and objectively interpretable by the subject of rational analysis?

Insofar as Levinas' work is concerned with metaphysics as that which precedes and makes possible, and at the same time exceeds and destabilizes, ontology, it provides an opportunity for a reorientation of philosophy. More particularly, I want to argue that it occasions a move away from the question of signification, which has dominated analyses of the marked body, and allows for a consideration of *signifiance* as an affective process of sensibility that both exceeds the subject/meaning, and constitutes its condition of possibility.

As I argued earlier, the Saying (the *signifiance* of signification) is understood by Levinas as exposure, as a condition for all communication. Whilst *signifiance* or the Saying is never fully present in the Said or signification, the latter constitutes the only access we have to the Saying. The Saying leaves a trace on the Said, but is never revealed in it. *Signifiance*, then, as a process of infinition, makes meaning and identity possible, and at the same time precludes the concretization or delineation of existence. Inasmuch as the theorists discussed in Chapter One focus primarily on the Said (the meaning of the marked body as text), it could be said that their work functions to reduce the other to an object of knowledge through a process of "designating identities". The methods of "dermal diagnosis" employed by these writers designate or represent the marked body as the intentional expression (conscious or unconscious, it makes little difference) of an innate ego. Representation in this case consists of a re-presentation of that which is supposedly latent and/or originary: namely, the subjective essence. Dermal diagnosis then could be thought of as a form of intellectual midwifery whereby the truth of the tattooed subject is (supposedly) brought to light through a process of textual extraction. But what is re-presented is nothing more than that which was (supposedly) always already present. Likewise, the dermal diagnostician "learns" nothing that he or she did not always already know from the textual body he or she reads. The tattooed body of the other merely provides an occasion for the replication or reaffirmation of the researcher's sense of self through a reconstitution of the body of the other, according to the normative criteria assumed by the subject of interpretation.

As would be expected, Levinas is critical of Socratic maieutics[23] as exemplified by the above-mentioned approach, since it reinforces the primacy of the Same by denying the Other's alterity, and thus constitutes what Levinas might call a "philosophy of injustice". According to Levinas, insofar as the Other is incommensurable with the self, to welcome the Other is to learn something from him/her. The encounter with the textual Other, then, is not understood in Levinasian terms as the revelation of univocal meanings or innate identities, but rather is an "event", a structural possibility that makes possible all subsequent experience, that inaugurates (un)becoming in ways that are beyond the subject's intention or comprehension, rather than reaffirming being.

Rather than conceptualizing the marked body of the Other as an epistemological object, a text to be deciphered, it is possible, drawing on the work of Levinas, to "read" the textual Other as the site of infinition in which the "whole" is revealed as inhabited by that which it cannot contain. The trace of the Other that marks (the body of) the self is not simply the product of authorial intention, but is always already something Other—namely, the trace of *signifiance*. To mark, and to be marked, then, is not merely an intentional act, but is rather an integral aspect of the inter-subjective and/or intertextual character of what we might call existence and existents—ineffable forms of (un)becoming that are beyond being or essence. Insofar as this is the case, the task of reconfiguring the marked/tattooed body consists not so much of a thematizing (what is it? what does it mean?) of the body of the Other, since this would inevitably result in a reduction of the Other to an Economy of the Same. Rather, my reading of Levinas' work provides the opportunity to consider the ineffability of the tattooed body as a literalization of the process of corporeal inscription affected in and through the face to face relation. If this is so, the focus shifts from the question of what the tattooed body *means* to what the process of marking and being marked *does*, a question of affectivity rather than one of intentionality and/or signification. This question will be explored in more depth in the following chapter, which focuses on the *signifiance* of textuality and pleasure as it is elaborated in the work of Roland Barthes.

NOTES

1. My use of the pronoun "he" here is deliberate, since both Freud's and Lacan's models of oedipalization are more applicable, or at least less problematic, in the case of the male.

2. It is important to note here that this nostalgia for a past that may have never existed is retrospectively imposed on the pre-oedipal stage. In effect, then, one of the problems with this model is its limited notion of temporality. Both past and future are understood solely in terms of the present—a theoretical gesture of which Levinas is sceptical, as we shall come to see in due course.

3. I am indebted to Elizabeth Grosz (1990b) for this reading of Lacan.

4. Similarly, in a provocative discussion of both Freud's and Lacan's notions of fetishism, Anne McClintock argues that psychoanalysis's "genuflection to the phallic economy of one rehearses the logic of fetishism—the disavowal of . . . difference and agency, . . . and repetitive fixation on a single organizing principle . . . which both conceals difference, and thereby ratifies it as transcendent and inevitable" (McClintock, 1993, 12).

5. Lingis (1994b).

6. The thinking behind this claim is that monotheism, or Christocentrism, consists of the worship of the corpse of Christ—a figure whose very essence is death. Thus religion could be thought of as a form of "spiritual necrophilia", in that it is a system of (de)valuation that debases sensuosity, the transient, the ephemeral, or, to use a Levinasian term, alterity, in its insistence on a model of self-other relations founded on a fundamental lack that the subject attempts to overcome through a reduction of the other

to an Economy of the Same. For an in-depth critique of Christocentrism that has been central to the development of the argument presented here, see Lingis (1978).

7.   Levinas uses the term "Other" to gesture toward a notion of the other as existing in a relation of alterity to the self. The Other is the metaphysical Other, whereas the other is the ontological other, which presupposes the former. Throughout the remainder of the text I will use these different terms in accordance with the way in which otherness is understood in the given context.

8.   For Levinas the *I can* denotes an intransitivity that is not the capacity of an already established I.

9.   For an extended discussion of this claim, see Lingis (1986).

10.   For an extended discussion of this claim, see Lingis (1979; 1986).

11.   See Levinas (1969, 50–51).

12.   Here Levinas is referring to a term associated with ancient Greek philosophy, meaning beginning, starting point, principle, ultimate underlying substance, and so on.

13.   See "Clivage" (Splitting) in *The Pleasure of the Text* (1994) in which Barthes formulates an account of what he calls the anachronic subject. This ties in with my reading of Levinas' understanding of the Saying and the Said, insofar as *jouissance* (the Saying) wells up in, and disrupts, pleasure (the Said), but at the same time Saying (*jouissance*) is impossible without pleasure (the Said).

14.   This is opposed to the view of the dermal diagnosticians and the practitioners of modern primitivism discussed in Chapter 1.

15.   The point I am making here is that exposedness is not an intentional act of dissimulation.

16.   Levinas uses this term, as does Barthes for whom *signifiance* is meaning insofar as it is sensually produced (Barthes, 1994, 61). Likewise, for Kristeva, *signifiance* is "precisely this uninhibited and unbounded generating process, this increasing operation of the drives towards, in and through language; towards, in and through the exchange system and its protagonists—the subject and his institutions" (Kristeva, 1984, 17). *Signifiance* then is the (non)site of exposure, of alterity, of infinity, and thus is in no way interpretable as significance, despite the fact that this is how Miller translates it in Barthes (1994).

17.   The I *is* this ability, the *I can.*

18.   For a critique of parousia in the Aristotelian sense, see Jacques Derrida's *Margins of Philosophy,* A. Bass (trans.), Sussex: Harvester Press, 1986.

19.   Jean-Luc Nancy makes a similar claim when he states that "present is that which occupies a place . . . it is not an essence. . . . The place is *place*—site, situation, disposition—in the coming into space of a time, in a spacing that allows that something to *come* into presence . . . something, some *one* comes ('one' because it 'comes' not because of its substantial unity: the she, he, or it that comes can be one and unique in its coming but multiple and repeated 'in-itself'. Presence *takes place*, that is to say it *comes into* presence. It is that which comes indefinitely to itself, never stops coming, arriving: the 'subject' that is never subject to itself. The 'ipseity' of presence lies in the fact that it engenders itself *into* presence: presence to itself, in a sense, but where this 'self' itself is only the *to* (the taking place, the spacing) of presence" (in Cadava et al., 1991, 7).

20.   This is the case even if the subject's intentions are latent or unconscious, as Freud's work on the analysis of dreams demonstrates.

21.   The reason for this is that Levinas focuses on a different order of being than Freud—namely, metaphysics, as that which precedes ontology. Consequently he is concerned with the inauguration of the self-other relation, rather than on the self's attempts to overcome it.

22.   Valerie Walkerdine argues that the observation/interpretation of the researcher, "like all scientific activity, constitutes a voyeurism in its will to truth; a will to truth which not only encompasses a desire for certainty and power, but also a terror of the other who is watched" (Walkerdine, 1986, 167).

23.   See for example, Levinas (1969, 43–48, 64–70).

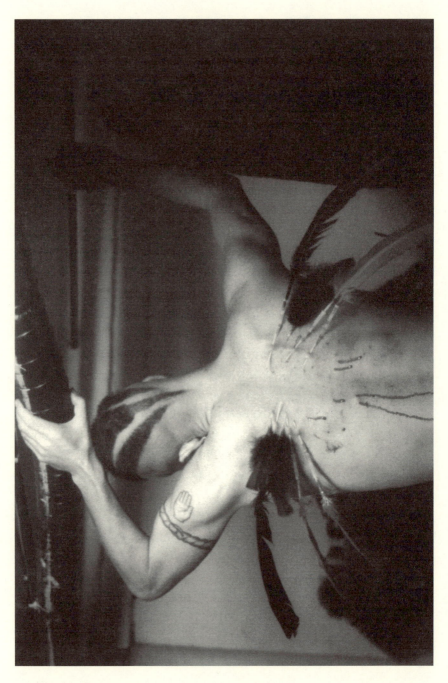

Steve in the dressing room (Hellfire Club), 1997. Photo copyright © Amanda James Photography

Chapter Four

Reading Body Writing: An Ethics of (Inter)Textual Pleasure

Language is a skin. . . . My language trembles with desire. (Barthes, 1990b, 73)

In the previous chapter, I argued that insofar as the self-other relation is founded in alterity, any attempt to know the Other functions to reduce the Other and difference to an Economy of the Same. The thematization of (the body of) the Other, according to the Levinasian model that was outlined, is a totalizing gesture that veils over alterity and disavows the subject's debt to the Other, or the intersubjective character of identity and difference. Dermal diagnosis, it was argued, constitutes just such a gesture. What motivates the research of the criminologists and psychologists discussed in Chapter One is the desire to know the "thing-in-itself", and the belief that such objective knowledge is possible. The textual body of the Other—in this case the subject in/of tattooing—is scrutinised, strip searched. The dermal diagnostician performs the role of what Roland Barthes calls the critic. In each case, the one who interprets the text scrutinises the (textual) body of the other in order to dis-cover what is inside it. The critic is "like those children who take a clock apart in order to find out what time it is" (Barthes, 1990b, 71).

But as Levinas argues, the imposition of meaning is always perspectival and secondary, or as Nietzsche puts it: "at the bottom of . . . the question "what is it?" . . . there always lies "what is it for *me?*" (Nietzsche, 1968b, #556, 301). In other words

coming to know means "to place oneself in a conditional relation to something"; *to feel oneself conditioned by something and oneself to condition it*—it is therefore under all circumstances establishing, denoting, and making-conscious of conditions (not forth-coming entities, things, what is "in-itself"). (Nietzsche, 1968b, 103, my emphasis)

Neither self nor Other, according to this model, is a "thing-in-itself", but rather is constructed, deconstructed, and reconstructed ceaselessly[1] in and through a disseminative relation of, or with, alterity.

As I have argued, Levinas provides a model of self-other relations that allows us to move beyond the solipsism and individualism inherent in Foucault's model of ethical self-(trans)formation, and thus can be said to offer a more fertile starting point from which to begin to elaborate a different economy of bodies and pleasures not founded on hermeneutic principles. For the subject in/of tattooing, the importance of Levinas' argument concerning the irreducibility of the Other to the Same appears in the irreducibility of the Saying to the Said. Yet, since Foucault's account of pleasure lacks an understanding of alterity, and Levinas' account of *significance* sidesteps the issue of pleasure altogether, we must now seek a reading of pleasure that embraces both the ethics of intersubjectivity and the complexities of (inter)textuality. It is in the work of Barthes that a complex of such ideas finds their articulation.

The aim of this chapter, then, is to formulate an understanding of the affectivity of textuality that shares resonances with the model of self-other relations developed in the previous chapter. Drawing on the work of Barthes, I will provide a critique of the notion of the (tattooed body as) text as a veil, "behind which lies, more or less hidden, meaning (truth)" (Barthes, 1994, 64), which informs the theses of the theorists discussed in Chapter One, and propose instead the idea of the textual body (the subject in/of tattooing) as a generative process of perverse productivity.

THE BARTHESIAN CORPUS

During the intense social, political, and intellectual upheavals of the 1960s and 70s, the work of Roland Barthes was argued vehemently, both for and against. However, over the last decade or so we have witnessed a considerable decline in engagement with what have come to be known as his later works[2], at least by English-speaking theorists. There have been numerous reasons posited for this "turning away", the most common of which is the claim that Barthes "sold out"; that his shift in focus from literature and other such social structures to textuality constitutes a turning away from politics and toward a form of self-indulgent aesthetics[3]. Whilst this line of argument seems to me decidedly limited in scope, there are, I believe, a number of reasons why it is worth mentioning here.

First, claims of this sort assume that the author (in this case Barthes) is the moral subject of his or her ideological positions, and is thus liable to judgment on moral or political grounds. Such judgment involves not only the attribution of the text to a unique individual, but, at the same time, the classification of the wo/man "behind" the text[4]. Thus both the text and the author are assumed to be perfectible. The text is "too much *this,* not enough *that"* (Barthes, 1994, 13); the author is bourgeois, an aberration, a revolutionary, a threat to society, and so on. As we witnessed earlier, it is not only the body of Barthes that comes under such close scrutiny from those who see themselves as having access to truth or knowledge. Yamamoto et al., Grumet, Lombroso, Curry, Idexa, and Jeffreys in their varying ways all read the textual body of the other as the external expression of the author's interior identity. In other words, the approach that both these theorists and those who judge Barthes' work adopt involves the unquestioned use of terms that Barthes' work sets out to problematize. I will go on to discuss both the dominant understanding of authors, texts, readers, and the relation between them, and the alternative model that Barthes proposes in due course, but for the moment suffice it to say that my approach to the corpus of writing that bears the signifier "Roland Barthes" does not involve a judgment of the moral character of the "man himself", the subject "behind" or in the textual body.

Nor, for reasons which will become apparent, do I intend to engage in a teleological mapping of the man or his work. Rather, and this brings me to my second point, I want to provide what Moriarty calls a kaleidoscopic perspective (Moriarty, 1991, 186–87) to certain elements or fragments of the Barthensian corpus, which itself is fragmentary. Whilst this may seem like a protracted justification of my decision to engage directly only with (some of) the texts—or parts thereof—published in and after 1968, it is rather an attempt to head off at the pass the assumption that such a focus is the result of a belief that the period 1968 to 1977 represents an epoch of enlightenment in Barthes' work, or in the man himself. Indeed, to view Barthes' texts as a progression from bad to good, a regression from good to bad, or even from bad to worse (or any other combination thereof) is to imply that the text has a particular purpose that it either achieves or fails in. This sort of functionalist approach is exemplified by Grumet's elaboration of the "love/hate ratio" discussed in Chapter One, the purpose of which is to unearth "the evolution of character development" (Grumet, 1983, 490). Consequently, I will refrain from pronouncing judgments in the name of Truth, Politics, Science, and Morality, since I do not read the Barthensian corpus as a transmissible object. Rather than discovering a meaning hidden in the text with which I must inevitably agree or disagree (a form of interpretation as evaluation), I want to explore what this body *does*—at least for, to, and/or with me. In other words, I want to acknowledge that my reading(s) of Barthes' body of work "reveals" as much about me as it does about the body of texts referred to as "Roland Barthes".

However—and this is my third reason for opening with such a discussion— during the course of this chapter it is hoped that the supposed opposition posited by some critics between Barthes' early "politicized" texts, and his later "depoliticized", or aesthetic texts will be destabilized. But, whilst I do not seek to honour this opposition, neither do I desire to annihilate it, to prove it wrong. Rather, I want to divert the stereotype of the good/bad text/author. I want to perform, as Barthes might put it, a "transgression of transgression" in order to allow the return of subjectivity, textuality, politics, and the body, but in "another place"[5]. Thus my aim in this chapter, as in the book as a whole, is not to gesture toward a possible future utopia exempt from meaning, a place where the tattooed body, like all texts, no longer signifies. Instead, what I propose is an extension of the Levinasian claim that disarticulation or dethematization is an inextricable aspect of the process of articulation, by focusing on the *affective* dimension of (inter)textuality[6]. Similarly, in a section of *Roland Barthes* entitled "Amphibologies", Barthes stresses the need to recognize the duplicity of language—the idea that *signifiance* simultaneously structures meaning and decomposes it—rather than attempting to either privilege one meaning over another, or seek out the radical polysemy of language according to which something can mean anything and thus nothing (Barthes, 1977, 72–73). In so doing, I hope to move beyond the tendency apparent in counter-cultural analyses of the tattooed body as text that simply celebrate it as one possible site of the production of an unassimilable, and thus (potentially) revolutionary, excess or *counter*-cultural force. For as Barthes argues in "Exemption of Meaning", both the positing of truth or doxa and the supposedly opposed desire to resist all meaning are in the end equally problematic insofar as both function to substantiate a "right way" (Barthes, 1977, 87).

THE DEATH OF THE AUTHOR

Since I am dissatisfied with the notions of textuality, subjectivity, and communication at work in the writings of the theorists discussed in Chapter One, let me begin my reading of Barthes' later works with an examination of the much discussed text, "The Death of the Author", first published in France in 1968. This text performs a critique of the modern figure of the Author, and in so doing suggests an alternative conceptualization of writers, readers, texts, and the relations between them. Barthes claims:

The image of literature to be found in ordinary culture is tyrannically centred on the author, his person, his life, his tastes, his passions, while criticism still consists for the most part in saying that Baudelaire's work is the failure of Baudelaire the man, Van Gogh's his madness, Tchaikovsky's his vice. This *explanation* of a work is always sought in the man or woman who produced it, as if it were always in the end, through the more or less transparent allegory of the fiction, the voice of a single person, the *Author* "confiding" in us. (Barthes, 1990a, 114–15)

If we cast our minds back for a moment to Chapter Two, we find interesting resonances between this quote and the Foucauldian understanding of confession, interpretation, and classification as aspects or technologies of self-formation. For Foucault, confession is at the heart of procedures of individualization. Given this, I would argue that the interpretation of the Author's text as his or her "confiding in us" plays into normalizing systems of classification and evaluation insofar as it individualizes the Author in accordance with the normative criteria assumed by the critic. Moreover, such a process reaffirms the critic's sense of him- or herself in relation to the other[7]. We have witnessed such a process at work in the approach taken by the theorists discussed in Chapter One. For example, Grumet begins his analysis of the tattooed body from the premise that "tattoos are a form of non-verbal communication that can often be deciphered" (Grumet, 1983, 489). His method of dermal diagnosis interprets the textual body as the external expression of an interior Author; the corporeal hieroglyphs are understood as a nonverbal "confiding in" the reader. What Grumet and those of his theoretical position offer us is an explanation of the tattooed body that is sought in the man or woman who produced or Authored it, and, moreover, is evidence of the individual's nature or intentions (whether conscious or unconscious), and thus his or her social (un)acceptability. What is more, such a reading is assumed to have no bearing whatsoever on the subject of interpretation since there is an assumed absolute distinction between self and other, subject and object, writing and reading.

"The Death of the Author", on the other hand, functions to disconnect textuality from an authorial source, or, to put it otherwise, deconstructs the assumed "I" of liberal individualism. I want to explore this claim, and the relation between the modern notion of the Author and the liberal humanist "I", via an examination of Sean Burke's critique of Barthes' text. In *The Death & Return of the Author* (1993), Sean Burke criticizes Barthes' targeting of the Author, since in his opinion the existence of critical approaches to literature such as New Criticism, Russian Formalism, and that of the Prague Structuralists imply that such a target has "long since retreated out of range" (Burke, 1993, 25). Indeed, Burke goes on to argue that "the Author in 'The Death of the Author' only seems ready for death precisely because he never existed in the first place" (27). Burke points out, and perhaps rightly so, that the concept of the death of the Author invokes the Nietzschean death of God. In fact, he suggests that it does so intentionally so as to lend force to the Barthesian stereotype of the deific Author, and the liberating consequences of its abandonment. But, he claims,

this analogy . . . is askew in one very broad sense. The attributes of omnipotence, omnipresence, of being the first uncaused cause, purpose and end of the world are all affirmed a priori in the Christian God: they inhere in his definition, without them He is not God. Not so for the author though: we can, without contradiction, conceive of authors who do not issue "single theological messages", who do not hold a univocal mastery over their texts. (25)

I am not entirely comfortable with, or convinced by, Burke's line of argument. In fact, it seems to me that there may be another way to view the analogy. In *The Gay Science* #108, entitled "New Struggles", Nietzsche states that

[a]fter Budda was dead, his shadow was still shown for centuries in a cave—a tremendous gruesome shadow. God is dead: but given the way men are, there may still be caves for thousands of years in which his shadow will be shown—And we—we still have to vanquish his shadow, too. (Nietzsche, 1974, 191)

What this aphorism suggests is that despite a shift in focus in philosophical reasoning from the figure of God as the measure of all things (as in the works of metaphysicians such as Descartes), to the figure of Man (as in the works of Kant, Rousseau, Mill and others), there nevertheless remains a universalizing system of evaluation that is no less delimiting in scope. We live life, Nietzsche claims, in the shadow of God—of a God that may not exist, or that may never have existed in any essential way—the representation (which at the same time constitutes the creation) of which nevertheless gives life to particular ways of being. Similarly, the Author of which Barthes is critical may never have assumed the status of a *fait accompli*, and yet we most certainly live in its shadow, as theorists such as Grumet, Yamamoto et al., Jeffreys, and so on demonstrate. This is not to completely dismiss Burke's claim that there is something askew with the analogy. Rather, it is to argue that whilst the death of God may have slightly different implications than the death of the Author, it could be said that neither has in fact taken place, at least not in any final way, which is the point stressed by Nietzsche. For as Jeffner Allen points out, "with the death of God the human subject stands in for the divine subject and takes its place as all that the divine subject once represented" (Allen, 1988, 287). Thus whilst the dominant system of interpretation and evaluation may have undergone quantitative changes, it nevertheless remains relatively unchallenged at a qualitative level. Anthropocentrism is simply another version of theocentrism, or, as Levinas might put it, thematization is a totalizing gesture insofar as it attempts to reduce alterity (or the Other) to an epistemological object that the subject (as God) can know.

Despite being in and of a world that is for the most part secularized, the characteristics of Godliness (meaning, order, autonomy, truth, knowledge, and so on), still cast a pervasive, if not monolithic, shadow that to some degree coheres in the figure of the (liberal) subject. As I will go on to argue, the death of the Author is not so much the destruction of an essential reality, nor the dismissal of an outmoded fiction, but more of a deconstruction, or as Barthes puts it, a decomposition of a historical formation. In *Roland Barthes*, Barthes asks us to imagine for a moment that the function of the contemporary writer or intellectual is to sustain and stress what he calls "the decomposition of bourgeois consciousness" (1977, 63). In order to do this, he says, "the image must retain all its precision" (63). In effect, what Barthes is suggesting is that we must not presume that we can critique the image from a position somehow/where outside of "bourgeois consciousness", or as Foucault might put it, outside systems of power/knowledge. Rather, we must "remain within this consciousness and . . . proceed to dismantle it, to weaken it, to break it down on the spot, as we would do with a lump of sugar by steeping it in water" (63). What Barthes makes evident in his discussion of the role of the contemporary writer and the notion of decomposition is, first, that intellectual work cannot take place in a space untainted by the logics of dominant culture, and, second, that decomposition is not synonymous with destruction, since the latter assumes the possibility of exteriority. The destruction of "bourgeois consciousness" (assuming for a moment that such a thing were possible) simply posits an alternative truth to the "doxa" of what Barthes refers to as "dogmatic language", and thus maintains, rather than deconstructs, dichotomous logic. Destruction, says Barthes, assumes that we are "able to *overleap*. But overleap where? Into what language? Into which site of good conscience and bad faith?" (63). Decomposition, on the other hand, is a process in which the subject who participates is simultaneously decomposed. He or she is de/re/constituted as something other than the author of knowledge and of his- or her own being.

Like Nietzsche, Barthes refuses to turn a blind eye, to flee from the cave of shadows into the less discomforting clear light of day where God, the Author, appears to no longer exist. Instead, Barthes calls us to participate in a game of shadow-play that fractures or disarticulates the articulation of that which is "tremendous, gruesome". Indeed, for Barthes, like Foucault, not only is there no outside of power, no (en)lightened place where shadows do not fall, but, moreover, shadows are necessary if the duplicity of meaning is to avoid concretization, if one is not to remain "deaf to one's own language"[8]. There are those, says Barthes, who long for a text without a shadow, "without the 'dominant ideology'"[9]. But this desire is, according to Barthes, ill-conceived, for to want a text without a shadow is to want an infertile text, a text without productivity, a text that is singular, autonomous, closed. "The text needs its shadow: this shadow is a *bit* of ideology, a *bit* of representation, a *bit* of subject: . . . subversion must produce its own chiaroscuro" (Barthes, 1994, 32). In effect, then, a dichotomous "black and white" approach to textuality veils over duplicity and thus becomes entrenched in the "violence of prejudice" (Barthes, 1977, 47) that the doxa/paradoxa dichotomy (re)produces, as I will demonstrate in due course.

THE SUBJECT IN/OF WRITING

In "The Death of the Author", Barthes replaces the traditional understanding of literature with an alternative model of writing and textuality. The Author too is de/re/composed, and we witness the emergence of the writer or scriptor[10]. For Barthes, there are important differences attenuated to these historically and culturally specific discursive formations. Unlike a work of literature, for example, which is traditionally assumed to be the unique and unequivocal expression of the individual soul or psyche of the Author who produced it, Barthes claims that "the text is a tissue of quotations drawn from innumerable centres of culture . . . a multi-dimensional space in which meanings blend and clash" (Barthes, 1990a, 116). It is wrong, he argues, to conceive of the notion of the text as synonymous with the notion of literature: "literature *represents* a finite world, the text *figures* the infinite of language" (Barthes, 1977, 119). Barthes' critique of the mimetic theory of literature, which relies on a distinction between reality and representation, makes way for a notion of performativity in which "reality" is always already fictional. Truth can never be discovered, only ever be un/re/made[11], and so on, in and through an infinite process of *significance*. Barthes calls this process intertextuality, and claims that it is impossible to live outside the infinite text.

The notion of intertextuality also has significant repercussions for rethinking subjectivity. Unlike the classical Author, the writer of texts—or the tattooed subject—who may wish to "express" him- or herself

ought at least to know that the inner "thing" he thinks to "translate" is itself only a ready-formed dictionary, its words only explainable through other words, and so on indefinitely . . . [the writer] bears within him . . . this immense dictionary from which he draws a writing that can know no halt. (Barthes, 1990a, 117)

Hence, there is no essential self as such that precedes and produces texts. The writer is not a parental figure who exists before, labours over, and nourishes his or her offspring. Rather, the writer participates in a non-unified process of productivity—writing, unwriting, rewriting, and so on *ad infinitum* fragments of the fictions of which he or she and his or her world are composed[12]. Thus insofar as the writer "accompanies" his or her de/re/composition of the infinite text, then his or her subjectivity could be said to exist only in its performance, its continual (un)becoming. This is what I would suggest is meant by Barthes' claim that "the modern scriptor is born simultaneously with the text, is in no way equipped with a being preceding or exceeding the writing, is not the subject with the book as predicate; there is no other time than that of the enunciation and every text is eternally written *here and now* . . . the temporality is different" (116). This is reminiscent of the Levinasian model of temporality outlined in the previous chapter. Just as the scriptor does not precede writing, the Levinasian "I", who enters language with the utterance "here I am", does not re-present himself in doing so. Rather, the utterance affects exposure. In both cases, one's existence forms in the trope the-one-for-the-other. And the utterance ("here I am", or in Barthes' case, writing) is not a phenomenal event that takes place in the present, but occurs (or has always already occurred) in and as an an-archial past that cannot be re-presented: a past "more ancient than every representable origin, a pre-original . . . *passed* . . . a past which was never present" (Levinas, 1978, 9, 24). Such a move beyond the presence/absence, self/other, subject/object dichotomy radically resists recuperation into an Economy of the Same.

Just as the writer is a plurality of texts (rather than a unique, unified, self-transparent, discrete, and autonomous individual—the *causa sine qua non*), it follows that the reader is also an effect of language (Barthes, 1977, 79). As Barthes states in the opening pages of *S/Z,*

"I" is not an innocent subject, anterior to the text, one which will subsequently deal with the text as it would an object to dismantle or a site to occupy. This "I" which approaches the text is already itself a plurality of other texts, of codes which are infinite, or more precisely, lost (whose origin is lost). (Barthes, 1995, 10)

The reader, then, is not so much an "individual" (in the liberal humanist sense), as a subject; a subject in/of language who, in and through the performative act of reading, (re)writes the text: and, here, "to read", which is also to (re)write, is an "(in)transitive verb"[13]. Performativity as (un)becoming does not seek truth or closure, but rather "ceaselessly calls into question all origins" (Barthes, 1990a, 116)[14]. We never find, says Barthes, "a state where man is separated from language, which he then creates in order to 'express' what is taking place within him: it is language which teaches the definition of man, not the reverse" (Barthes, 1990c, 135)[15]. The subject then, as text, is superficial, unstable, dispersed, a multiplicity of (inter)texts "to be ranged over, not pierced" (Barthes, 1990a, 117). As I have attempted to demonstrate, what Barthes' writings offer us is a decomposition of the traditional distinctions between reader and writer, dermal diagnostician and tattooed body, subject and object, reality and fiction, cause and effect, producer and product, production and consumption, active and passive, and so on.

Before I go on to discuss in more depth the Barthensian notion of textual affectivity, what he calls "the pleasure of the text", let me first ponder for a moment or two the implications of my reading of "The Death of the Author" for (re)reading the tattooed body. As has been said, the theses of the theorists discussed in Chapter One rely on particular notions of subjectivity, textuality, and communication, all of which could be said to be inherent aspects of liberal humanism. It seems to me that what drives such analyses is the question, "what does that mean?"[16], and the desire to provide an unequivocal answer. This search for certainty, for knowledge, involves "something like a game of hide-and-seek in which every investigator is a private eye and every investigation becomes a detective story" (Taylor, 1997, 17). This is a story in which the principal character (the criminologist, the psychologist, the critic) enacts the role of the hero of his or her own epic narrative, his or her own being[17]: he is a Jason-like figure, attracted by danger, who, with the gods on his side, is confident of retrieving the Golden Fleece, and thereby taking his rightful place as king[18] Jason is the leader of an illustrious band of heroes (the Argonauts) and captain of the *Argos*, the ship that gave name to their quest. But this pursuit of the *etymon*—true or original signification[19]—is perilous, and, as Jason comes to know only too well, ends in murder, in the killing of the other, which the Levinasian focus on alterity seeks to avoid, or at the very least, to prove misdirected.

What I want to suggest is that my analysis of the Barthesian understanding of (inter)textuality provides another way to read and write this story. In *Roland Barthes,* Barthes suggests that the figure of the *Argo* (each piece of which the Argonauts gradually replaced, thus forming an entirely new ship) "affords the allegory of an eminently structural object, created not by genius, inspiration, determination, evolution, but by two modest actions . . . *substitution* . . . and *nomination*" (Barthes, 1977, 46, emphasis in original). In substitution one thing replaces another, as in a paradigm, whilst nomination refers to the fact that the name of something does not indexically refer to the stability of the parts of that thing. Thus Barthes concludes that "by dint of combinations made within one and the same name, nothing is left of the *origin: Argo* is an object with no other cause than its name, with no other identity than its form" (46, emphasis in original). The *Argo* then could be said to give name, not to the attainment of truth or origins, but to the alteritous character of (inter)textuality. Thus the textual subject of this nonlinear voyage has neither origin nor destination; it does not grasp the other, the etymon, and in doing so attain rightful sovereignty, but rather encounters, or is exposed to, alterity in the Levinasian sense, and partakes in the infinite performativity of (un)becoming, or, as Barthes would have it, (de)composition.

Given this, it seems no longer necessary, or for that matter tenable, to conceive of the role of the critic—or the dermal diagnostician—as the canny detective of deeply hidden truths or origins. Or as Mark Taylor so lucidly puts it:

In the end, it all comes down to a question of skin. And bones. The question of skin and bones is the question of hiding and seeking. And the question of hiding and seeking is the question of detection. Is detection any longer possible? Who is the detective? What is detected? Is there anything left to hide? Is there any longer a place to hide? Can anyone continue to hide? Does skin hide anything or is everything nothing but skin? Skin rubbing at skin, skin, skin, skin, skin. (Taylor, 1997, 11)[20]

For Barthes, like Taylor, everything is superficial, one-dimensional, like the shadows that flicker on cave walls. But the question is how to read/(re)write these shadows. Shall we continue to interpret them as signifiers of a Transcendental Signified, as the source of our deification, or, following Barthes, will we "agree" to accompany their decomposition through the dramatization of a game of shadow play that knows no beginning, no end?

THE PLEASURE OF THE TEXT, OR WHAT TO DO WITH BARTHES

In an article published in 1978 entitled "Doing and Not Doing Things with Barthes", Steven Ungar identifies a response to Barthes' later writings that is still apparent twenty years later: a response I am faced with surprisingly regularly when I mention my fascination with the texts discussed in this chapter. But perhaps this puzzlement, the question of what to do with Barthes, is not such a surprising response after all. Ungar argues that Barthes' later works "function less as commentaries on literary objects than as literary objects in their own right which require a suitable critical response of their own" (Ungar, 1978, 91). This so-called change, then, in what Barthes does, and in the way he does it, necessitates a different approach to reading (Barthes), or, as Ungar puts it: "one [can] no longer 'do things' with Barthes as one might have done before" (Ungar, 1978, 91). Similarly, Andrew Brown suggests that it "is as if Barthes dedicated one decade, the 1960's, to putting a lot of hard work and political passion into a scientific and combative science of semiology, then spent another decade, the 1970's, throwing it all away" (Brown, 1992, 5). But as Brown's thesis demonstrates, this shift constitutes not so much a turning away from political concerns, but rather a more self-reflexive and complex approach to theoretical discourse: an approach to writing as a signifying excess, as that which is never entirely reducible to the signified that theory so often desires. In effect, Barthes' later writings could be said to dramatize what in *The Pleasure of the Text,* he refers to as "drift". That is, the *intractable* that "occurs whenever . . . the sociolect, *fails me*" (Barthes, 1994, 1809).

Given this, it perhaps comes as no surprise that whilst "The Death of the Author" provides a critique of the dominant form of critical activity engaged in prior to, or at the time of, its publication, it nevertheless refuses to posit an explicit alternative methodological approach to textual analysis. As the text draws to a close, the reader may well feel quite confident about "what not to do", but may find him or herself in something of a quandary as to what *to do* with texts, with Barthes. Turning to *S/Z, The Pleasure of the Text, Roland Barthes, Camera Lucida,* and *A Lover's Discourse,* we find, not answers as perhaps we might have hoped, but examples of, or attempts at, "textual" reading/writing; performative combinations of theory and practice that move beyond the distinction between literary object and critical subject. For example, *S/Z* is comprised of 561 fragments of Balzac's *Sarrasine,* punctuated with, interrupted, and generated by, 93 "divigations" in which Barthes comments on his own (experience of) reading the text[21]. Inasmuch as Barthes' reading/writing of *Sarrasine* refuses to posit an objective and definitive explication of the text it could be said to perform a renunciation of meta-language, and thus to exemplify the critical approach to textuality outlined earlier in this chapter. Moreover, Barthes' reading/writing of *Sarrasine*, of *S/Z*, of him"self" from the (non)site[22] of *dramatis persona*   (rather than the exalted position of critic/truth), draws attention to (or *affects*) an aspect of (inter)textuality that nonreflexive practices of literary criticism have turned a blind eye to, that is, the affectivity of *enonciation*. Let us now consider the possible significance of Barthes' affective dramatization of (inter)textuality, of the irreducibility of his reading/writing to conventional critical discourses.

But let me first confess that I am by no means immune to the quandary of doing and not doing things with Barthes. For a number of years I have been fascinated, inspired, enraptured even by Barthes' writings, particularly those discussed here. At the same time, however, I was, and at times still am, perplexed as to what to do with Barthes. How does one critically engage with that which is performative rather than descriptive or proscriptive? If we no longer wish to approach the text as would the detective, searching for what is presumably deeply hidden (truth), or as the endorser of cultural values, deciding in all our wisdom what is good, what is bad, then what part do we perform? The question remains, what do we do with Barthes, or analogously, what do we do with the subject in/of tattooing whose (bodily) writing could be said to be both a signifying excess and a historically and culturally specific form of "social language"? There are a number of possible responses to the question, the most obvious being, nothing at all—an option many have probably taken. Alternatively, one could emulate the Barthensian approach without any mention of Barthes whatsoever. But neither of these responses satisfies my need to articulate, or to put into circulation, the affects of the texts that bear the signifier "Roland Barthes" on "me". Nor do they provide an opportunity to perform a reading/writing of Barthensian pleasure, in which the texts of my "self", of Barthes, of the reader/writer are (trans)formed. The following section offers one possible attempt to respond to this dilemma.

SYNCOPIC ENCOUNTERS: BARTHES MEETS BEVERLEY

In this section I want to explore the possible connection between Barthes' notion of (inter)textuality as performative and affective and the irreducibility of reading/writing to conventional critical discourses, by way of an articulation of the association of reading body writing with the perverse. More specifically, my aim is to consider body marking—especially as it is "performed" in a film starring Beverley D'Angelo entitled *Marks*[23]—in terms of what Barthes calls "the pleasure of the text". For Barthes, pleasure (as affect) *is* intertextual:

intertextuality being the necessary presence of other textual bodies in the body of the text. Every textual body is marked by its encounters with other bodies; with bodies as texts, texts as bodies, the word as flesh, the flesh as word[24]. Consequently, when I read *The Pleasure of the Text,* I read Barthes' body not as an object to be known, but as a proliferation of other bodies, which then become an inseparable aspect of my body. Given this, it is not my intention to construct a coherent or unified theory of Barthesian pleasure. I concede that I am not a Barthes expert: Barthes "is what comes to me, not what I summon up; not an "authority", simply a *circular memory*" (Barthes, 1994, 36).

When approaching texts such as *Marks, or The Pleasure of the Text,* the reader is faced with the possibility of various roles (or aspects thereof) to perform, two of which are the confidant or voyeur[25]. For Barthes, the confidant of critical pleasure puts herself in the position of the critic, agrees with or disputes what the critic says, and thus becomes ensnared in a barren dialectics; a sure way to miss critical pleasure (Barthes, 1994, 17). A text *on* pleasure that describes or represents pleasure does not necessarily affect pleasure. Alternatively, the voyeur clandestinely observes the critic's pleasure in writing (a pleasure that is without function or utility), and, in doing so, enters perversion—perversion being a search for pleasure that is not motivated or dominated by social ends or reproductive goals, a pleasure, then, that is without function or utility—that is intertextual (17–18). Insofar as this doubling and trebling of perversity is an open-ended process, the text can no longer be seen as a product endowed with hidden meaning or truth, but rather is understood generatively as a perpetual interweaving, by and through which the subject continuously unmakes herself (64). Thus the relation between readers, writers, and texts, which Barthes articulates, shifts an analysis of subjectivity from the notion of being to what I want to call perverse (un)becoming.

What I want to do then in this section is to play the voyeur, to perform perversity, to create a scene, to "articulate impressions, not affidavits" (Barthes, 1982, 7), "to stage an utterance, not an analysis" (Barthes, 1990b, 3). And what I hope you will do is take pleasure, in my taking pleasure, in Barthes' pleasure, in D'Angelo's pleasure, and to indulge in voyeurism, to be moved by these textual bodies, to be marked by these fleshly encounters.

Marks is a short monologue performed by Beverley D'Angelo[26]. It is the story of a woman whose life is (trans)formed in and through encounters with others who both mark and are marked. But rather than mapping D'Angelo's existence, her picturesque body—as a map—affects connections between existents. In short, Beverley D'Angelo's *Marks* is both an articulation of the function of pleasure/*jouissance*, as outlined by Barthes, and a seductive account of body marking, of the subject in/of tattooing, that provides the possibility of moving beyond the limitations of the accounts of the subject in/of tattooing offered by the theorists discussed in Chapter One.

Pleasure/*jouissance* functions in Barthes' text in complex and varying ways. At one level there may appear to be a distinction between the two, with pleasure, on the one hand being linked to a *comfortable*, self-confirming practice of reading, and *jouissance*, on the other hand, being associated with loss and disease, a conformist versus a radical heterogeneous force (Barthes, 1994, 51–53). However, at the same time Barthes draws attention to, and plays with, the ambiguity of the term *plaisir*, which he claims denotes a "particular pleasure" distinct from *jouissance*, and a "general pleasure" that at once refers to pleasure and *jouissance*, contentment and rapture (Barthes, 1994, 19). Moreover, *plaisir* is precarious, slippery, uncertain, affected by emotion, circumstance, and so on (52). Indeed, *jouissance* "wells up in [pleasure] like a scandal, an irregularity, that is always *the trace of a cut*, of an assertion (and not a flowering)" (20, my emphasis). Thus the reader/writer of the text is an "anachronic subject", for he or she participates in the profound hedonism of culture, and simultaneously in its destruction. He or she at once enjoys the cohesion of his or her selfhood and desires its loss (14). Thus becoming and unbecoming, pleasure and *jouissance*, are inextricably linked in the same way as are the Saying and the Said, or, as Irigaray might put it, one cannot exist without the other. However, this process can be, and is, disavowed by focusing on the interpretation and classification of pleasure, of meaning, and of the self as missible object as is the case in the Foucauldian understanding of sadomasochism and the ethics of self-(trans)formation discussed in Chapter Two.

The passionate process of (un)becoming that D'Angelo's performance affects desires me without knowing where I am: it cruises me. And in and through this encounter a site of *jouissance*, ephemeral, transitory, and atopical is created. My body reads D'Angelo's as a body from which radiates the other bodies she has encountered. Just as these other bodies have become part of D'Angelo's textual body, they now become part of mine, and so on *ad infinitum*. This is the pleasure of the text.

Until I was 35 there was nothing remarkable about my life. . . . My days were very like one of those baroque string quartets, soothing, placid, repetitive, without protest or excess. Not so much as a single evenings anarchy . . . At my eighteenth birthday my uncle . . . proposed a toast which described me—positively he thought—as unsurprising. . . . In college, an unexceptional college, I appreciated, appreciated art, appreciated music[27]. . . . I majored in a subject whose point or content escapes me . . . cultural geography. . . . Had I died at that time perhaps of acute boredom as I sat in the school cafeteria eating peas, it would have been agreed by all that my epitaph might have read "she did as she was told", or blander yet, "she did as she supposed she might be told". . . . I met my husband Arthur at a festive tea to honour the retiring head of the Christian Youth Centre. . . . We dated for two years . . . had two children, two job transfers. . . . On our fifteenth anniversary Arthur left me . . . saying I was unmarked by life. . . . In the months that followed I suffered most because I could not seem to suffer. . . . I became an acolyte to sangria. . . . I made brief nervous forays to singles bars, and one night was walked to my car by a musician who suggested we make love there in the parking lot, between two yellow lines, as he was, as he so delicately put it, between sets. . . . I resisted and he, much annoyed, cut me. . . . When the scar formed . . . I noticed that for the first time people looked at me, not unkindly, and with interest, and these were not the sort of people I'd known. . . . These people were interesting, these people were marked by life. . . . It occurred to me then that it might be best to wear our lives upon our skin, and so I do[28].

The pleasure of the text, suggests Barthes, is not the pleasure of the corporeal striptease, the gradual unveiling of the truth of the text or the author behind it (Barthes, 1994, 10). Rather, the text is a fetish object, lost in the midst of which is the Other whom I desire but cannot grasp. I desire his or her *figure,* (which is neither a representation nor an expression of his or her "self"), as he or she likewise desires mine (27). For Barthes, figuration denotes the various ways in which the erotic body may appear in the profile of the text: "a body split into fetish objects, into erotic sites" (56). Figuration, unlike representation, creates an erotic rather than a specular relation between reader and text. The figure of the body is more a sort of a textual operator than a concept.

In *Camera Lucida,* Barthes again formulates an erotics of the text in terms of figuration and representation, but this time he describes the elements of the photographic text as the *studium* and the *punctum.* Whereas the representation or *studium* of desire never leaves the frame, the figure or *punctum* breaks up representation, it leaps out of the frame "like an arrow and pierces me" (Barthes, 1993, 26). "The erotic photo . . . draws the spectator out of its frame [out of his frame] . . . and it is in this way that . . . I animate it and it animates me" (59).

This seems to me to be an interesting way to approach D'Angelo's text; a way around the difficulties I experienced when considering how to dramatize, and not simply describe, the pleasure of this text. It allows the possibility of reading the textual body not as an account of the truth of the narrator's or Author's being, but as a staging of intertextual pleasure, of affectivity: a passionate (un)becoming, which is/was never simply hers nor mine—I animate it and it animates me. This then is to see the text as a figure of the erotic body, a body of *jouissance* consisting of erotic relations that supersede distinctions between writer and reader, active and passive, subject and object.

If, as Barthes, following Lacan, suggests, *jouissance* can only be said between the lines, then perhaps in true voyeuristic fashion, it would be best to turn to the moment in the first part of *Marks* that most impassions me; that is, D'Angelo's encounter with the musician in the parking lot. An encounter, which interestingly takes place between two yellow lines, between sets; a syncopic encounter that in many ways parallels the blissful convergence that is the meeting of my body with the textual bodies of Barthes and D'Angelo—an encounter with bodies that mark and are marked. The term "syncope" designates an eclipse, an interval, an absence followed by a new departure (Clément, 1995, xviii). In medical discourse syncope denotes fainting, swooning, a loss of consciousness or irregularity in heartbeat (1). Syncopation is also a musical term used to define an element of rhythm whereby the shifting of accent gives birth to a harmonious and productive discord (4). Etymologically speaking, syncope derives from *syn* meaning with and *kopto* meaning to cut (4). For Barthes, syncope is an element of the physics of *jouissance*, whereby the "truth" of language, the solidification of old metaphors, as Nietzsche puts it, is exploded[29]. A syncopic encounter, then, could be understood as an intersubjective and/or intertextual process of passionate (un)becoming, in and through which one both marks and is marked. Or as Catherine Clément puts it, insofar as they are struck by love, the lovers "will have earned some scars" (17).

To voyeuristically "read" the car park scene as a syncopic encounter is to enter into perversion, to participate in the *jouissance* of the text, which, as Barthes says, "unsettles the reader's historical, cultural, psychological assumptions, the consistency of [her] tastes, values, memories" (Barthes, 1994, 14). It is in and through this encounter with the body of another (the musician) that D'Angelo momentarily loses her "self", and acknowledges the dizzying schism that is the subject. And it is in and through interpretation, as process, as (un)becoming, as passion, that the subject (D'Angelo) returns as *fiction*—a fictive identity that is no longer the illusion of a unity, but on the contrary is the staging of the plurality of a self that is born simultaneously with the text (62), a brief encounter, "an eclipse followed by a new departure; life recommences, but it is no longer altogether the same" (Clément, 1995, 4).

D'Angelo reads her life, prior to this episode, through the optic of a posterior encounter. But insofar as intertextuality knows no chronology as such, this is not simply a retrospective reconstruction of the past through the truth of the present. Rather, it is an example of the circulating relations between life and text, which for Barthes is the process of perverse productivity, and thus of pleasure/*jouissance*. D'Angelo tells how, after the breakdown of her marriage, she suffers most because she can not seem to suffer. She becomes an "acolyte to sangria", which, besides being a kind of wine, in Spanish literally means bleeding: a disciple of passion, in all senses of the word. She desires the figure of the musician as a site of unpredictability; she cruises him, and, in turn, he desires her. And in and through this encounter, which takes place between two yellow lines, between sets, she is marked. Thus what we have here is a syncopic encounter, a "cutting-with". The rhythm of life changes with the shifting of accent. The baroque string quartet, soothing, conformist, and repetitive, is ruptured by syncopation, and we witness the birth of a "fascinating rhythm".

For Barthes, the *jouissance* of the text proceeds from the collision of antipathetic codes that is achieved by cutting: the creation of two edges; a conformist edge and a subversive edge, neither of which is erotic in itself. Rather, it is the fault between them, the cut, which becomes so. What pleasure/*jouissance* wants, says Barthes, is "the site of a loss, the fault, the cut . . . it is intermittence . . . which is erotic: the intermittence of skin flashing between two articles of clothing . . . between two edges . . . the [alternation] of appearance and disappearance (Barthes, 1994, 7, 9–10).

Thus it seems to me that what is erotic or affective about the car park scene is precisely the syncopic character of the encounter; the redistribution of meaning achieved by cutting; the intertextual staging of intermittence in which I, the voyeur, am implicated. It is not, then, the comfortable conformity of D'Angelo's history, nor its or her destruction that cruises me, but rather the cut, the *punctum* that leaps out of the frame and pierces me, that causes the heartbeat to falter, that marks. D'Angelo's "history" is less a historical fact than a mode of writing, which is itself a historical act, and the textual body is the name and emblem of that intertwining[30].

Before I go any further, perhaps I should stop for a moment and dispel a fear that has been relentlessly tugging at me for quite some time now. What worries me is the possibility that in focusing in the way I have, on the encounter in the parking lot, it may seem that I have romanticized an act of nonconsensual violence, namely, D'Angelo's being marked for life, her being marked *by* life. I may have implied—albeit inadvertently, and despite my critique of Foucault's analysis of sadomasochism in Chapter Two—that masochism is somehow liberatory. Again Barthes comes to me. I am reminded that judging a text according to pleasure cannot involve the use of categories such as "good", and "bad", since what this would imply is that the text of pleasure (or the pleasure of the text) has a definable social function that is achievable. But according to Barthes, one should not imagine that the text is ameliorable: "The text can wring from me only this judgement, in no way adjectival: that's it! . . . *That's it for me!* This "for me" is neither subjective nor existential, but Nietzschean (basically it is always the same question: What is it *for me?*)" (13)[31]. So, what is it for me? What is it about the cut that impassions me? I am loathe to attempt to force this encounter to fit into a chain of cause and effect in order to render passion meaningful, to rescue it from perversion; to minimize the dis-ease that the marked body often invokes, and thus to make it more palatable. And yet at the same time, the aim here is to gesture toward a rethinking of the ethics of perverse pleasure, of textuality, and in particular of body marking or of the subject in/of tattooing.

As I suggested earlier, Barthes' notion of an erotics of reading presupposes an understanding of intertextuality, whereby every textual body is marked in and through its encounters with other bodies. Just as my body is marked by my encounter with D'Angelo, and by her encounter with the musician, so too is yours. And this perpetual interweaving of bodies/texts, wherein the subject makes and unmakes herself, goes on *ad infinitum*. What I am suggesting is that the distinction between the marked and the unmarked, the proper body and the improper body, self and other, reading and writing, is tenuous, to say the least, since, morphologically speaking, it is only through the marking of the body, the encounter with the Other, that the subject as such comes into being. Textual violence then does not so much consist of marking and being marked, but rather is the result of disavowing such a process in the search for absolute knowledge. Or as Levinas might put it, Western ontology, like war, is a systematic form of violence that reduces the Other to the Same, and disavows the call to responsibility that the face to face relation affects. In *Totality and Infinity*, Levinas states that the "primordial *expression* of the face of the Other, his or her 'first word' to me, is you shall not commit murder" (Levinas, 1969, 199). This commandment is not something imposed on an already constituted subject, but rather is an intertextual affect that precedes and overflows, makes possible and impossible, any attempt on the part of the subject to make a conscious decision whether or not to respond.

What puzzles me, then, is why the literalization of this intersubjective or intertextual process of marking and being marked, of (un)becoming, is so often met with disdain, with premature judgments spoken in the name of Truth, Science, Politics, Morality, and so forth. Like you, "I" am marked by life, and like D'Angelo, "I" too wear my life on my skin. Thus for me this question is one of passion. Let us turn to D'Angelo's textual performance, more specifically to her "discussion" of her tattooed body, in order to explore the question of the subject in/of tattooing.

This serpent is Mohammed Mustafah, who coiled his life around mine and taught me that there are pleasures and dangers so delightful that it seems ungrateful to resist . . . this bird, in flight, horror-struck is my mother, this scythe, the ritual likeness of my musician in the parking lot . . . this lily which blooms and dies is Mary who taught me with her death . . . this crucifix is Brother Lawrence who reached out a hand to save me—so he thought—and was repaid with pain . . . a rising sun for Alex . . . Charybdis and Scylla for Virginia and Cath. . . . May I advise you please, . . . let them mark you because you see, the best among us have had so many life imprints left upon us that it is like embroidery and these people, life engraved, are drawn to each other, pass the time interpreting their signs, and these moments of sharing are the best in life. . . . This unravelling of hieroglyphs, personally I call it love, lasts only as long as there are marks to read and then it's gone.

As I have argued throughout this book, the tattoo is most often read ideographically, that is, as a graphic that signifies to others something of the subject's integral interiority. As I said earlier, for proponents of subcultural praxis, tattooing is "a political act and sign of dissent"[32]. For example, in an interview in *Body Play and Modern Primitives Quarterly*, Idexa, a self-confessed "radical primitive she/boy", replies to the question of what her tattoos and piercings mean to her: "They make me more whole; it's my act of completion. I am part of this culture but I don't believe in it. My body modifications are a way to say that" (Idexa, 1993, 11). Ironically, the same model of meaning and of identity is apparent in the interpretation of tattoos by criminologists such as Lombroso. In a move that simply reverses the discourse employed by Idexa, Lombroso argues that tattoos signify a pathological need for attention and an atavistic propensity to crime. Similarly, tattooing and scarification are often unquestioningly interpreted as self-mutilation as is evidenced in the works of Favazza and Jeffreys discussed earlier. Jeffreys' understanding of tattoos as "stigmata of body abuse" brings to mind an article by Marc Blanchard in which he too makes an association between tattoos and stigmata. But unlike Jeffreys, Blanchard reads the stigmata/tattoo not as a sign of the internalization of abuse, but rather as a *figure* of desire and pain—of passion. Thus he asks whether "to seek the tattoo is the modern equivalent of seeking the stigma in our lay theology: a postmodern sainthood?" (Blanchard, 1993, 295), a question that brings me back to the figure of D'Angelo, the acolyte to sangria, the disciple of passion, of (un)becoming passion, and also to the figure of Drycome.

What I find provocative about D'Angelo's dramatization of body marking is that it provides an opportunity to think about the question of how to read tattoos otherwise. Perhaps this is best illustrated by returning for a moment to the distinction between representation and figuration discussed earlier. According to Barthes, representation, is hindered figuration, "encumbered with other meanings than that of desire: a space of alibis (reality, morality . . . truth, [politics,] etc)" (Barthes, 1994, 56). Representation, then, is the relation between mime and the model: the text mimics a model in referential reality and represents it. This is the way the marked body as text is read by Idexa, Lombroso, and Jeffreys. Despite their very different political agendas, all three read body inscription as *significant*, that is, as a representation of the truth of the body-subject, or Author.

Figuration, on the other hand, is the name Barthes gives to the relation of desire that goes both ways, from text to reader and from reader to text, a process of perverse productivity whereby "'I' animate the text, and it animates me"[33]. Insofar as representation hampers figuration or overlooks the relation of desire, the question of body marking becomes "what is it?" or "what does it mean?" rather than a question of the erotics of reading, or of intertextuality. Representational models of textual analysis are concerned with questions of truth, with the thing-in-itself, rather than with what the test *does*. And here I am reminded of Nietzsche's claim that "the criterion of truth resides in the enhancement of the feeling of power" (Nietzsche, 1968b, #534, 290). If we consider for a moment the attempts by Idexa and Lombroso to define what the tattoo *is* (and in turn what or who the subject *is*), we find that they illustrate Nietzsche's claim nicely. Whereas for Idexa the tattoo represents her opposition to society positively, as a setting apart by and through which she becomes complete unto herself, for Lombroso the reverse is the case. For Lombroso the tattoo is both an antisocial act and the sign of a menacing attitude that threatens the well-being of the body politic. Thus in both cases, the one who interprets reaffirms his or her identity against the body of the other, and in accordance with the normative criteria he or she assumes, as I demonstrated in Chapter Two. As a result, the two become ensnared in a barren dialectics of what Barthes calls doxa/paradoxa, whereby identity can only be understood in terms of opposition or complementarity: a battle for power, as futile as it is repetitive.

The texts of Lombroso and Idexa, then, constitute an opposition between conformity and dissent, doxa and paradoxa, neither of which is erotic in itself. Alternatively, the staging of intertextual pleasure affected by D'Angelo's (inter)text overflows interpretation and evaluation, and attests to the *process* of perverse productivity that exceeds both the subject and the communicative function of language. This overflowing, or force of suspension that counters evaluation, is the third term that is necessary if we are to move beyond the doxa/paradoxa dialectic. It is what Barthes calls *signifiance*. It is sense/meaning (*sens*) only "insofar as it is sensually produced" (Barthes, 1994, 61). It is what precedes and exceeds, makes possible and impossible, signification. *Signifiance* disturbs the logics of representation; "it baffles [and] subverts . . . the entire practice of meaning [as doxa]" (Barthes, cited in Jefferson, 1989, 173). In a discussion of *signifiance* that shares resonances with Levinas' understanding of the term, Julia Kristeva states that "this heterogeneous process [*signifiance*] . . . is a structuring and de-structuring *practice*, a passage to the outer *boundaries* of the subject and society" (Kristeva, 1984, 17). *Signifiance*, then, is the affective aspect of language, or, as Levinas might put it, the Saying.

What I have attempted to suggest is, that for me at least, D'Angelo's text opens up the possibility of reading the marked body perversely. Like the *punctum,* the figure of the marked body in this text erupts out of representation, "shoots out . . . like an arrow, and pierces me" (Barthes, 1993, 26). Thus it becomes less a question of what the marked body *means* than of what it *does.* Insofar as the text diagrammatically (and not imitatively) stages an encounter with other (textual) bodies, it affects the intersubjective process of marking and being marked, of perverse productivity, of (un)becoming passion. Thus tattooing can be seen as a textual practice rather than as an intentional act of self-confession, whereby the tattoo, like the cut, is not a sign of presence, but, as Levinas might put it, is the an-archic trace of the *other-in-me*: an emblematic figure of the intertwining of bodies and texts, of the ambiguous, open-ended, and inter-relational character of meaning and thus of identity.

The "unravelling of hieroglyphs", to which D'Angelo refers, could be understood not as a gradual unveiling of the truth of the (textual) Other, but as a generative productivity; a perpetual interweaving of texts, in and through which "the subject unmakes [herself] like a spider dissolving in the constructive secretions of its web" (Barthes, 1994, 64). The spider—interestingly the only tattoo of which D'Angelo tells us nothing—is a figure of fascination and fear, of passion, of that which cannot be said, except of course between the lines.

Sometimes the unmarked are attracted to me . . . fascinated and a little frightened . . . and in parking lots I cut them, just a little mark, like this. . . . It is then their lives begin, with a little pain . . . that is if there's any understanding in them. . . . You understand. . . . Yes, I think you do.

TO COMMUNICATE: AN INTRANSITIVE VERB?

D'Angelo's performance draws to a close, but the invocative and imperative words, "You understand . . . yes, I think you do", barely whispered in the exhalation of cigarette smoke, resonate, reverberate in the hollows of one's body like the sonorous chains of hungry ghosts in the chiaroscuro of the cave that is one's history. I read this section ("Syncopic Encounters") sometime later, view *Marks* again (and again), and what I "hear" is not so much the truth of these texts, or of my"self", D'Angelo, or Barthes, but rather the *Dasein* (as Barthes following Heidegger puts it) of Barthes, D'Angelo, my"self"; it is the being-there, which is a bodily-being-with[34]—the trace of a (re)markable encounter with the Other that can be heard only in absentia. Such an encounter, it seems, renders me decidedly un-Jason-like. It could hardly be described in heroic terms, as a voyage of discovery that culminates in the retrieval and consequent exhibiting of the luminous grail of truth; there are no accolades; no exultant voices raised in unison, declaring "victory to the critic" (Barthes, 1990a, 117). If this is the case, then what has this encounter, this entering into conversation with Barthes, with D'Angelo, "achieved" if not the conceiving [35] of (the truth of) the Other?

In order to respond to this question, I will now examine the role and function of the interlocutor, in particular the notion of communication. Thus the discussion that follows has resonances with the analysis of the relation between readers, writers, and texts developed earlier, but shifts the focus in significant ways, and in doing so provides a critique of the notion of communication unquestioningly assumed by the theorists discussed in Chapter One. In an article entitled "Platonic Dialogue", Michel Serres claims the notion of communication embraced by modern logicians assumes that

in order for dialogue to be possible, one must close one's eyes and cover one's ears to the song and beauty of the Sirens. In a single blow, we eliminate hearing and noise, vision and failed drawing; in a single blow, we conceive the form and we understand each other. (Serres, 1982, 70)

Serres states that the act of eliminating both the "accidental" plasticity of graphic signs and the background noise internal and external to language and communication is "at the same time the condition of the apprehension of the abstract form and the condition of the success of communication" (68) and, thus one would presume, of community. In other words, the necessity of a rational community founded in and on shared linguistic systems, experiences, and values inevitably involves the elimination of the adumbral specificity of carnal materiality, and, more particularly, the privileging of abstract idealized knowledge over aesthetic experience. Or as Lingis, summarizing Serres, puts it:

To recognize the words [or any signs] of another as the words one used or would use, one departicularizes these words of their empirical particularities: their pitch, timbre, rhythm, density, and volume—their resonance. One disengages the word [sign] from its background noise and from the inner noise of its utterance. The maximal elimination of noise would produce successful communication among interlocutors, themselves maximally interchangeable. (Lingis, 1994a, 78)

To put it another way, according to modern logics signifiers and referents function as abstract idealized entities that universalize meaning and identity, and veil over difference, or what Levinas calls alterity. It is this model of communication that informs the work of the theorists discussed in Chapter One. As I have demonstrated, the dermal diagnostician glimpses the tattoo and sees the sign of personality disorder, of an atavistic propensity to crime, of an infectious threat to the salubriousness of the body politic. He or she closes his or her eyes, covers his or her ears, and conceives the (truth of the) other; in "a single blow" the other is reduced to a variant of the Same. In and through this process, we come to understand each other, concludes Serres. But do we? Does understanding necessarily call for the extraction of the abstract form from the noise internal to the message and the background noise in which it is emitted? Or perhaps a more salient question to ask is whether we want to promote a notion of understanding, of knowledge, that seems inextricably bound to what Levinas would call violence: in a single blow we eliminate specificity, in a single blow we conceive the form of the other. It appears to me that what is being performed in this scenario is something closer to a totalizing monologue, an attempt at closure, than a dialogue with the Other that opens up a space of learning in the Levinasian sense.

What is it then that motivates modern logicians to attempt to curtail sensuous enjoyment with incessant negatives: *don't* touch, *don't* look, *don't* listen, *don't* even consider stepping outside the bounds of rational discourse, for there monsters lurk, Sirens, tattooed bodies, mutant half-beings whose sensuosity is a guile to lure unsuspecting heroes to their death. Like Jason, modern logicians—and dermal diagnosticians—supposedly save themselves by thwarting the Sirens, by closing their eyes, stopping up their ears, dealing a single deadly blow to what Serres calls "the *demon*, the prosopopoeia of noise" (Serres, 1982, 67). But, as we know, the voices of the Sirens did not die with them, but still abide in the whispering of the wind, the crashing of the waves, the flickering shadows of ghosts, the vibrancy of life's cacophony. "Thou shalt not kill" (Levinas, cited in Westphal, 1993, 493), says Levinas, quoting from the Bible, and this it seems is less a commandment than a radical insight.

It is not my intention here to attempt to define exactly what it is that motivates the desire for abstract knowledge in and through the interpretation and classification of the other and the signs his or her body emits, beyond claiming that such processes function to reaffirm the critic's sense of self in relation to the other; a proposition outlined in more depth in Chapter Two. Rather, what I want to explore is the possibility that communication may entail something other than that which Serres outlines, something that is performatively affected (and was explained) in the previous section of this chapter ("Syncopic Encounters"). For, as Lingis asks, "is it not false to suppose that only the meaning attached to words [to signs] by a code, fixed or evolving, communicates?" (Lingis, 1994a, 90). "Not believing in the separation of affect and sign, of the emotion and its theatre" (Barthes, 1977, 177), my body refuses to focus simply on the meaning of the textual/tattooed body, and ignores what it does to and for me. The Sirens call, and unlike modern logicians and dermal diagnosticians "I" am moved by their songs, the caressing, grating, crackling cadences of their voices, the "pulsional incidents, the language lined with flesh" (Barthes, 1994, 66–67).

Like Zarathustra, "I want to speak to the despisers of the body" (Nietzsche, 1978, 34), to those who seek to silence the vibrancy of carnal materiality. But how will they hear me if not with their bodies? There may just be a chance that somewhere, sometime too long ago to remember[36], they too encountered the mythological poet-prophet who muttered the words, "body I am entirely, and nothing else . . . 'I' you say, and you are proud of the word. But greater is that in which you do not wish to have faith—your body and its great reason: that does not say 'I', but does 'I'" (Nietzsche, 1978, 34). What Zarathustra offers us is a model of identity as performative rather than essential, of the body as a sensuous surface event rather than as the expressive surface of a depth, the vehicle of conscious rational intent. If we "hear" this cacophonous and irrecuperable voice it may be possible to understand the subject in/of tattooing as something other than an object of cognition, a sign that emanates out of the depth of the tattooed body and that the subject—the interlocutor who interprets—receives and recognizes. It may no longer be necessary to read or hear the tattooed body as the reiteration of the same old story of a Platonic imaginary, whereby inscription functions as a copy of a copy: "a visual imitation of a phonic stream of vocal signs, which itself is a copy or imitation of the logos" (Lingis, 1983b, 24). For to do so is to efface the carnal specificity, sensuosity, the alteritous vibrancy of the body of the Other, to idealize and universalize the sign and its referent. And as Lingis warns us, "[i]n the measure that what [is] received [is] what [is] emitted, and that what [is] communicated [is] the abstract, departicularized message, each partner in conversation becomes the same for the other" (Lingis, 1994a, 86). As I argued in the previous chapter, drawing on the work of Levinas, such a disavowal of alterity results in an hegemony of the Same that is tantamount to an act of violence, to a single blow in and through which "I" become master of all that I (blindly) survey.

THE CARNAL PLEASURE OF THE (INTER)TEXT

Earlier (in "Syncopic Encounters"), I attempted to dramatize the affective aspects of my encounter(s) with Barthes, with D'Angelo: a visceral encounter with bodies, with texts, that mark and are marked. I argued that intertextuality denotes the necessary presence of other textual bodies in the body of the text, and that every textual body is marked in and through this infinite encounter with other bodies, with bodies as texts, texts as bodies, the word as flesh, the flesh as word. In effect, "Syncopic Encounters", I would argue, provides an alternative model of communication to that proposed by the logicians discussed by Serres and uncritically assumed by the theorists discussed in Chapter One, insofar as the relation between interlocutors evoked here is founded in and through what Levinas calls exposure. Exposure, says Taylor in an article on Levinas, "establishes a 'communication' that cannot be understood simply in terms of sending and receiving messages" (Taylor, 1987, 202). Communication in this sense is a becoming open to the vibrancy and excess of the world, in and through which "one is exposed to the Other as a skin is exposed to that which wounds it" (Levinas, 1978, 49). And as I demonstrated, this "wounding" generates an infinite process of (un)becoming, rather than destroying or castrating an already constituted subject, as Freud would have it. Communication then, is not first a modality of cognition that serves to reaffirm the ego through the incorporation and annihilation of the other. Rather, communication as exposure to carnal materiality (to the Other or alterity) "seeks out and affirms otherness, while protecting it" (Irigaray, 1993, 174). Insofar as it allows for the recognition of the sensuous and affective dimension of communication as that which is "antecedent to the verbal signs it conjugates, to . . . linguistic systems" (Levinas, 1978, 5), this model "decomposes" the distinction between abstract knowledge and ephemeral "non-signifying" materiality, and also between politics and aesthetics—a point I will return to in due course.

The Barthesian emphasis on pleasure as a force of suspension (the *signifiance* of signification), that interrupts the narrative drive toward closure, combined with the notion of intertextuality as the absent presence of the Other's materiality—what Lingis calls the "indefinite discernability of empirical particulars" (Lingis, 1994b, 91)—provides an understanding of communication concomitant with the Levinasian model outlined in Chapter Three and mentioned briefly above. Here the intertext, the Other, is not simply an idealized entity that I can call forth to agree with or dispute, to incorporate and annihilate in the process of self-affirmation. Rather, the textual Other figures, as I have said, the impossibility of living outside the infinite text (Barthes, 1994, 36), the impossibility of silencing the sonorous "rumble of the world", in and through which the utterances we make, the subjectivities we perform, are formed and transformed *ad infinitum.* The notion of intertextuality then, gestures toward alterity, infinity, articulates the guttural vibrancy of the Sirens whose timeless voices we cannot entirely fail to hear no matter how hard we try to stop up our ears—despite our most heroic attempts at selective hearing. Or, as Barthes puts it, "[t]he intertext . . . is a music of *figures* . . . it is the signifier as *Siren*" (Barthes, 1977, 145, my emphasis). As I have said, for Barthes, following Lyotard[37], the figural is that which discourse never entirely manages to bind, to re-present, that is, the aleatory or alteritous substratum of language. The (inter)text then, as the previous quotation suggests, is the tonal basis of communication, a primal melody that sends no message—at the level of meaning—but that makes meaning both possible and impossible, and that can only take place through that which it calls into question. The intertext, or textual Other, is something like a "mana-word", a drifting ineffable "signifier taking up the place of every signified" (Barthes, 1977, 129); it is the signifier as Siren, as that to which the heroic defenders of rational knowledge must turn a deaf ear, a blind eye. But, as I have argued, the pleasure of the (inter)text (the primal melody) overflows; it interrupts "the taking of power by adjectives" (Barthes, 1994, 13), that is, the "funereal" power to judge, to assign value and concretize meaning that the desire to idealize wants.

In effect, then, Barthes convincingly rejects the assumption that pleasure is hedonistic and politically bankrupt, and in fact demonstrates that pleasure can and does function as an ethical figure. Pleasure in the Barthensian sense generates the possibility not of a universalizing morality (*la moralé*) but of an ethics of alterity (*une Moralité*). *Une Moralité,* writes Barthes, "is the thinking of the body in the state of language" (Barthes, 1977, 145), and it is this connection between pleasure, the body, and the *signifiance* of signification that leads Hill[38] to use the term an "ethics of enonciation" to describe the Barthensian project. Insofar as "body I am entirely", it seems aesthetics need no longer be construed as that which is opposed to, or impedes, ethics or politics. Consequently, the charge made by those critics who interpret Barthes' later works as exemplifying a turning away from politics and toward a form of self-indulgent aestheticism appears somewhat misguided. It is precisely the carnal sensuosity that is at the heart of the notion of an ethics of alterity. This idea is at work in Barthes' later texts and I find it particularly conducive to a rethinking of the subject in/of tattooing. Indeed, one could argue that the inextricability of the fleshly and communication reformulates subjectivity, textuality, ethics, and politics, and at the same time subjectivity, textuality, ethics, and politics, can be seen as various modes of (re)writing the body.

THE GRAIN OF THE VOICE: FLESHLY WRITING

In the final section of *The Pleasure of the Text,* entitled "Voice", Barthes proposes that an aesthetics of textual pleasure would necessarily include writing aloud (Barthes, 1994, 66). Writing aloud, he says, is not expressive; it belongs to the geno-text[39], to *signifiance* rather than to the pheno-text. Writing aloud is affected in and through what Barthes calls the grain of the voice. As the distinction between the geno-text and the pheno-text suggests, the grain of the voice "is an erotic mixture of timbre and language" (66) rather than a medium through which messages are imparted. The grain of the voice figures carnality, sensuosity; it searches for "the pulsional incidents, the language lined with flesh, a text where we can hear the grain of the throat, the patina of consonants, the voluptuousness of vowels, a whole carnal stereophony: the articulation of the body, of the tongue, not that of meaning" (66–67).

It is precisely the geno-text, Barthes so lovingly evokes here, that the logicians whom Serres discusses argue must *not* be heard if communication is to be "successful", if closure is to be achieved. If, according to such logics, the subject is to understand the signs that the other emits, he or she must inevitably close his or her ears to the tone, the volume, the tempo, the resonance of the voice; to the susurration of the breath, the succulence of saliva, the corporeality of the lips, mouth, tongue (67); to mispronunciations, stammerings, the lilting of accents, half-words. But far from wanting to silence the fleshly materiality of the Other and of communication and become the hero who finally grasps the infamously elusive Signified, Barthes wants the pleasure of "writing aloud". Indeed he heralds it, albeit "silently", as that which manages to shift the signified, to cast the carnal sensuosity of the Other's voice into my ear; it granulates, it crackles, it *caresses*, it grates, it *cuts*" (67, my emphasis).

In other words, the grasping of meaning veils over the ambiguity of language, and at the same time constitutes the other as nothing but the anonymous tool of cognition with which the subject reaffirms his or her authority. Similarly, the tattoo, at least as it is understood by the theorists discussed in Chapter One, functions as an "anonymous" sign that, as Serres puts it, evokes a "class of objects having the same form" (Serres, 1982, 68). The carnal specificity of the graphic is lost in and through the focus on the signified: "I", the subject or dermal diagnostician, become the Author of both my own and the other's being. Alternatively, writing aloud figures the relation of *differánce*, or alterity, and this is the way I want to think of the subject in/of tattooing. Writing aloud succeeds in shifting the signified a great distance—"I" cannot grasp it, at least not without a struggle, as Serres demonstrates. Writing aloud generates the process of (un)becoming whereby "a signifier take[s] up the place of every signified" (Barthes, 1977, 129); the signifier as mana-word. And for Barthes "this word-as-mana is the body" (130). It is the body of the Other as performative event, as *énonciation*, that marks me ("it caresses . . . it cuts"), that leaves behind the trace of a trace in the resultant utterance (*énonce* or meaning). The voice (of the Other) is a bodily performance or productivity, the sonorous trace of alterity that always wells up like a scandal[40] (Barthes, 1994, 20) in any attempt to concretize meaning and thus identity; it is, as I said earlier, always the trace of a cut, of an assertion (20).

The fragment of *Roland Barthes* entitled "His Voice" begins with the words: "(*Il ne s'agit de la voix de personne—Mais si! précisément: il s'agit, il s'agit toujours de la voix de quelqu'un*)" (Barthes, 1975, 60). Richard Howard translates this as "[n]o one's in particular. Yes, in particular! It is always someone's voice" (Barthes, 1977, 67). But it seems to me that the ambiguity of the aphorism is somehow lost in this translation, and perhaps this is because, for the most part, translation involves interpretation. It is an attempt to grasp, or re-present, the signified, as I will demonstrate in more depth in Chapter Five. As Naomi Schor points out, Howard's translation re-presents a theoretical statement rather than a bodying forth of Barthes' voice (Schor, 1986, 32), which is always already past/passed or dead, (is nothing but the trace of a trace), but which "lacerates me by dint of having to die" (Barthes, 1990b, 114). Consequently I want to propose an alternative translation that is no less problematic, or no more "correct" than Howard's, but one that attempts to gesture toward the *figure* of the Other-in-me. The triple anaphora of *il s'agit,* a reflexive verb, is both particularly difficult to translate and highly significant here, as is the repetition of the word *voix,* and the cleavage with which the quote begins, and which in Howard's translation is reduced to a contradiction[41]. My translation, then, goes something like this, although at the same time that I propose it I want it to remain under erasure, drifting: "He doesn't disturb himself, is not disturbed, through the voice of no-one—But yes! (or 'if only!'), he disturbs himself, he is always disturbed through the voice of someone". What I am trying to evoke here is the sense in which the voice, like the face in Levinas' work, is not so much a thing that belongs to someone or everyone and thus no-one, but rather functions as a performative event that is *simultaneously* idealized and alteritous. The voice that the "I" encounters is always the voice of the Other; yet, it is never simply an object of the self's perceiving consciousness. Rather, the voice of the Other is invocative and imperative, a carnal resonance; it precedes and exceeds (the function of emitting) meaning. Whilst the voice of the anonymous idealized other (of no-one, and thus everyone) may appear not to disturb the subject *qua* subject, the ambiguity of the quotation, at least as I have translated it, suggests that at the same time, the Other's voice (the voice of some*one*) is affective; it cuts, it disturbs the self. And the self that is disturbed, that disturbs him- or herself in and through this process of "hearing" what cannot be pronounced let alone defined (of marking and being marked) is constituted in and through this encounter with the (inter)textual Other that caresses, cuts.

In "His Voice", Barthes tells of the impossibility of the adjectival approach to *render* the voice of the Other, to obtain by force that which has always already "past" through the fingers of the prehensile subject. To re-present the voice of the Other says Barthes, one would have to invent the perfect metaphor; a metaphor which stop, for all time, the flux of alterity. For Barthes, such an accomplishment is at best unlikely, at worst, impossible, and, more to the point, undesirable since it would result in rendering (inter)textuality sterile and unproductive (67–68). In short, such a move would be deathly, funereal.

For Barthes, the descriptive quality of the adjective is a tool of illusion that attempts to render living or present that which is intractable, "inordinate, doesn't enter into the present, and inverts the *arche* into anarchy" (Levinas, 1978, 177). The Other's voice is less the instrument of a subject who speaks in the present— for here "to speak" is "to be"—than "a way the Other has of manifesting himself without manifesting himself (Levinas, 1987a, 66), which designates a nonintentional but active participation in the process of (un)becoming. Given that the tattoo is for the most part traditionally understood as a form of nonverbal communication, it is seen to perform an analogous function to that of the voice. But insofar as the voice, as it is outlined here, is not simply the anonymous vehicle of the exchange of truth(s) between subjects, but rather is something like an infinite carnal resonance that makes meaning possible and disallows its concretization, then the notion of the tattoo as the idealized signifier of a universal referent is significantly undermined.

Likewise, the "hearing" of the voice is not simply the consumption of a message, but rather the caress, the being moved, the being marked, the hearing "what we do not understand" (Barthes, 1994, 25). The text produces in me the best pleasure, writes Barthes, if it succeeds in making itself listened to indirectly, if, whilst reading it, the reader is moved to avert his or her gaze away from the text, to hear something else (24). This is reminiscent of the lovers in "To Speak/to Embrace" (Barthes, 1977, 140), whose delight in the erotic encounter is generated by "that play of meaning which opens and breaks off: the function *which is disturbed*: in a word: *the stammered body"* (141). The "stammered body" figures the "non-signifying" glossolalia of life, the unbounded generative process of perverse productivity that can be said, heard, and felt only "between the lines". It is the atopic site of a sensuous exposure to the Other, of *signifiance*.

What Barthes' notion of writing aloud offers us then is a model of communication that does not simply involve the idealization of signifiers and referents through the elimination of carnal sensuosity, of the alteritous noise internal to the message and the background noise(s) in which it is emitted—a process which, as I have argued, attempts to universalize both meaning and identity, thus reducing the Other to an Economy of the Same. The relation between *énonciation* and *énoncé* in Barthes' work functions similarly to the Levinasian understanding of the Saying and the Said, but insofar as it is developed in alliance with the notions of (inter)textuality, pleasure, and the body, it provides us with a means of critically analysing the ways in which the marked body (as text, or as a form of nonverbal communication) is ontologically both read and (re)written. However, Barthes' notion of writing aloud is, for the most part, formulated in and through his analysis of the voice and music, and thus in one sense is limited to the audible, a gesture that could be seen as privileging one sense over what are traditionally categorized as the other four: sight, touch, taste, and smell. Whilst I would argue that Barthes does not "intend" to separate the senses in this way, there is little suggestion in his work as to how we might formulate, for example, the olfactory dimension of (inter)textuality. But perhaps in putting it this way I may also be seen to be positing a distinction between the olfactory, the audible, the ocular, the palpable, and the oral.

Perhaps one way around this problem would be *not* to attempt to elaborate a theory of the olfactory affect(s) of the tattooed body, but rather to suggest that, insofar as the senses are inextricably bound, one cannot separate the tattooed body from the olfactory dimension of one's bodily engagement with it, and with the world in which the encounter between bodies takes place; one should focus on the whole sensorium of carnal exposure in and through which the process of (un)becoming is generated *ad infinitum.* In the following chapter I will draw on the work of Alphonso Lingis and Jean-Francois Lyotard in order to (re)formulate an understanding of the ways in which the (tattooed) body is continuously written and rewritten in and through exposure to the alteritous Other, and to the sensuous vibrancy and excess of the world.

NOTES

1. This is not to suggest a linear temporality whereby being is transformed through the encounter with the other into an-other form of being, but rather that both self and Other exist in an infinite relation of (un)becoming.

2. By later works I am referring to those published in and after 1968. This classification of his texts into "earlier" and "later" works has also been noted by numerous critics including Michael Moriarty (1991); Andrew Brown (1992); and Gregory Ulmer (1978).

3. For examples that take such a position with varying degrees of vehemence, see Graham Hough (1977); Philip Thody (1977); Jonathan Culler (1974; 1983); and Annette Lavers (1982).

4. This could be said to be true of Susan Sontag, who begins the preface to *A Barthes Reader* (1983) with the following eulogism: "Teacher, man of letters, moralist, philosopher of culture, connoisseur of strong ideas, protean autobiographer . . . of all the intellectual notables who have emerged since World War II in France, Roland Barthes is the one whose work I am most certain will endure" (vii).

5. For an extended discussion of this concept and its function see "Transgression of Transgression" in Barthes (1977, 65–66).

6. As I will go on to argue, for Barthes the question of pleasure, as affect, is essential to any consideration of textuality, since it prevents theories of the textuality from "revert[ing] to a centred system, a philosophy of meaning" (Barthes, 1994, 65).

7. Or as Barthes puts it, the conception of the Author that furnishes the text with a final signified "suits criticism very well, the latter then allotting itself the important task

of discovering the Author beneath the work: when the Author has been found, the text is 'explained'—victory to the critic. Hence there is no surprise in the fact that, historically, the reign of the Author has also been that of the Critic" (Barthes, 1990a, 117).

8. See Barthes (1977, 170).

9. For Barthes, the dominant ideology is not so much the false truths that the bourgeois propagate and that the proletariat must throw off in order to reclaim the essential truth or liberation. Rather, says Barthes, "the expression is a pleonasm: ideology is nothing but an idea insofar as that idea dominates" (Barthes, 1977, 47). Thus the dominant ideology is not opposed to truth, but rather is the notion of truth itself. This is a similar claim to that made by Foucault in *The History of Sexuality Volume One*. Therefore the Author is not a false truth (a lie), the death of whom allows the "true" truth to emerge.

10. This is not to imply that there is a discernible and essential distinction between literature and texts, or between authors and writers, but rather that these different discourses and/or discursive practices give life to different ways of being.

11. What I am outlining here is not a Hegelian dialectical movement from thesis to antithesis to synthesis. The claim is that every making is at the same time an unmaking and a remaking, and this process of perverse productivity has no beginning and no end— it is an-archic as Levinas might put it.

12. Perhaps this suggests an alternative nonlinear paradigm for understanding parenthood. It could be said that the "parent" is born in and through the child, and, thus, rather than producing an essential thing, participates in the productivity of both the child's and his or her own (un)becoming.

13. In "To Write: An Intransitive Verb?" Barthes argues that the historically changing notion of the writer from one who writes *something,* to one who *writes*, is not simply a shift from the transitive to the intransitive, since no writer "whatever age he belongs to can fail to realize that he always writes *something*" (1990c, 49). Drawing on the work of Benveniste, Jakobson, and others, and particularly the diathetical analysis of the "middle voice", Barthes argues that the subject remains inside the action, or to put it another way, affects him- or herself in acting. Thus, he concludes, the middle voice does not exclude transitivity. But given my understanding of the notion of (inter)textuality and of the voice developed in his later works, I want to suggest that whilst "to write" is not simply a transitive verb (it is an action that *does* pass over to an object insofar as to write is always to write *something)*, at the same time the something that is written is never a complete idealized object. Rather, my reading of the Barthesian notion of intertextuality suggests that writing is always a re-writing with and through the Other, and, moreover, that in writing the subject does not merely affect him- or herself, but is always already affected in and through "his" or "her" relation with the (inter)textual Other. Thus "to write" is a transitive verb insofar as it does pass over to an object, or produce meaning, whilst at the same time "to write" is an intransitive verb inasmuch as it is a process of perverse productivity that overflows both the subject who writes and the "object" it supposedly produces. Thus the distinction between subject and object, self and other, is destabilized.

14. See Barthes (1990b, 116).

15. See also "The Voice of the Reader," in Barthes (1995, 151–52).

16. For a critical discussion of this question, see Barthes (1977, 151).

17. See Barthes (1990a, 117).

18.   My use of the pronoun "he" here is deliberate, since as feminist critiques of the subject have argued, the characteristics that are said to constitute the subject are exclusively associated with the "masculine".

19.   See Barthes (1977, 139).

20.   Taylor claims that "since the organism as a whole is formed by a complex of dermal layers, the body is, in effect, nothing but a strata of skin in which interiority and exteriority are thoroughly convoluted" (Taylor, 1997, 12). For further development of this thesis, see especially the first two chapters of *Hiding,* entitled "Skinsc(r)apes" and "Dermagraphics".

21.   For a discussion of this phenomenon see Richard Howard's preface to *S/Z.*

22.   In *A Lover's Discourse* (1990b), Barthes elaborates the notion of "atopos" (an alternative to the Aristotelian concept of *arche* as origin, essence, or primary principle), as that which decomposes the stereotype of the subject as Author and origin (site, or topos), of meaning and identity, and as that which is generated in and through the "ceaselessly unforseen originality" and unclassifiability of the relation between self and Other (Barthes, 1990b, 34–36).

23.   "Marks", in *Talking With,* produced by Great Performances, New York, 1995.

24.   See Leslie Hill (1988, 108).

25.   This is not to suggest that the distinction between the critic and the voyeur is in anyway absolute. Rather, I want to deconstruct the opposition by unveiling the debt to the other, the affectivity, that the critic disavows.

26.   In using D'Angelo's name here I am not so much referring to her as the Author in the humanist sense, but rather as the Other whose existence is performative and is at once inextricably bound with or to my own, but at the same time is unknowable in any absolute way.

27.   Appreciation in this sense is linked to normalizing techniques and evaluative categories. The pleasure (read retrospectively) of appreciation reproduces within the subject the cultural values and ideals that he or she has embodied, reinforcing the subject's (illusory) sense of being a unique individual, and thus "veiling over" the role of the Other, or of culture, in the constitution of the self.

28.   Perhaps I should reiterate here that I do not read D'Angelo's text, her body, as a mapping of the truth of herself and/or her history, for, as Barthes claims, "in the field of the subject there is no referent" (Barthes, 1977, 60). Like *Roland Barthes by Roland Barthes,* D'Angelo's text is rather the exploration of identity as fiction. For further discussion of this idea of identity as fiction, see Barthes (1994, 61–62).

29.   My reading of Barthes' notion of *jouissance* is influenced by Mortimer (1989).

30.   For a more in-depth discussion of the relation between history and writing as it is outlined in Barthes' *Michelet,* see Leslie Hill (1988).

31.   In an article entitled "Fetishism in Roland Barthes's Nietzschean Phase" (1978) , Gregory Ulmer describes the Nietzschean *for me* as a response, not to the meaning of words, but to their desires, their *jouissance.* Thus the *for me,* he argues, is associated with the affective (or in Levinasian terms, sensible) basis of language, its "primal melody", rather than the communicating of an essential meaning. Similarly, in "Misunderstood Ideas", Barthes tells how M. D. finds the phrase "one writes in order to be loved" imbecilic, and claims that first and foremost the sentence touches and is then circumscribed, or interpreted as "imbecilic" (Barthes, 1977, 103–4)—a second degree

response that fails to capture what precedes and exceeds it. See also "Idea as Delight" (Barthes, 1977, 103).

32. For example, see Curry (1993, 82).

33. This distinction is informed by Barthes' reading of the Brechtian critique of conventional or "culinary" theatre, which attempts to represent and thus concretizes history, inducing in the viewer an attitude of passive acquiescence, and "narrative" theatre, in which the audience actively participates in the (dis)articulation of meaning. Again, this is not to suggest that there exist two essential forms of theatre, but rather that there are different ethical systems, or states of theatre, that give life to different modes of being. However, as Levinas' work on the Saying and the Said would suggest, the act of the Saying and the Said, of figuration and representation, are by no means mutually exclusive.

34. Nancy makes a similar point in his critique of the traditional understanding of community that assumes that subjectivity precedes social relations. Nancy develops the term "being-in-common" to connote a metaphysical being-with that is not "an experience that we have, but an experience that makes us be" (1991, 26). See also Secomb (1997), 2000).

35. Here I want to evoke both senses of the verb "to conceive": to apprehend, and to become pregnant, that is, to create the other in one's own image (a reproduction of the Same), since it seems that the two are inextricably bound.

36. Serres describes the mathematician as becoming impatient with the philosopher who may want to reconsider the cacophony of writing, of language, because the former "thinks inside a society that has triumphed over noise so well and for such a long time, that he is amazed when the problem is raised anew" (Serres, 1982, 68).

37. For an extended discussion of Lyotard's understanding of figuration see Bennington (1988).

38. In a section of *Roland Barthes*, entitled "Ideology and Aesthetic", Barthes poses the question of how ideological analysis (counter-ideology), given its tendency to its *consistency*, its validity, can avoid becoming itself an ideological object. One possible solution, he suggests, is the *aesthetic* one. "[P]erhaps the role of the aesthetic in our society . . . [is] to provide the rules of an *indirect and intransitive* discourse (it can transform language, but does not display its domination)" (Barthes, 1977, 104).

39. In *Revolution in Poetic Language* (1984), Julia Kristeva says, "even though it can be seen in language, the genotext is not linguistic (in the sense understood by structural or generative linguistics). It is, rather, a *process*, which tends to articulate structures which are ephemeral . . . and nonsignifying. . . . The genotext can . . . be seen as language's underlying foundation. . . . [T]he term phenotext . . . denote[s] language that serves to communicate, which linguistics describes in terms of 'competence' and 'performance'. The phenotext is a structure . . . it obeys rules of communication and presupposes a subject of enunciation and an addressee. The genotext, on the other hand, is a process; it moves through zones that have relative and transitory borders and constitutes a *path* that is not restricted to the two poles of univocal information between two full-fledged subjects. . . . The signifying process . . . includes both the genotext and the phenotext; indeed it could not do otherwise" (Kristeva, 1984, 86–89).

40. Here "scandal", which is of Hebrew origin, denotes something that causes "one" to stumble.

41. I am grateful to Naomi Schor, whose article "Roland Barthes: Necrologies" brought this problem to my attention.

Megan at home, 2000. Photo copyright ©Amanda James Photography

Chapter Five

Bodily Inscription: Figuration and the Discursive Production of Imaginary Bodies and Social Imaginaries

We need a corpus: a simple nomenclature of bodies, of the places of the body, of its entry ways, a recitation enunciated from nowhere, and not even enunciated, but announced, recorded and repeated, as if one said: . . . belly, mouth, nail, wound, beating, sperm, breast, tattoo, eating, nerve, touching, knee, fatigue. . . . Of course, failure is given at the outset, and intentionally so. And a double failure is given: *a failure to produce a discourse on the body, also the failure not to produce a discourse on it.* A double bind. (Nancy, 1993, 190, my emphasis)

In the previous chapter I argued, drawing on the work of Roland Barthes, that reading and writing are not simply functional tools with which to discover or re-present meaning or truth, but rather that these open-ended processes are both affective and intersubjective or intertextual. This led to a critique of the notion of the body assumed by the theorists discussed in Chapter One, as a symptomatological text that is written (on), either consciously or unconsciously, by the subject or Author who inhabits it, and that in turn can be interpreted by others. Such a representational understanding of the body as text is characterised by a movement from surface to depth, from the fleshly to the conceptual, from the material to the immaterial. The body comes to matter in the process of dermal diagnosis only insofar as its matter or materiality is veiled over in and through the extraction of abstract and immaterial truths. As Taylor observes, "true knowledge, it seems, . . . appears when surface gives way to depth" (Taylor, 1997, 17). For Barthes, on the other hand, reading and writing is inextricable from the fleshly, or as Jean-Luc Nancy so aptly puts it, it is necessary to understand writing/reading as "touching, as being touched . . . [as] matters of tact" (Nancy, 1993, 198), rather than as something that involves decipherment. In this chapter, I will draw on the work of Alphonso Lingis, and Jean-Francois Lyotard, and refer back to previous discussions of Foucault, Levinas, and Barthes in order to elaborate in more depth on the possible ways in which the (tattooed) body is continuously (re)read and (re)written in and through a perpetual interweaving with others and with a world. In particular, I want to consider the relation between the constitution of the "individual" body and the social body or body politic, and explore how this might challenge traditional conceptualizations of knowledge.

EVERY PICTURE TELLS A STORY

There is an age old adage that "every picture tells a story". Such myths and maxims are everywhere present in our culture and yet their origins are long forgotten. In Nietzschean terms they are metaphors that have solidified into truths become "second-nature". They (in)form, often at an "unconscious" or visceral level, our social imaginaries. Metaphors, maxims, images, and symbols provide us with what Moira Gatens refers to as ready-made grids of intelligibility (Gatens, 1996, viii) with which to make sense of our "individual" bodies, and the social bodies that we inhabit, and of which we are, as Foucault might put it, both agents and effects. Moreover, social imaginaries determine, at least in part, the value and status of both my body and the body politic, and the possible relations between them[1].   Following Gatens, then, I use the term "imaginaries"[2] in a "loose but nevertheless technical sense to refer to those images, symbols, metaphors and representations which help construct various forms of subjectivity" (viii).

If maxims, such as the one with which this discussion began, are not simply truths, neither are they merely lies; ideological falsehoods contrived by a contemptible elite in order to distort the consciousness of the masses[3]. This, as Gatens points out, would be to assume that social imaginaries exist in contrast to "reality", and likewise that bodies exist prior to the processes of enculturation that inscribe them. Foucault makes a similar point when he suggests that what is called for is

an analysis in which the biological and the historical are not consecutive to one another, as in the evolutionism of the first sociologists, but are bound together in an increasingly complex fashion in accordance with the development of modern technologies of power that take life as their objective. Hence, I do not envisage a "history of mentalities" that would take account of bodies only through the manner in which they have been perceived and given meaning and value; but a "history of bodies" and the manner in which what is most material and most vital in them has been invested. (Foucault, 1980, 152)

Given this, the notion of imaginaries at work here rejects the traditional distinction between ideology and reality, mind and body, and replaces it with an understanding of *embodiment* as an effect of systems of power/knowledge that morphologically create the body's "capacities, its desires and its actual material form" (Gatens, 1996, 12). Or, to quote Foucault again, "power relations can materially penetrate the body in depth, without depending even on the mediation of the subject's own representations. If power takes hold on the body, this isn't through its first having to be interiorised in people's consciousness" (Foucault, 1980c, 186). Like Gatens, Diprose, and Foucault, I want to examine the relation between embodiment and systems of power/knowledge, that is, between imaginary bodies and social imaginaries, between "individual" bodies and social bodies for, as Le Dœuff puts it,

imagery and knowledge form, dialectically, a common system. Between these two terms there is a play of feedbacks which maintains the particular regime of the discursive formation. . . . [T]exts offer images through which subjectivity can be structured and given a *marking* which is that of the corporate body [or body politic]. (Le Dœuff, cited in Gatens, ix, my emphasis)

The aim of this exercise is to develop an open-ended ethics of embodiment that avoids the tendency toward universalism apparent in traditional conceptions of ethics, and of *the* human body.

I want to take up the often unquestioned notion that "every picture tells a story", not in order to substantiate its falsity, but rather to play with it, to tease out the resonances of imaginary understandings of bodily illustrations and dominant imaginary accounts of signification, subjectivity, and social relations. The aim of questioning long-established notions of signification and subjectivity is neither to replace erroneous models with "true" ones, nor to gesture toward the possibility of a utopic limitless polysemic future in which the sign and/or the subject is, or can be, entirely open-ended or free from the constraints of social convention. To assume that there is an *outside of representation,* a *beyond* that is immune to the effects of power, is, in the end, tantamount to determining an alternative domain of truth, to imagining a thing that replaces the sign, but itself becomes a sign (Lyotard, 1993, 47). Consequently, I want to retain the adage that "every picture tells a story" in order to examine the embodied effects that social imaginaries produce, and at the same time to show that social imaginaries, as systems of ideas and relations that morphologically produce subjects in culturally and historically specific ways, are never unified or static but are heterogeneous and in a constant state of (trans)formation (Gatens, 1996, ix).

The picture that concerns me here is the tattoo, and, as we have seen, tattoos are more often than not conceived of as pictures that tell stories, as intentional external expressions that tell of the desires, and thus of the internal psyches, of those whom they adorn. But if we accept that both imaginary bodies and social imaginaries are heterogeneous, nonunified, and in a constant state of (trans)formation, then we must also recognize that pictures such as tattoos never simply tell *a* story. As Pasi Falk puts it, "what is . . . written in flesh is much more than mere body-decoration, or simply marking one's status in the community. The human body . . . its surface, is filled with hieroglyphs telling one of the stories of corporeality in history" (Falk, 1995, 95). And as I have argued throughout this book, the "human" body and its history presuppose one another. What I want to suggest is that (tattooed) bodies may be *duplicitous*— that, on the one hand, the stories they appear to tell function in conjunction with dominant social imaginaries, and yet, on the other hand, we can listen to these stories, and hear, as Barthes puts it, *something else*[4]. In effect, then, this bringing together of social imaginaries and pictorial bodies is an attempt to draw pictures in the sand, to provide a transitory or ephemeral pattern(ing) of linkages and transformations that does not cohere into a unified and static picture—at least not in any absolute way.

I want to conceive of tattooed bodies as imaginary bodies, that is, as body-morphologies that are "socially and historically specific [insofar as they are] constructed by: a shared language; . . . and common institutional practices and discourses which act on and through the body" (Gatens, 1996, 12). As I have demonstrated throughout this book, tattoos are most often read ideographically, that is, as pictures or graphics that tell an unambiguous story of the subject's integral interiority. For example, for proponents of subcultural praxis such as David Curry, tattooing is "a political act and *sign* of dissent" (Curry, 1993, 82, my emphasis). Such a position is exemplified by Idexa (as discussed in the previous chapter) who claims that her body modifications signify her belonging to a culture whose values and norms she does not believe in. Ironically such a claim dovetails nicely with the arguments put forward by criminologists such as Cesare Lombroso, who, as we saw in Chapter One, is of the opinion that tattoos tell the story of the subject's pathological need for attention, atavistic propensity to crime, and antipathy to the health and well-being of the body politic. Similarly, for Sheila Jeffreys, the Valkyrian saviour of womankind whose work was referred to in Chapter Two, tattoos are "stigmata of body abuse", corporeal confessions of the subject's internalization and perpetuation of the intrinsic violence of patriarchal relations and structures (Jeffreys, 1994, 21). Whilst in each of these cases tattoos tell somewhat conflicting stories informed by different, yet connected, social fictions (i.e., criminological, counter-cultural, and radical feminist discourses), they nevertheless share with Grumet a conceptualization of the imaginary body as a canvas on which psychological themes are portrayed. In other words, each draws on aspects of a particular social imaginary that we might perhaps call liberal humanism, and links these in various ways with other available discourses.

So let me begin with a story; a story about pictures. A story that, for me at least, does not either simply reproduce or entirely escape the dominant imaginary relation between representation and reality, between pictures and stories of, or as, truth, but rather offers imaginary alternatives, or alternative imaginaries. This is the story of Molly, an imaginary woman, who, along with a bevy of equally anomalous beauties, inhabits the pages of Michael Westlake's *Imaginary Women* (1989). One evening, whilst Molly is taking a stroll beside the canal she comes across a girl who has a red rose tattooed on her upper arm. The rose is at once discreet and provocative. This chance encounter convinces Molly that she too will become tattooed, and raises the question of what image Molly will choose. Sometime later we find Molly afloat in a steamy bath. It is here that the image of a brightly coloured tropical fish comes to her. And thus begins Molly's foray into the world of tattooing.

On her initial visit to the dingy little upstairs studio located on the seedy side of the tracks, Molly emerges with an angel fish on her upper arm. But the picture of the little jewelled fish is not merely an object that ornaments Molly's body or signifies to others something of her inner being. Nevertheless, the little fish does invoke curiosity in others. As her diary entry tells us, people cast her surreptitious looks. They saw the fish, "and they didn't, like it was there and not there at the same time" (Westlake, 1989, 12). This ambiguous (in)attention makes Molly all the more aware of the tattoo herself. It was "*her* little fish, for all to see but no one to [know]" (12). Molly finds this discovery exhilarating, and feels as if she too is a polychromatic sea creature swimming in the sea of life. In a sense then, this image is reminiscent of the oceanic feeling that I discussed in Chapter Three, of an affective sensuosity that is irreducible to an epistemological object that the subject or interpretation can know.

As I have demonstrated, liberal humanist representations of the subject in/of tattooing assume a depth model of the subject that embraces a distinction, and at the same time a causal connection between interiority and exteriority; the notion of an autonomous subject whose relations with others and with a world are secondary; and an expression-reception model of communication whereby the intentional expression of a sign designating the thought of an innate "I" is simply cognitively perceived by another as a sign of the truth of the subject. Keeping this in mind, let us imagine for a moment some of the stories that Molly's little fish might possibly be said to tell. My aim in doing this is not to claim that these interpretations are erroneous, but rather that they are symptomatic of the ways in which imaginary bodies are discursively produced in and through the relation with dominant social imaginaries.

For those who take up the position outlined by Curry and Idexa, the angel fish may tell the story of Molly's "counter-cultural" commitment to ecological politics. Perhaps for disciples of Lombroso, this oceanic creature could be said to represent Molly's retarded primeval position in the evolutionary chain, whereas for followers of Jeffreys, the fish might well signify Molly's association with the degraded and abused feminine body, and her subsequent abuse of her self and her thalassic[5] body. But perhaps at the same time there are other unspeakable stories at work within and against these discourses, disrupting the rule of representation on which they rely. Perhaps if, as I suggested in the previous chapter, we reconfigure the notion of communication and refrain from the desire to extract abstract forms from the noise internal to the messages and the background noise in which they are emitted, we may just, as Barthes puts it, "hear" *something else,* that is, the alteritous "rumble of the world" in and through which the utterances we make, the subjectivities we perform, are intertextually generated or perpetually interwoven.

LIBIDINAL INSCRIPTION, SAVAGE IMAGINARIES

If bodily illustrations do not function simply as a representative reflection or image of the author's psyche, then what Other kinds of imaginary stories could Molly's picturesque body be said to tell? And if hearing is not simply the consumption of a message, how can we "hear" these stories otherwise? Bodily inscription as a variety of practices that includes tattooing is described by Alphonso Lingis as palpable (sensuous) rather than simply significatory. As he puts it in an analysis of various forms of body marking in a paper entitled "Savages":

What we are dealing with is inscription where writing, graphics, is not inscription on clay tablets, bark or papyrus, but in flesh and blood, and also where it is not . . . narrative. Where it is not significant, not a matter of marks whose role is to signify, to efface themselves before the meaning, or ideality, or logos. For here signs count: they *hurt.* Before they make sense to the reader, they give pain to the living substrate. Who can doubt, after Nietzsche and Kafka . . . that before they informed the understanding of the public, this pain gave pleasure to its eyes. . . . The eye that looks at them does not read them; it winces, it senses the pain. . . . [B]efore historical—narrative, signifying, phonocentric, logocentric—inscription, there is a savage inscription not yet despotic, not serving speech. It pains rather than signifies. (Lingis, 1983b, 23–24, 34)

The "savage"[6] imaginary body that Lingis elaborates here is significantly different from the imaginary body of liberal humanism. "It is not . . . the . . . expression, moment by moment, of an inward spirit, or a person belonging to him- [or her]self" (Lingis, 1983b, 25), as classical theories of intentionality would have it. Bodily inscription, then, is not always read simply as a form of nonverbal communication or representation as assumed by the theorists critiqued in Chapter One. Rather, Lingis argues that the incisions and corporeal markings of the "savage" body create an erotogenic surface; "they create *not* a map of the body, but the body precisely as a map" (Grosz, 1994, 139). In other words, rather than reproducing or mapping what already is (i.e., the body-subject), bodily inscription can also be conceptualized as an active process of perverse productivity, of (trans)formation, that is always already intertextual or intersubjective. This is the idea that Lingis gestures toward when he asks "are not all these scarifications, perforations, incisions bound up somehow with the exorbitant pleasure the savage takes in himself?" (Lingis, 1983b, 24). It is not that the "savage" subject exists prior to these inscriptions, but rather "it is the inscription *that makes* the savage" (24). Elsewhere, Lingis ponders whether the eddy of subjectivity that feeds off the excess potential left on the surface at the conjuncture of Masai testes and lion pelt is an ego(ism) attached to the warrior or the beast (32), and implies that not only is the question unanswerable in any absolute sense, but more importantly its asking tells us more about the ontological status of the subject in/of Western capitalism than it does about ("savage") subjectivity *per se*. Inscriptive mapping then—in the Lingisian sense—has no finality; the subject is not so much its source or destination as that which is continuously (re)born in and through processes of int(ert)extuation. As Deleuze and Guattari put it, "[t]he map does not reproduce an unconscious. . . . The map has to do with performance . . . [it] is open and connectable in all its dimensions; it is . . . susceptible to constant modification. It can be torn, reversed, . . . reworked by an individual, group, or social formation" (Deleuze and Guattari, 1987, 12). However, inscription as a sort of cartographic effectuation that is always already intertextual is not necessarily particular to "savage" bodies. Rather, Lingis' elaboration of a "savage" imaginary offers us a way of rethinking the relation between reading, writing, and the body (of both the subject and the socius), of inscription as the writing of a *corpus*", as a separation and sharing of bodies, sharing their being-body, shared out by it, and thus divided from itself and from its sense, exscribed all along its own inscription" (Nancy, 1993, 197).

Inscription, according to Lingis, could be thought of as the codification of excitations, of libidinality. Drawing on the Freudian notion of libidinality, the distinction between freely mobile excitations and bound excitations, Lingis proposes an understanding of libidinality that is multiplicitous rather than directed toward unification and stability, which is superficial rather than topographical. Lingis, like Lyotard, claims that "the libidinal zone in the body is the skin—skin and the mucous orifices which prolong it inward, but where the finger, tongue, or penis will make contact [only] with more skin" (Lingis, 1983b, 27). The libidinal surface[7] then, is something like a Möbius strip that destabilizes the distinction between inside and outside, surface and depth. Moreover, "[t]he movement of libidinal excitations is horizontal, from one contact point on the skin to another" (Lingis, 1983b, 28), rather than vertical, from depth to surface, from "hyletic datum to its meaning" (27). In other words, the body is not simply the surface *of* a depth as suggested by the theorists discussed in Chapter One, nor is it, as Foucault sometimes seems to imply, a pre-social *tabula rasa* on which libidinal excitations occur, "[f]or through the free excitations which intensify and discharge, *a body surface first extends . . .* excitations, in their ephemeral and passing multiplicity, distend a zone which is all surface" (27, my emphasis). Similarly, Lyotard—exemplifying the position of the "libidinal economist"—is suspicious of the supposed distinction between inscription and its site. Rather than thinking (through) the body, Lyotard suggests that we

strengthen our . . . palpative potential . . . until we forge the idea of an intensity which far from setting itself up on a producer-body, determines it; the idea of a passage over nothing, which produces, one instant beyond countable time, the being of its proper passing, its *passage*. . . . Therefore not a surface first, then a writing or inscription over it. But the libidinal skin of which, *after the event,* one will be able to say that it is made up of a patchwork of organs, of elements from organic and social bodies, the libidinal skin initially like the *track* of intensities, . . . *the surface crossed and crossing.* (Lyotard, 1993, 16–17)

In other words, neither Lingis nor Lyotard conceive of libidinality as a transcendental vitalism that civilization attempts to control, as is possibly implied by Freud's distinction between primary and secondary processes, or, as I discussed in Chapter Three, between the program of the pleasure principle and that of the reality principle. Rather, as Lyotard's reading of Freud suggests, force or energy as libido struggles with what he calls the theatre of representation, but also accounts for its constitution. And for Lyotard this ambiguity or "incandescent duplicity" provides the possibility of avoiding dichotomous accounts of subjectivity[8] and libidinality, of the tendency to propose *either* a rationalist semiotics or a form of transcendentalism. This ambiguity is apparent, according to Lyotard, in Freud's account of desire, which, despite its tendency to reduce the implications of primary process libido through recourse to the doctrine of representation, simultaneously implies that secondary processes presuppose primary processes, or at least that the "two" are inextricably bound. Lyotard says:

In Freud himself there is a profound and not merely circumstantial hesitation (it is probably even of decisive importance) as to the position and function of the term desire. There are two poles: . . . desire-wish, which implies a negativity, which implies a dynamics, which implies a teleology, a dynamics with an end, which implies object, absence, lost object, and which also implies accomplishment, something like the fulfilment of a wish. All of which forms a set-up implying the consideration of *meaning* in desire. The other pole of the category of desire in Freud is desire-libido, desire-process, primary process. (Lyotard, cited in Bennington, 1988, 15, my emphasis)

What we have here, at least as Lyotard sees it, are not two competing or opposed forms of desire, but rather "two" inextricable "regimes" of force or energy which are mutually constitutive and at the same time incommensurable. Desire-wish is a particular configuration of desire-libido, but this is not to suggest that the former constitutes something like alienation; the reduction of pure energy to meaning. Rather, the relation between primary processes and secondary processes shares resonances with the relation between the Saying and the Said as outlined in Chapter Three. As I argued, the Saying can only take place in and through the Said (the very language the Saying calls into question) and the Said presupposes something it cannot incorporate, namely, the Saying. Likewise, primary processes are "known" only through effects in the secondary sphere, which presupposes them but which at the same time can never entirely incorporate them.

Let me explore this configuration a little further by returning for a moment to the notions of figuration and representation outlined briefly in the previous chapter. As I said, for Barthes, figuration is not simply opposed to representation, but rather is internal to, and breaks up, representation. In *Discourse, Figure* (1971), Lyotard develops a similar thesis, claiming that discourse, as the condition of representation to consciousness by a rational order of concepts, is inextricably bound to the figural (as an unspeakable other necessarily *at work* within and against discourse), and vice versa, despite the fact that the discursive claim to accurate representation or truth involves the repression or disavowal of figurality (Readings, 1991, xxxi). For Lyotard and Barthes, figurality, like libidinality, is neither opposed to representation nor is it presumed to precede representation in terms of a temporal dialectic. Rather, as Bill Readings puts it, "[f]igure and discourse are necessarily and impossibly co-present, as constitutive and disruptive of representation" (Readings, 1991, 7). Thus in *Libidinal Economies* Lyotard claims that ultimately there is no discernible difference between a discursive formation and a libidinal formation since they are both formations (Lyotard, 1993, 25).

In effect then, given that both individual and social bodies or imaginaries are libidinally and discursively (in)formed, and that figuration simultaneously constitutes and exceeds representation, the project of (re)thinking the subject in/of tattooing must necessarily avoid the desire to either establish meaning or truth, or alternatively to romantically assume that "irrationality" or meaninglessness is the liberatory goal of ethics. Rather, what is needed is an examination of the ways in which incommensurable elements are held together, impossibly, in the "same" space. Given this, my aim is not to produce a more coherent reading of the tattooed body as text by rendering audible the silent, the unspeakable. Rather, I want to confuse the traditional readings of the stories that tattooed bodies supposedly tell, have made distinct, to strengthen our palpative potential, to forge an idea of bodily reading/writing as matters of tact. This is in keeping with Lyotard's notion of deconstruction as the possibility of performing an ethics of reading; a refusal to allow claims to know the truth of a text to disavow the demands that the sensible, the figural, makes; a (re)affirmation of heterogeneity or duplicity. As Lyotard puts it:

The deconstruction of the articulations of language, bringing with it the subversion of the most deeply hidden categories, is the work of affirmation (*Bejahung*) if one understands by it not a crude affirmation which would place itself *before* language, but a secondary affirmation, a reaffirmation which comes to cover again what language had placed in the open, to block together[9] what it had separated, to confuse what it had made distinct. (Lyotard, 1971, 296)

Let me attempt to perform such a task, then, via an examination of the relation between social imaginaries and imaginary bodies.

As Lingis' account of "savage" inscription demonstrates, the recording, channelling, regulating, and coding of libidinal impulses occur in differing ways in various cultural and historical contexts; social imaginaries produce particular kinds of imaginary bodies, and vice versa. For example, Freud's story of oedipalization and Lacan's notion of the Mirror Stage tell of the ways in which libidinal impulses are (trans)formed into intrinsically generic signs through processes of enculturation particular to Western capitalism, and morphologically produce specific kinds of imaginary (sexed) bodies. According to Lacanian theory, it is the imaginary body, or gestalt, that allows the subject to orient his or her body in time and space, and in relation to other bodies and to a world. According to Foucault, insofar as we embody social imaginaries, subjects or imaginary bodies are both agents and effects of socially and historically specific practices and relations of power. The imaginary body of liberal humanism, then, as the surface articulation of an innate and autonomous depth, is the morphological effect of particular discourses and discursive practices; it is neither a truth nor a lie[10]. As Lingis puts it in "The Society of Dismembered Body Parts",

The closed plenum upon which organs are attached, producing surface effects, pleasure surfaces, and eddies of egoism, reduces to the individual mass of the body only in the discourse and practices of our epoch. That the closed plenum upon which our organs are attached is identified with the mass of our individual bodies is the residue of a historical process of deterritorialization, abstraction, formalization. . . . The notion of the integral man, the privatized body, is a moment of the capitalist coding. (Lingis, 1994c, 291, 301)

Although Lingis is drawing on the work of Deleuze and Guattari here, the point is similar to that made by Foucault in *Power/Knowledge,* when, in a critique of the liberal humanist notion of subjectivity, he states:

The individual is not to be conceived as a sort of elementary nucleus, a primitive atom, a multiple and inert material on which power comes to fasten or against which it happens to strike, and in so doing subdues or crushes individuals. In fact, it is already one of the prime effects of power that certain bodies, certain gestures, certain discourses, certain desires, come to be identified and constructed as individuals. (Foucault, 1980c, 98)

As my analysis of *Dead Man Walking* (Chapter One) illustrated, the flesh is (trans)formed into a *body,* in and through processes of inscription, reading, and writing. Poncelet's body, gestures, desires, and capacities are the truth-effects of social imaginaries or systems of power/knowledge and are read, in and through socially and historically specific grids of intelligibility, as signs of delinquency. The delinquent body-subject is both written and read in accordance with social conventions, and thus confirms and reinforces the disciplinary archipelago insofar as it is inscribed with the civil code and signs of its transgression. Social imaginaries are incarnated in the movements, actions, and desires of imaginary bodies. But at the same time, imaginary bodies (trans)form social fictions since, as Butler points out in *Gender Trouble*, subjectivity is "structured by repeated acts that seek to approximate the ideal of a substantial ground of identity, but which, in their occasional *dis*continuity, reveal the temporal and contingent groundlessness of this 'ground'" (Butler, 1990, 141). And it is this possibility of a failure to repeat that "reveals" subjectivity to be a regulatory fiction that is open to change.

The representational model of "the delinquent" embraced by the criminologists and psychologists discussed in Chapter One is premised upon the disavowal of the figural in the discursive processes of subject formation. In other words, the imaginary body of liberal humanism is a body that expresses itself, and that (supposedly) makes sense. And here sense is nothing more than meanings that discourse may speak. But if we take into account the work of Lingis, Lyotard, Foucault, Barthes, and Levinas, we can no longer speak simply of bodies that make sense, of pictures that tell singular and static stories of/as truth. At the same time as we may read (tattooed) bodies as stories that make sense, as paradigmatic of dominant social and political fictions, we must also forge the idea of reading/writing (the body), as Nancy puts it, as a body of sense that refrains from reducing the body to a sign. Thus what we have is not a body that makes sense, but rather

sense that engenders and shares bodies. . . . Bodies are first masses . . . offered without anything to articulate, without anything to discourse about. . . . Discharges of writing, rather than surfaces to be covered by writings. . . . No "written bodies", no writing on the body, nor any of this graphosomatology into which the mystery of the Incarnation and of the body as pure sign of itself is sometimes converted "modern style". . . .[T]he body is not a locus of writing. No doubt one writes, but it is absolutely not where one writes, nor is it what one writes—it is always what writing exscribes. In all writing, a body is traced, is the tracing and the trace—is the letter, yet never the letter, a literality or rather a lettericity that is no longer legible. A body is what cannot be read as writing. (Nancy, 1993, 197–98)

This is obviously not to suggest that subjectivity as we know it occurs as a dialectical reversal from plenitude to lack. The point, rather, is that insofar as time and space are not already given *a priori*, but are temporalized moment by moment by the marking (out) of the intensification and discharge of libidinal impulses, of sense, then what occurs is not (a) being as pure presence or lack, but an infinite process of (un)becoming that transgresses the boundaries that dichotomous logic assumes. Such a formulation provides a conception of subjectivity "as a constituted *social temporality*" (Butler, 1990, 141).

In other words, the bodily illustrations or inscriptions of which Lingis speaks do not simply reiterate the same old story of a Platonic imaginary, whereby inscription functions as a copy of a copy, "a visual imitation of a phonic stream of vocal signs, which itself is a copy or imitation of the logos, the chain of ideas" (Lingis, 1983b, 24). The tattoo is not merely an object of cognition, a sign that emanates out of the depth of the subject and that the other interprets, but first and foremost it is an intensive point, an aesthetic mark or site of what Barthes might call intertextual affectivity. Given this, these pictures that tell stories cannot, or at least need not, be limited to the gaze alone. What is implied is an imaginary relation that encompasses "a whole sensorium", a veritable "passion of the senses" (Muecke, 1997, 90) in and through which both self and Other are (trans)formed *ad infinitum*. I will discuss this point at more length in due course, but for the moment let us return to Molly.

It is said amongst those who frequent the alchemical realms of back-street parlours that tattoos can be addictive, and, as we shall see, Molly is no stranger to either the parlour or the addiction. Over a period of months, Molly's body (which *is* Molly, not something she simply inhabits) undergoes, or perhaps more specifically dramatizes, a process of transubstantiation. Her tattooed breast, for example, reconfigures, rather than reiterates, the imaginary female body as the locus of reproduction and infantile sustenance. It becomes the habitat or dwelling of two aggressive Siamese fighting fish, ready, as Molly writes in her diary, "to defend [her] honour" (Westlake, 1989, 11). Thus one could possibly argue that this graphic marks the site of an alternative imaginary relation between Molly, the breast, femininity, and the body politic, but one that, like Luce Irigaray's "two lips", actively engages with the morphological construction of the imaginary body, rather than painting a "true" picture of Woman.

This process of (un)becoming continues with the appearance of a clouded moray eel coiled languidly around Molly's right leg and a manta ray covering her upper back and shoulders, chased by a shoal of tiny fleet-finned mauve and green moon wrasses.

Molly was being transfigured into a coral reef. Across her body there swum . . . brilliantly coloured fish . . . that glided, darted, hovered as she moved. . . . Along her ribs dozens of butterfly fish, on her belly . . . a whitethroated surgeonfish, on her back [and] buttock[s] . . . a mass of lyretails, jewelfish, labyrinth-fish . . . in an endless profusion of form and colour. . . . Her feet became flat fish . . . whose dark . . . topsides contrasted with pale cream undersides on the soles of her feet. . . . A Portuguese man-of-war . . . floated behind an ear, its trailing strands mingling with her hair. . . . And behind all these lay the living coral reef itself, [a multi-coloured] intricate architecture. (Westlake, 1989, 15)

As she drifted into sleep at night Molly heard the distant sound of waves pounding against coral reefs and the cries of seabirds who inhabited lands unknown to her. She dreamed of the shifting of continents, submarine squalls, and the creation and extinction of all manner of life forms. To put it simply, Molly's body (and thus "Molly") undergoes a "sea change". Her imaginary body could be said to perform—or at least potentiate—"a revolution in thought and ethics . . . a reinterpretation [of] the . . . relationship between subject and discourse, the subject and the world . . . the microcosmic and the macrocosmic" (Irigaray, 1991, 166), as is called for by Luce Irigaray in *An Ethics of Sexual Difference* (1993).

OCEANIC IMAGINARIES/ FLUIDENTITIES

In a fascinating account of his journey into the oceanic depths, in a paper entitled "The Rapture of the Deep", Lingis articulates an oceanic imaginary that has resonances with Molly's story, and at the same time provides a critique of the appropriation and negation of the other in the constitution of the "I" of liberal individualism. In order to explicate his claim that "the deep is all in surface effects" (Lingis, 1983a, 7)—a claim that challenges the depth model of the subject uncritically assumed by the theorists discussed in Chapter One— Lingis critically reconsiders functionalist explanations of the fluctuating patterns and colours that are at play on the body surface of various sea creatures. Such understandings, he argues, in claiming that the phantasmagoric "performances" of fish, octopi, anemones, and so on function as camouflage, means of species identification, or ostentatious warning signals to potential predators, become entangled in an exhaustive cryptic/semantic impasse. In effect, then, such a vision of the deep is

profound, penetrating; one would in seeing the color and patterns of the skin comprehend the fish in its functional relationship with species it devours and those that devour it, or comprehend the relationship of recognition with those it does not devour, its species-fellows, or comprehend its expressive-aggressive index. (Lingis, 1983a, 8)

This critical insight could equally well be applied to the theses expounded in Chapter One, whereby tattoos are thought to signify a relationship with a particular group such as the Hell's Angels, which at the same time constitutes a potentially threatening gesture to other social groups or institutions. Thus a depth model of subjectivity is not only problematic insofar as it reifies a notion of the *a priori* subject, but inextricably links identity to an antagonistic notion of self-other relations in which difference can only be understood in hierarchized dichotomous terms, as my discussion of the Freudian notion of subjectivity and social relations demonstrates.

Lingis also engages with the idea, introduced by Adolf Portman, of "organs to be looked at". The thesis of Portman's book, *Animal Forms and Patterns,* is that the patterns, colours, and display behaviours of both sea and land creatures demand a specific explanation on the level of the phenomenal and not simply of the functional. For Portman there appears to be "a logic of ostentation over and beyond camouflage and semantic functions" (Lingis, 1983a, 9), which explains the glorious theatrics that take place in the deep in terms of "the spectacle". But even this sort of approach is problematic since, as Lingis aptly points out,

[g]lory is for its witness, the spectacle is for the spectator. . . . [Thus] one makes even the gloss of appearance intelligible, and one posits oneself as an essential and necessary factor in the sphere [of the other] which one enters . . . I am the eye all this spectacle was inventing itself for in the depths, the dark, for millions of years. (9)

Here we have a specular economy in which the picturesque body of the other is nothing but an object that serves to reaffirm the glorification of the (liberal) subject who interprets, or at least enjoys, the splendour of the spectacle, and this is reminiscent of the position taken in relation to tattooing by the theorists critiqued in Chapter One such as Edgerton and Dingman, who identify one of the five main reasons for the preponderance of tattooing in Western culture as the desire to beautify or ornament the body-self. Again, the I/eye "and what is to be looked at form a functional unity" (Portman, cited in Lingis, 1983a, 8). The proximity of self and other is veiled over in a deft sleight of hand that reduces difference, yet again, to an Economy of the Same.

But if we cast our minds back to Molly we may just be able to sense the echoes of another story, of *something else.* In the diary entry that I mentioned earlier, Molly tells of how people cast her surreptitious looks of puzzlement. They saw the angel fish and yet they did not, as if it were simultaneously there and not there. It was *her* little fish, for all to see but no one to know. Thus perhaps we could think of Molly's tattooed body (and thus her "self"), as inalienable, as a "sphere of resplendent phenomena whose glory, utterly disinterested, calls for no acolyte" (Lingis, 1983a, 9). Whilst the I's/eyes that cast surreptitious looks at Molly's picturesque body cannot entirely apprehend its sense, subject it to sense perception, they are nevertheless affected by it, moved by it, subject to its sensuosity[11]. This validates the proposition made earlier that our readings of the stories such pictures tell cannot be limited to the gaze alone, since sensibility involves "a whole sensorium", a veritable "passion of the senses". Reading and writing as inseparable processes are, as Nancy points out, matters of tact, or, as Lingis argues, perception presupposes sensibility as affective.

In contradistinction to occularcentric explanations of spectacular bodies, Lingis proposes a sensuous account of imaginary bodies and the relations between them that involves the notion of the "voluptuous eye" as opposed to a liberal humanist eye/I. He says:

Denuded of one's very postural schema, of one's own motility, swept away and scattered by the surge, one does nothing in the deep. One takes nothing, apprehends nothing, comprehends nothing. One is only a brief visitor, an eye that no longer pilots or estimates . . . that is moved, with nothing in view. . . . The eye adrift in the deep is not penetrating, examining, interrogating, surveying, gauging. It passes over surface effects, caresses . . . is caressed by the laps of brine, the magnesium networks of light, the evanescent slidings of the fish. . . . [The eye] is not seeking to grasp . . . the foundation beneath the attributes, the substrate beneath the surface effects. . . . The caress that passes over the surface . . . makes contact only to expose itself. . . . The organ that caresses . . . is moved, affected, affectionate, moves to be in contact with [the inalienable other]. (1983a, 10–11)

The imaginary relation between Self and Other that Lingis formulates here, as in his analysis of "savage" inscription, is something like an incompossible intertwining, or what he calls "couplings". It foremostly affects palpability in and through proximity to the Other, rather than producing knowledge in and through a rational distancing, or incorporation, of the Other as other. In other words, cognition and signification, Self and Other, are not opposed to sensibility or affectivity, but rather presuppose it; discourse and figure, meaning and sense, the speakable and the unspeakable are mutually constitutive yet incommensurable. The relation is one of duplicity rather than duality.

As I said in Chapter Three, the exposure to the inalienable Other, which is the caress, is not so much an event situated in time and space, but "a structural possibility that [exceeds] and makes possible all subsequent experience" (Davis, 1996, 45). Levinas conceptualizes the caress as sensibility. He says, "[t]he caress consists in seizing upon nothing, in soliciting what ceaselessly escapes its form towards a future never future enough, . . . what slips away as though it *were not yet*" (Levinas, 1969, 257–58). Or perhaps to put it more simply, sensibility "opens us . . . upon an extension without determinate frontiers" (Lingis, 1986, 222); it affects an infinite process of (un)becoming.

This encounter with the inalienable or with alterity then is not the convergence of discreet beings that could be configured according to the mathematical equation $1+1=2$. Rather, exposure exceeds the ontological categories characteristic of Western philosophical social imaginaries insofar as it affects modes of existence in terms Levinas might call "otherwise than being". The Other is not an object of perception whose meaning I can sense, and who would thus reaffirm my sense of self and place in the world. The Other who moves me, affects me, calls me forth as an "I" remains unassimilable. But as Deleuze and Guattari put it, there is no such thing as self and other, subject and object, human and animal, prior to their interaction, "only a process that produces the one within the other and couples the machines together" (Deleuze and Guattari, 1983, 2). Nevertheless, insofar as we embody the ontologies of our specific cultural and historical epoch, we live our bodies as discrete individuals who seemingly own these bodies, and read the graphics with which we "adorn" them as expressions of our inner being. As I have argued, following Lingis, the thematic separation of the hand that writes from inscriptive surfaces is paradigmatic of the privitization of organs and flows which constitute the private, integral individual of the socius as the body of capital(ism). As Lingis puts it, in this way, "inscription becomes graphics coupled with the phonetic, taxonomical, syntactical, semantical laws of significant language" (Lingis, 1994b, 298). The caress of that which touches and that which is touched (and the "two" are inextricable) is disrupted by a violent rending asunder by "the *one* of form, of the individual, . . . of the proper name, of the proper meaning" (Irigaray, 1985, 26), as Irigaray puts it in her critique of the phallic imaginary.

Let us call once more upon the figure of Molly in order to (re)consider the notion of the imaginary body in terms of this analysis of bodily inscription, subjectivity, and self-other relations. Earlier I spoke of Molly's body as a performative process of transubstantiation. Given the formulation of (inter)subjectivity proposed above and in Chapter Three, as a nonreproductive process of perverse productivity, of (un)becoming, generated in and through exposure to alterity (the Other), I want to suggest that the story Molly's pictorial body tells could be thought of, not simply as a determinate tale in itself that confirms, or conforms to, linguistic systems, but as that which simultaneously articulates and disarticulates meaning. The process of transubstantiation that is affected in and through the relation between "Molly", various forms of subaqueous life, the tattooist who draws them, and those in whom they provoke awe and puzzlement is not one that unites disparate and discrete entities into an homogenous whole or that replaces one mode of being with another. Rather, the term "transubstantiation" implies an infinite process of (un)becoming; it is a (re)affirmation of the figural at work within and against discourse, of the sensual as that which is "beyond every possible project, beyond every meaningful and intelligent power" (Levinas, 1969, 266); it is "otherwise than being, or beyond essence" (Levinas, 1978). Molly's imaginary body, then, could be said to dramatize the Lingisian notion of the voluptuous eye adrift in the inalienable deep that does not simply seek to gratify desire in and through the incorporation of the Other—a gesture that reduces the Other to a tool with which to reaffirm or complete one's being—but also engenders affectivity, (un)becoming, the figural. Thus in one sense, Molly's pictorial body tells stories that provide a key to "the decipherment of the social and personal significance of [tattooed bodies] as [they are] lived in [contemporary Western] culture" (Gatens, 1996, 12), and at the same time, articulates something else, that is, an "uncontained ability to affect and be affected" (Massumi, 1993, 35). This is the reason behind my claim that tattooed bodies are duplicitous: they tell of the ways in which linguistic systems or social imaginaries (in)form bodies, they speak of meaning, identity, and social relations, *and* simultaneously they affect a disarticulation of such thematics.

SPEAKING THROUGH THE BODY? VOICE IS SILENCE, FLESH IS VOICE

If, as I have argued, tattooed bodies could be said to tell duplicitous stories, to evoke or (re)affirm an incommensurability at work within and against discourse that narrative attempts to disavow, then should we conclude that the marked body performs some sort of political function? If our answer is affirmative, then what does this suggest about our understanding of the materiality of the body (as text), in and through which the figural silently speaks? Or for that matter, what does it suggest about our conception of politics? I want to explore these questions, which I have already touched upon throughout the book, because there is a tendency amongst some writers who, whilst disagreeing with the simplistic approach of reading the body as an unambiguous representational text—the approach outlined in Chapter One—nevertheless (re)inscribe the materiality of the body that speaks what language cannot say as an object of signification. Connected to this is the (sometimes implicit) assumption that politics is a matter of knowledge.

In an article entitled "The Voice on the Skin: Self-Mutilation and Merleau-Ponty's Theory of Language" (1996), Janice McLane claims that self-mutilation[12] can be understood as a form of speaking one's pain:

When hidden pain starts to speak, it will speak silently. Its voice may appear as a cut on the leg, a burn on the arm, skin ripped and scratched repeatedly. There will be no sound . . . only unfelt and silent pain which makes its appearance in another pain, self-inflicted, and when that second, collateral pain emerges, it will articulate in blood and blisters the open definition you desire, although it may not be in a language you care to see. This, it says, is pain, and this is real in any language you care to speak. (McLane, 1996, 111)[13]

McLane defines self-mutilation as the intentional self-wounding of the body as a response to physical and/or psychological abuse (McLane, 1996, 109), and states that it is a phenomenon most often practised by survivors of various kinds of childhood abuse, and is more common amongst women than men. According to McLane, the pain of abuse is impossible to discern as such, but it (in)forms the bodily and psychological integrity of the abuse survivor, and creates an enforced silence that must be broken if "healing" is to be possible. Drawing on the work of Maurice Merleau-Ponty, she argues that the possibility of an openness to others and to a world, which is the precondition of (inter)subjectivity and of communication, is what recedes when a person is silenced in and through abuse. Both the corporeal schema and the structure of the world are "experienced" as pain, yet pain and thus the abuse survivor's sense

of self are impossible for her to discern as such, and therefore to express.
However, McLane argues that the abuse survivor's bodily being-in-the-world,
her corporeal and psychological schema, is a lived expression of her embodied
history:

a primary pain is absorbed into itself and becomes the living body. . . . A spine of bone
becomes a spine of pain. A beating heart, which looks like any other heart, becomes an
injury-circulating mechanism. (110)[14]

Due to the lived contradictions of abuse, the subject cannot openly
communicate her dilemma, not even to herself, and thus she must learn to speak
again in and through her body (110), since in McLane's reading of Merleau-
Ponty's theory of language, "speech is a lived structuring of what is new" (109),
the possibility of an openness to others and to a world. Consequently, McLane
characterizes self-mutilation, irrespective of the form it takes, as "the creation of
a voice on the skin" (115), a mouth-like wound that can utter what the literal
mouth has been prohibited to speak (115). This bodily-speaking, it seems, both
articulates—albeit silently—the carnal "experiences" of the abuse survivor and
at the same time literally rewrites the material (existence) of the body-subject.
Thus, unlike Jeffreys, for whom self-mutilation unequivocally signifies the
perpetuation of the intrinsic violence of patriarchal structures and practices,
McLane sees self-mutilation as an ambiguous "speaking through the body" that
does not simply express subjectivity, but more importantly (re)formulates
bodily-being. In other words, McLane is wary of the tendency to pathologize
bodily inscription, but as a result attempts to reclaim it as something of a virtue
that, in an unconventional way, has emotional and political import.

Self-mutilation, McLane claims, "reinstates a unified lived structure for the
abuse survivor, stabilizing a chaotic existence" (112). It achieves this in three
connected ways. First, self-mutilation (re)establishes the difference between
pain and the pain-free by situating pain in one particular injury and thereby
allowing the rest of life to be constituted through a process of inversion, that is,
as pain/wound-free. Second, self-injury reinstates the boundary between the
existence and nonexistence of the self since it constitutes an act(ion) that renders
the subject's existence present to itself: *I cut, I feel, therefore I am*. Third, self-
mutilation enables the self to restore firm boundaries between self and other by a
literal carving out of self-possession: it is the self, rather than the other, that
inscribes the self. In effect then, the subject who marks herself, heals her "self",
becomes unified, through the (re)construction of her "self", the world, and the
relation between them, in terms of dichotomous and seemingly absolute
distinctions: self/other, pain/nonpain, existence/nonexistence, and so on.

Drawing on Merleau-Ponty's notion of reversibility as that which structures
the world, the self, and the relation between them, McLane argues that abuse
severs, represses, or deadens interconnectedness, and the expression of

experience as such. But insofar as "the reversibility and the emergence of the flesh as expression are the point of insertion of speaking and thinking into the world of silence" (Merleau-Ponty, cited in McLane, 116), then self-mutilation as the creation of a voice on the skin expresses the lived contradictions of abuse, and at the same time (re)tells or (re)inscribes bodily-being as an openness, as the possibility of being otherwise. "The self-mutilator . . . hear[s] herself through her own body. [Her] voice . . . vibrates upon her skin, her very flesh" (117), and in doing so "becomes" reversibility, so to speak[15]. And as McLane stresses, this corporeal "voice" is the precondition for language, rather than its vehicle (117). In other words, self-mutilation as the creation of a voice on the skin is not the *intentional* expression of experiences that the subject does not or cannot verbalize. Rather, it is, at least as McLane sees it, the corporeal expression and recognition of interconnectedness, of the flesh of the wor(l)d, and is therapeutic insofar as it generates "the possibility for another, more *authentic* voice [to] emerge" (117, my emphasis).

Unlike the theorists discussed in Chapter One, McLane does not "forget" the corporeal engagement of the body in the production of meaning and in the constitution of identity and sociality. Indeed, her reading of Merleau-Ponty's notion of gesture as the basis of language, and at the same time as that which is distinct from language, allows her to claim that the flesh is voice—a corporeal voice that does not speak in language, but vibrates in wounds, cuts, burns, tattoos. However, whilst this voice is literally inaudible—which is not to suggest that it cannot be sensed—it metaphorically, and by a process of substitution, makes heard what the physical mouth has been forbidden to utter, what has been silenced by abuse, that is, the abuse survivor's embodied history, her subjectivity, the uncontrollable and chaotic nature of which she cannot bear to face, or speak, directly. Thus, whilst the marked body is not simply a canvas on which psychological themes are intentionally expressed, it is nevertheless the site of a confession, albeit a complex and ambiguous one. In effect, then, McLane posits what Readings calls a "sensible real" that is at once distinct from language as a seemingly decorporealized and abstract system of meaning, and the precondition of such language. There are a number of problems with this, the first of which I will elaborate upon by returning to Lyotard's *Discourse, Figure*.

As I said earlier, Lyotard formulates the relation between discourse and figure as one of duplicity rather than duality[16]. It is not the case then that representation (as the rule of discourse) is bad or erroneous, whilst figuration is good or true. Thus the aim of deconstruction, as I have already suggested, is not to produce superior readings of texts, but rather, to (re)affirm the duplicity, the heterogeneity, that figurality raises, to confuse what discourse—through a process of disavowal—has made distinct. Lyotard exemplifies such a task by juxtaposing Saussure's model of structural linguistics and Merleau-Ponty's writings on vision in order to demonstrate that "vision appears as a figure in the textual conception of space[17], and that textuality appears as a figure in the phenomenological understanding of perception" (Readings, 1991, 12).

Drawing on the works of Merleau-Ponty—particularly *The Primacy of Perception* (1964), and *The Visible and the Invisible* (1968)—Lyotard argues that vision does not merely involve a passive object and a distanced subject. Rather, the seeing eye is imbricated in the world it views and vice versa. Vision is something like an affective and fleshly intertwining, rather than an intentional action performed by an autonomous "I". However, as Lyotard makes clear, vision (as perception) also involves "reading" (as a process of "making-distinct"), and thus the distinction of gesture from language, and of seeing from reading in Merleau-Ponty is itself dependent on language as a system of meaning[18]. Rather than embroil myself any further in Lyotard's analysis, I want to (re)consider McLane's argument—and its implications for her project and for my own—in light of this discussion of textuality, sensibility, and the relation between them.

Let me begin by briefly recapping her thesis. McLane's article is a critical reply to the commonly held belief that self-mutilation is a *negative* response to trauma and/or abuse. She claims that abuse traumatizes the subject and thwarts or forbids both the conscious recognition, and the expression, of pain (as the bodily-being of the abuse survivor). Thus other forms of communication become necessary. Drawing on Merleau-Ponty's theory of language, McLane argues that as "gestural communication, self-mutilation can reorganize and stabilize the trauma victim's world, providing a 'voice on the skin' when the actual voice is forbidden" (McLane, 1996, 107). Self-mutilation generates the possibility for the abuse survivor of hearing a voice that vibrates in her own flesh, and insofar as this constitutes a possible pre-condition for language, and for what Merleau-Ponty calls "reversibility", then self-mutilation (re)generates—at least potentially—an openness to the world and to others. Thus McLane concludes that the fossilization or petrification of bodily-being as pain, dissolves through the healing vibration of a voice that is the intertwining of breath, and flesh, and life.

Whilst McLane's analysis offers a refreshing alternative to accounts of bodily inscription as either antisocial and therefore aberrant, or counter-cultural and therefore liberatory, it nevertheless exemplifies a trap that is easily fallen into when one attempts to theorize the vicissitudes of the marked body as text. McLane's analysis offers a picture of the inscribed body as an ambiguous text which ultimately can be read, rather than as an affective site of (un)becoming that is thematizable only insofar as thematization presupposes *signifiance*. In her account, the figural—as the unspeakable—becomes another kind of representation insofar as it is conceived as a sensible, inaudible voice through which a more authentic voice may emerge (117), that is, as meanings that discourse may speak. But as Lyotard would argue, the figural is not another kind of representation, but rather is other to (and internal to) representation. It is not an other that can be represented *as other*, as the negative of representation. For McLane the fleshly materiality of the inaudible voice (on the skin) is other to language, and yet insofar as it constitutes a kind of sensible real, it can be *represented* as other—it can be read, as McLane demonstrates. What we witness is the fleshly incarnation of materiality, of a sensible real, and inasmuch as the materiality of the inaudible voice (on the skin) can be made to make sense, to tell a story—albeit an ambiguous one—then the materiality of body-language becomes its literal truth: materiality as transcendental signified. Such an understanding of materiality, as the property of an object, a body, functions to disavow the figural rather than to evoke it—as McLane's analysis makes apparent.

What this article brings to light is what Readings identifies as the potential danger of implying that the materiality of the body is *either* the pure negative of representation, and thus refuses the possibility of reading, or that it is *the* property of being that generates the possibility of meaning. In each case materiality is the object of a signification: a (non)meaning. Thus the relation of discourse and (the) figure (of/as the body) is conceived of in terms of a duality, rather than—as Lyotard formulates it—in terms of duplicity. There occurs a dialectic movement from thesis to anti-thesis, to synthesis. It is my contention that materiality, the gestural, the sensible, must not be represented as other to meaning, but rather as an unspeakable Other at work within and against discourse. As I, following Lyotard, have argued, discourse and figure are at once mutually constitutive and incommensurable. And given this we need to forge an idea of the marked body as "the site of an aporetic clash of incommensurable languages, a site that has the performative effect of provoking further discussion" (Readings, 1991, 37), rather than that which either makes sense or refuses sense, since both of these positions effect closure. What I am calling for, following Jean-Luc Nancy, is "the body of a sense that would not give signification of the body, and that would not reduce it to being its sign" (Nancy, 1993, 198); a corpus of tact. I want to problematize the presumed notion of bodies that make sense, and instead forge the idea of sense that engenders and shares bodies (197).

Earlier, I suggested that tattooed bodies could be said to tell stories that provide a key to the decipherment of the social and personal significance of embodied being as it is lived in contemporary Western culture, and, at the same time, to articulate "something else". This "something else", as the discussion above implies, is not a property of the (marked) body—its carnality or materiality—in and through which meaning is made either possible *or* impossible. I do not want to define this "something else" as an other to representation that can be represented *as other*. The best I can do is to evoke the figural coexistence of materiality, or the sensible, and meaning—and the two are never separate or distinct—as what Lyotard describes as the "blocking together" of the incommensurate. Given this, my task is more complex, and possibly less satisfying—at least to those who want definitive answers—than McLane's.

POLITICS AND/OR ETHICS: A QUESTION OF JUSTICE?

In this section I want to explore what it is that makes McLane's analysis vulnerable to the pitfalls that I have identified above. Whilst McLane's attempt to reclaim self-mutilation or bodily inscription from the realms of psychopathology may be well intended, it nevertheless dis-figures the body of the Other, not because it distorts the reality of that body, but because ultimately it apprehends—that is, reads and writes—the voice on the skin in terms of meanings that discourse may speak: it is perhaps an example of what Nietzsche describes as "the hand that in a considerate fashion—kills" (Nietzsche, 1984, 73). McLane desires, for reasons that I will go on to discuss in due course, to hear *the* story that the mutilated body tells, despite the horror involved in doing so. She says:

This voice is so appalling that even the self speaking in wounds cannot stand to hear it. For who can really bear to . . . look into their own eyes and see . . . [a] freak that . . . carve[s] their own body into wounds? Some people can . . . call their self-wounding tattoo-art, body-piercing, religious ecstasy, a drug-trip. . . . But these terms themselves are an artful arranging of cooked bits on a plate to disguise the fact that one is eating pieces of bloody dead animal. . . . This voice is too terrible to contemplate. *But we must.* (McLane, 1996, 111, my emphasis)

This passage raises a number of interesting and perhaps telling questions. First, *why* must we contemplate the apparently appalling voice on the skin? Second, *who* is the "we" that must listen? And third, whence comes the voice(s) of this commandment? It seems that this "we" refers to both the self-mutilator— who must necessarily hear her own vibration from within in order to experience her bodily-being as her own, and simultaneously as structured in and through the relation with others and with a world—and to the "non-mutilator". But whilst the incentive for the self-mutilator to do so resides in the possibility of (self)healing, what might motivate the (supposedly) unmarked subject is less clear. The implication of McLane's argument is that there is a political imperative for the cultural theorist, the clinician—and there is a sense in which both are assumed *not* to self-mutilate—to assist the other in the process of healing, rather than to simply pathologize such practices and the subjects who participate in them. "We" must listen in order to hear, to make audible, the truth that has been silenced, in order to know, to cure, to produce closure.

What bothers me about McLane's claim that we must listen to the voice on the skin is that it seems driven by a desire for altruism. Whilst an altruistic concern for others may appear, from a common-sense perspective, to be a "good thing", there is a sense in which it functions to reaffirm normative notions of self, Other, and the relations between them. As I argued earlier, citing Wyschogrod, common-sense notions of altruism assume that "one can enter into another's feeling so that, from the outset, the Other is another myself whose interests can be reduced to my own: the starting point of my affect is my ego" (Wyschogrod, 1990, 239). Or, as Nietzsche points out in *The Gay Science,* altruism functions to reify the subject *qua* subject: the motive of self-sacrificial morality stands opposed to its principle. If we look carefully at McLane's argument we can see such a phenomenon at work. Whilst the unspeakable voice of the other can be sensed, it is only in and through the intervention of McLane's own voice that the voice on the skin comes to *make sense*. Despite the horror involved in listening to the voice that is, for McLane at least, too terrible to contemplate (McLane, 1996, 111), she bravely reads the wounded body of the other, and finds it to be representative of its author's psyche, her history, and thus renders it/her audible, knowable. Like Heracles, "the greatest of legendary heroes . . . the strongest man who ever lived (Evslin, 1975, 96), whose deeds (the twelve labours) transcended mortal possibility and thus signified godlike powers, McLane fearlessly undertakes a journey into the perilous underworld of self-mutilation and returns triumphant, with the head of that which was once too monstrous to face directly.

Given this, it seems that the incentive to obey the command "we must" resides in the promise of self-gratification: "I" become the godlike Author, whose voice speaks the being of both my self and the other—an understanding of obedience to ethical commandments that shares resonances with Freud. And insofar as this "we must" is assumed to be a political imperative, then politics is both the cause and the effect of knowledge. Politics becomes a metalanguage that authoritatively determines the literal meaning of the voice on the skin, of the subject who translates it, and the other whose otherness is once again constituted as an object of knowledge.

This tendency is also apparent, in one sense, in the latter part of Molly's story. The day after her full-body tattoo is completed with the appearance of a translucent and barely visible flying fish on her face, Molly returns to the tattoo parlour with a bunch of flowers for the old man who has so changed her life— only to find that he is dead. Molly is devastated, and spends the sluggish hours of the ensuing months thinking about the old man whose very being had been poured into her coral reef with its abundance of life. Molly finally decides that she too must do something that will make a difference, "a creation herself, she must also create" (Westlake, 1989, 176), and so she embarks on a journey that results in the opening of her own business: Redemption Tattoos. Upon securing premises close to what was once the old man's studio, Molly sets to work repainting her surroundings, and collecting furniture from public auctions, her most precious find being a worn leather psychoanalyst's couch. On this, she decides, "her customers [will] bare their bodies just as Freud's patients once bared their souls" (176).

Unlike your everyday run-of-the-mill tattoo artist, Molly refuses to originate tattoos, and instead only supplements those that already exist, and which, for one reason or another, have ceased to please those whose bodies they embellish. Since tattoo removal is a relatively unsuccessful procedure, Molly tells her customers that a preferable alternative is to supplement the existing image and thereby change its meaning. She goes on to say that if in time these revisions also become unpalatable, they too can be (re)inscribed ad infinitum. The traces are indelible she says, "but the possibilities for re-interpretation are unlimited (Westlake, 1989, 117): hence her business card reads: "Redemption Tattoos: Reparation, Restoration, Restitution" (176).

Over the years Molly's reputation spreads, business booms, and in due course she is acclaimed as the city's greatest living artist and is given its freedom—a strange and somewhat implausible accolade for a tattoo artist, unless of course we recognize the resonances that Molly's redemptive vocation shares with the atonement of Christ. And there is a sense in which this symbolic association is preempted by Molly in her allusion to Freud. As is well known, Freud is (in)famous for "discovering" that symptoms such as dreams, slips of the tongue, and hysteria are ways of speaking what cannot be said directly. As Freud tells it, the role of the analyst to whom the patient bares his or her soul—just as Molly's clients bare their bodies—is to translate what is allusive or elusive, to direct speech: a process that will supposedly help to cure psychosomatic illness, or, in the case of Molly's customers, "suffering". Translation then does not simply turn something from one language into another, but more importantly transports a person from one condition or state to another[19]. Or as the *Shorter Oxford English Dictionary* states, one definition of the verb "to translate" is "to carry or convey to heaven without death" (1973, 2347). But as my critique of McLane's translation of the elusive voice on the skin to direct speech (to meanings that discourse may speak) shows, it is not the (marked) other who is conveyed to heaven without death, but rather it is the subject who translates, that is immortalized as the altruistic redeemer of suffering. In (re)reading/(re)writing the body of the other, Freud, Molly, and possibly McLane are (re)incarnated as the saviour *par excellence:* the Jesus Christ(s) of hysterical flesh.

This tendency is exemplified in the following story Molly somewhat smugly tells during a globally networked TV program to commemorate half a century of her practice. The client, a filthy-rich banker of questionable moral standing, comes to Molly in a state of sheer desperation. The head of his penis has been tattooed to represent a Nazi military helmet, whilst on the underside of the shaft, is a skull which stares blindly at the object of his lust. The rest of the shaft has become a ballistic missile with three tail fins bearing the signs $, £, and F. Molly insists that before she decides whether or not to undertake the task of restitution the banker must tell her how he acquired the tattoo—he must confess his sins. As Molly tells it, the banker had been taken prisoner in an un-named country in the southern hemisphere, whose recently formed government was involved in a struggle with a neighbouring racist state. The mercenary banker had capitalised on the current state of affairs by providing loans to the racist state to finance the continuation of a covert war. However, the banker had been captured and handed over to a group of peasant women whose families had been slaughtered in a so-called pacification raid. The women then inscribed the banker's body, the tattoo being "their comment on his existence" (181). In time, the banker was released after a ransom of $100,000 (0.1% of his personal wealth) had been paid.

Molly agrees to help the financier on one condition: that he transfer the remaining 99.9 percent of his wealth to those whose struggle for life his money has opposed, and that he provide her with evidence of having done so. This condition is fulfilled and within a week Molly completes her redemptive re-interpretation, which consists of a flourishing vine with an abundance of fruit and new growth covering his entire body. The roots of the vine are firmly planted in the "recycled, soil-filled, well-manured containers of helmet, skull, and missile cylinder" (181). The moral of the story, at least as Molly tells it, is that "the emblems of death can become the material of life" (181). Molly's translation of the banker's body constitutes a retelling or re-inscribing that functions to make amends for the mercenary wrongs done to those she interprets as "innocent" victims of post-colonial civil war and capitalist self-interest. At the same time Molly (re)writes her self as the saviour of the underdog by making audible the silent voice(s) of a group of anonymous peasant women from a country somewhere in the southern hemisphere. But the voice that travels via satellite to billions of viewers in countless locations across the globe is Molly's voice, and the stories it tells are presented in the context of a celebration of Molly's work, her politics, her subjectivity.

In Molly's account of her redemptive undertakings and McLane's response to the imperative to listen to the voice on the skin, politics is implied to be both a matter of knowledge and one of judgment. Indeed, what seems to motivate both texts is the assumption that truth and justice can, or at least should, be united. However, as Lyotard stresses throughout *Just Gaming*, injustice and totalitarianism result from just such an assumption. He claims that cognition and/or determinate judgment function, in and through the application of preexisting structures of meaning, to (re)constitute the Other *as other*, as an object whose truth or essence it is then (seemingly) possible to know. Consequently, as Lyotard sees it, a politics founded on determinate judgment and formulated in reference to truth is inherently unjust insofar as it disavows the figural at work within and against discourse, and thus prohibits—or at least attempts to prohibit—"that the question of the just and the unjust be, and remain, raised" (Lyotard and Thébaud, 1985, 66–67).

Similarly, in *Totality and Infinity*, Levinas argues that "being" (in the existential sense) "reveals itself as war to philosophical thought", and that politics, as the "art of foreseeing war and winning it by every means . . . is . . .

the very exercise of reason" (Levinas, 1969, 21). Thus he concludes that such a notion of "being" is a totalizing conception that is symptomatic of the kind of (onto)logics that dominates Western philosophy (21). Levinas posits as an "alternative"—to the antagonism of "being" that an ontology of totality issuing from war and politics and founded on absolute notions of the True and the Good maintains—what he calls an eschatological notion of judgment. Eschatology, he claims, establishes a relation with "being" that is beyond totality.

It is a relationship with *a surplus always exterior to the totality,* as though the objective totality did not fill out the . . . measure of being, as though another concept, the concept of *infinity*, were needed to express this transcendence with regard to totality, non-encompassable within a totality and as primordial as totality. (22–23)[20]

Eschatological judgment, then, like the face to face relation discussed in Chapter Three, calls existents forth to responsibility, rather than judging existence through the totalizing lens of the jurisdiction of history as meaningful and knowable. Eschatology—at least in the Levinasian sense—is neither a philosophical method nor an object whose essence can be philosophically demonstrated. Rather, eschatological judgment, like the face to face relation, can be thought of as the infinite engendering of being(s), rather than as something an already constituted subject can apprehend, can decided to participate in or not to participate in. To claim that we are just because we know what justice is is a totalizing gesture that functions to disavow alterity as that which precedes and exceeds, makes possible and impossible, meaning and identity. In effect, then, insofar as eschatological judgment (as an ethics of infinition) affects beings as always already in relation, and not on the basis of totality, then Levinas shows that totality presupposes infinity, and that politics presupposes ethics.

Levinas' aim is not to prove that what Lyotard calls determinate judgment is wrong or bad, and that eschatological judgment is good or true, since the apprehension (and therefore constitution) of being in terms of an absolute or essential dichotomy is again totalizing. Rather, Levinas wants to develop a critique of totality that would lead back to the situation that constitutes totality as always already fractured, that is, the encounter with alterity of which the face to face relation is exemplary (24). This shares resonances with Lyotard's notion of deconstruction as a secondary affirmation that "blocks together" what phallogocentric language has separated and that confuses what rational logic aims to make distinct.

Given this, I, following Readings, want to suggest that an ethics of reading consists *not* of the abandonment of any attempt to explore the (political) significance of cultural texts such as tattooed bodies, based on the assumption that doing justice to texts is ultimately a matter of loyalty to an essentialist understanding of their meaning or content. Rather, I would argue that an ethics of reading is not something we, as already constituted subjects, can choose to do or not to do based on a notion of justice and truth as united and knowable. I want to conceive of this "we must" (listen to the voice on the skin) not as a prescriptive commandment, but as an ethical invocation in the Levinasian sense, to "strengthen our palpative potential" as Lyotard puts it: to "allow" the figural—as that which disrupts previously established criteria by which texts have been understood, re-cognized, judged, assigned meaning—to evoke what is necessarily and impossibly co-present, as simultaneously constitutive and disruptive of representation. An ethics of reading, then, is not, as Readings points out, "a hermeneutic method, but [the affective] insistence [of] reading as a *crisis of judgement*" (Readings, 1991, 128, my emphasis).

Any encounter with the (textual) Other both will and will not, can and cannot, do justice to the Other, since ethics is the point at which the determinate grounds for judgment are made possible and withdrawn; it is the site of an aporetic clash of incommensurable elements—of totality *and*   infinity, of discourse *and* figure. What we are faced with then is not a choice between determinate and indeterminate judgment, between injustice and justice, but an ethics of reading as that which affects (in)determinate judgment, (in)justice, and thus has the performative effect of provoking further discussion. This is not, of course, as Readings emphasises, to suggest that an ethics of reading as the invocation of (in)determinate judgment should be understood as a "relativist refusal to judge, [nor as a] pluralist insistence that all judgments are equally valid" (Readings, 1991, 125), since both these positions are founded on the assumption that since justice is indeterminable (rather than determinable *and* indeterminable), we have no obligation to justice. But as Levinas would argue, obligation—at least if it is understood as an ethical response-*ability*—is something that affects being(s) rather than something that can be reflected upon by a subject(ivity) that pre-exists it, and is external to it.

RE-READING MOLLY AND McLANE, OR "WE ARE ANSWERABLE BUT WE CAN NEVER HAVE THE LAST WORD"[21]

As I argued earlier, the accounts of marked bodies given by Molly and McLane are informed by a notion of social justice as an act of redemption. Both seem driven by a desire to unite the good and the true, and thus to effect closure: a gesture that both Lyotard and Levinas would probably describe as totalitarian, or totalizing. But insofar as an ethics of reading could be said to affect injustice *and* justice, determinability *and* indeterminibility, discourse *and* figurality, then tattooed bodies, and the stories they seemingly tell, are duplicitous—which is not to imply, as McLane's analysis seems to, that they are simply ambiguous. Let us pay one last visit to Molly in order to listen to another of her stories, which, it seems to me, testifies—albeit silently—to alterity or heterogeneity as that which cannot speak its name, but nevertheless bears the trace of a trace which affects the possibility of re-interpretation, but not of a final word. Molly tells how one day an old man who had been born in a Nazi death camp came to her, rolled up his sleeve, and uttered the following words:

I have carried this number all my life, that I and others should never forget. Now, before I die, I wish to expunge it. Not through any technique that would eliminate it, but through a superabundance in which it will be lost. It will become just one grain of sand upon a beach. I wish to be covered, from head to toe, in one mighty number. *This* number [indicating the number on his arm], in becoming just six consecutive digits within the greater number will be relieved of the weight of evil it has borne until now. Yet [simultaneously] the greater number will be what it is through the presence of that part within its whole. That is inescapable. (Westlake, 1989, 178)

Molly sets to work, and with the help of her state-of-the-art pocket calculator begins tattooing the number, which, "when it is written, *will never be spoken, will remain blessedly silent*" (178, my emphasis)[22].

This story interests me first, because it is the voice of the old man that we "hear", and not that of Molly[23]. Second, and connected to the first point, the story focuses explicitly on what the marked body does rather than on what it means. The old man demands not that Molly retell or judge his story as determinate in the service of truth and justice, but rather that their encounter affect an (inter)textual and infinite (un)becoming that will testify—albeit silently—to the mark of the death camp as a site of incommensurability, of justice and injustice, of totality and infinity. Or as Readings puts it, "[a] point of difference where the sides speak radically different . . . languages where the dispute cannot be phrased in either language without, by its very phrasing, prejudging the issue for that side, being unjust. . . . Between . . . two little narratives . . . there is always [such a point] which must be encountered" (Readings, 1991, xxx). And as my analysis of Lyotard's formulation of the relation between discourse and figure illustrates, these "two little narratives", the six-digit number and the unspeakable number, are simultaneously mutually constitutive and incommensurable. Perhaps then we should, or at least could, re-read McLane's analysis of the voice on the skin and Molly's translation of the marked body of the banker, and recognize that both Molly's voice and McLane's voice are always also the unspeakable voice of the figural Other. And that despite their tendency to judge, to read, the marked body of the Other with reference to justice and truth as determinate and united, they nevertheless fail to silence the figural voice of the Other, to rewrite the marked body as/with the final word. The marked body remains duplicitous because like "my" body it both affects and is affected by a trace of the Other-in-me that presupposes the possibility of reading, and interrupts it.

NOTES

1. Both Michele Le Dœuff and Luce Irigaray have deployed the notion of "imaginaries" in their works. However, my use of the term is most influenced by the work of Moira Gatens (1996), who develops an extended analysis of imaginary bodies, social imaginaries, and the resonances between them.

2. Like Gatens I use the term "imaginaries" rather than imaginary in an attempt to avoid the impression that there is a singular unified discourse that, like the notion of ideology, is opposed to "reality".

3. For an extended discussion of the Nietszchean notion of truth and lies, memory and forgetting, and the role these play in the constitution of both individual and social bodies, see Rosalyn Diprose (forthcoming).

4. See for example "Amphibologies" in Barthes (1977, 72–73).

5. See Sandor Ferenczi's notion of the Thalassa Complex, in *Thalassa, A Theory of Genitality* (1968). According to Ferenczi's model of the Thalassa Complex, of the libido itself, *the* sex act, that is, heterosexual intercourse, functions as an attempt on behalf of the ego to attain some sort of pre-oedipal unification. But since, as Ferenczi puts it, "the individual identifies himself with the phallus inserted in the vagina, and with the spermatozoa swarming into the body of the female" (49), then what is implied is a notion of sexual difference whereby the subject of phallic law is inevitably male and where the imaginary body of woman functions metonymically as a foundation upon which the (male) subject's sense of self (or imaginary body) is (re)constituted in phallic terms. Thus feminine subjectivity is oxymoronic and woman's alterity is denied or covered over, which in Levinasian terms is tantamount to attempted murder.

6. The term "savage" is used by Lingis to explore a mode of bodily and social being that is (in)formed through processes of inscription that libidinally marks out belonging according to social conventions and values that differ significantly from those of Western capitalism. For example, Lingis claims that "savages do not belong to society as persons, individuals, juridic subjects, but as organs attached to the full body of the earth. The society is the marking of this attachment" (Lingis, 1994b, 293). Thus whilst inscription could be said to mark out belonging in culturally and historically specific ways, the relation between social bodies and "human" bodies is nevertheless affected in and through processes that mark. As Deleuze and Guattari put it, "Society is not first of all a milieu for exchange where the essential would be to circulate or to cause to circulate, but rather a socius of inscription where the essential thing is to mark and to be marked" (Deleuze and Guattari, 1983, 142).

7. In *Libidinal Economies* (1993), Lyotard uses the term "libidinal band" to refer to that which has neither inside nor outside, and which in a sense remains Other to all discursive attempts to conceptualize difference in oppositional terms. Thus, Lyotard stresses that the term should be understood as a kind of persuasive fiction rather than a "true" description, since its function is to gesture toward what is necessarily excluded by a representational economy that is indifferent to differences except in terms of binary oppositions. Any attempt to describe the libidinal band, or to posit it as a real thing, would inevitably collapse back into a representational model in which libidinality (as that which is opposed to representation) becomes the signifier of an alternative morality, or liberatory politics.

8.   This is not of course to suggest that this duplicity can be grasped or represented in any definitive way, or that it is "beyond" or opposed to representation. Rather, representation is itself libidinal, or, as Bennington puts it, it is "a local effect of the modifications or metamorphosis of the libido, or, in the language of *Économie libidinalé*, a particular configuration of the libidinal band" (Bennington, 1988, 25).

9.   In *Discourse, Figure*, Lyotard formulates the notion of "blocking-together" to examine the relation of incommensurable elements at work in art. Unlike critics who demand that art or literature synchronize incommensurability into a harmonious and autonomous unity, Lyotard argues that the text is the point at which the inevitable figurality of discourse, and the discursivity of figure, arises. For example, he says, "This book-object contains two objects: an object of signification . . . which says 'there is no notion (signified) abstracted from the sensible'. We *hear* this object. And in addition, there is an object of *signifiance,* made of graphic and *plastic* signifiers . . . made, really, of writing disturbed by considerations of sensibility. . . . The first object makes us understand the second, and the second object makes us see the first" (Lyotard, 1971, 71, my emphasis). For a more in-depth discussion of "blocking-together", see Readings (1991, 23–28).

10.   For further elaboration of this claim, see, for example, Foucault's reservations regarding the concept of ideology in *Power/Knowledge* (1980c, 118).

11.   For an extended discussion of the double-edged character of sensibility, see Alphonso Lingis, (1986, 219–30).

12.   I find the term "self-mutilation" to be highly contentious, since it does seem to imply the existence of a "proper" body prior to its disfiguring, as well as a system of values that regards such practices as inherently aberrant. However, since this is the term McLane uses I will also do so whilst discussing her article.

13.   Sections of McLane's text (such as this one) are written in italics, and differ in style from the rest of the paper. However, McLane offers no explanation of why she uses this technique, or of whose voice it is that is speaking these words. At times it appears to be the "silent" voice of the self-mutilating body-subject, whereas as at others it seems to be a less academically "authentic" voice, which McLane uses to explore her own less conventional ideas. Whilst this ambiguity is interesting, given her overall thesis, there is a sense in which it could be felt to cover over a tendency to take up the position of redeemer, and its ensuing implications.

14.   Again, this passage is italicised in the original.

15.   The reversibility that *is* me is not consciously or transcendentally created *by* me, as McLane points out, but rather is the precondition of the possibility of being.

16.   This is also the way Lyotard characterizes the relation between thought and libidinality, the relation between eros and thanatos, and the relation between primary and secondary processes in *Libidinal Economies*. See especially the section entitled "Duplicity of the Two Pulsional Principles" (1993, 25–32).

17.   Lyotard argues that Saussure develops an account of textual space as two dimensional, a space of pure opposition, whereas Merleau-Ponty's account of visual space involves something like an intertwining of elements that are never distinct.

18.   See, for example, Lyotard (1971, 56–57).

19.   In an analysis of Walter Benjamin's "The Task of the Translator", Eduardo Cadava states that "[i]f translation is not a matter of communication, not a task aimed at

imparting sense to the original, it is also because the essential quality of the original . . . does not itself belong to the domains of communication or meaning" (1998, 17). This is why Benjamin makes the claim that "translation must in large measure refrain from wanting to communicate something, from rendering sense. . . . The original is important to it only insofar as it has already relieved the translator and his translation of the effort of assembling and expressing what is to be conveyed" (Benjamin, cited in Cadava, 17). Consequently, Cadava concludes that the "task of translation is not to render a foreign language into one we may call our own, but rather to preserve the foreignness of this language" (17), that is, to testify to figurality, as Lyotard might put it.

20.   Levinas stresses that this "beyond" totality should not be described in a purely negative relation, since it is reflected within the totality and history. See Levinas (1969, 23).

21.   This phrase is taken from Readings' account of ethics as the imperative to be just without knowing in advance what it is to be just. See Readings (1991, 139).

22.   In *Heidegger and "the jews"* (1990), Lyotard argues that the impossibility of speaking or writing about "Auschwitz" is itself a sign of the obligation or responsibility of critical thought to talk about it, to write about it, but not in a representational mode. Lyotard's aim in this text, then, is not to make audible what has been silenced, but rather to testify to the *differend*, to the figural, to remember that which rational discourse and/or representation "forgets", whilst at the same time acknowledging that this "something else" cannot be remembered since it is an Otherness that thought cannot think but cannot not think either.

23.   Of the seven cases that Molly discusses in the TV program celebrating her work, it is interesting that this is the only story that is told in its entirety by the tattooed subject.

Conclusion

For me, as for a number of the theorists discussed throughout this book, tattooed bodies evoke ambiguous feelings of fascination and fear. As social texts they appear to demand to be read, and yet at the same time they remain elusive, or at best, duplicitous. The reader who has been searching for a way to master the mysteries of the subject in/of tattooing will not have found one here. And this is because, as I have demonstrated, analyses of the subject in/of tattooing tell us more about the ways in which subjectivity, textuality, ethics, and pleasure are understood and experienced in accordance with culturally and historically specific discourses and discursive practices than they do about tattooed bodies *per se*. But whilst I have argued that the tattooed body as text does not express an innate essence that can be discovered via the well-honed skills of the cultural critic, I have nevertheless suggested that to therefore conclude that such texts are anti-assimilationist and/or meaningless and thus potentially liberatory is highly problematic since as such a position constitutes an alternative domain of truth by imagining the tattooed body as a thing that replaces a sign but that in fact actually becomes a sign. Given this, the subject in/of tattooing could be said to have functioned throughout this text as a *figure* for the understanding of understanding.

Given that we live in an increasingly complex and heterogeneous "global economy" it is perhaps not surprising that we desire to know the world, and thus to secure our position in it. But as I have demonstrated, such knowledge and mastery are tenuous and can only be (seemingly) achieved in and through processes that delimit the possibility of being otherwise. Moreover, any attempt to designate identity as Levinas puts it, is tantamount to an act of violence that reduces the other to an Economy of the Same and disavows alterity as the very grounds of the self's possibility. Thus the subject, as it is ontologically defined by liberal humanist discourses and discursive practices, finds itself forever caught in a contradictory web of its own making. This is exemplified by Freud's model of the subject who at once desires to return to a state of symbiotic completeness, and to attain absolute autonomy; both of which are ultimately impossible. Likewise, the analyses posited by the dermal diagnosticians discussed in Chapter One are motivated by a desire to know the truth of the tattooed other. The assumption is that such knowledge is not only possible, but, perhaps more importantly, is essential if the ethical subject is to ward off the threat of contamination to the self and to the body politic that the aberrant other poses. But as I demonstrated in my critique of essentialist accounts of delinquency, the discursive production of the delinquent as other to the "norm", functions to reaffirm the subject of interpretation's sense of self and normative position, rather than re-presenting the truth of being.

In short, the notion and function of knowledge as the successful extraction of that which stands under—that is, essence or origin—has been shown to be at best misleading, and at worst a detrimental price to pay for a tenuous and blinded form of self-conceit. But if, as I have argued, the ontological thematizing of the tattooed other as an object of knowledge presupposes a metaphysics of transcendence in and through which self and Other are (re)constituted *ad infinitum*, then in the very effort to know itself and/or the Other the subject will repeatedly encounter something that is ungraspable (Taylor, 1987, 204). "Through an unexpected reversal, the condition of the possibility of dis-guising turns out to be the condition of the impossibility of detection" (Taylor, 1997, 17). However, as I have suggested, to claim that the tattooed body does not provide us with access to the truth of being is not tantamount to supposing that the tattooed body can or does exist somehow beyond systems of representation. Rather, drawing on various aspects of the work of Foucault, Levinas, Barthes, Lingis, and Lyotard, I have demonstrated that the tattooed body is duplicitous, and moreover that it could be said to literalize (un)becoming as an infinite intertextual process of marking and being marked.

I have argued that in and through processes of social inscription the corporeal substance is (trans)formed into a textual body, "and is fictionalised and positioned within those myths that form a culture's social narratives and self-representations (Grosz, 1990a, 65–66). Given that phallogocentric discourses inscriptively produce bodies that signify the law on and through the body, it is not surprising that, as Foucault points out, we read the surface of the body as the expression of an innate core. But insofar as interiority is produced "on *the surface* of the body, through the play of signifying absences that suggest, but never reveal, the organizing principle of identity, as a cause (Butler, 1990, 136), then subjectivity is shown to be a social fiction rather than an essence. Moreover, since identity and social relations are constituted in and through the repetitive performance of gestures and acts that are never self-identical, then it is necessary to conceive of existence and existents as a continuous process of (un)becoming rather than being.

Consequently, on the one hand, it is possible to read the tattoo as a picture that tells stories, whilst at the same time recognizing that the stories tattooed bodies could be said to tell are never simply stories of/as truth. Tattooed bodies are symptomatic: they tell of the ways in which identity and difference are morphologically produced in culturally and historically specific ways. On the other hand, insofar as reading and writing are, as Jean-Luc Nancy puts it, "matters of tact" (Nancy, 1993, 198), bodily inscription as an intertextual and affective process of sensibility generates the grounds of (im)possibility that meaning presupposes. In effect, then, the subject in/of tattooing is constituted in and through a (re)markable encounter with that which transcends it, "is exposed to the Other as a skin is exposed to that which wounds it" (Levinas, 1978, 49). And this relation of (un)becoming is what Levinas calls ethics.

Given this, an ethics of tattooed bodies and pleasures should consist *not* of a universalizing attempt to either define tattooing as an aberrant or resistory mode of self-(trans)formation through the use of pleasure, nor as a liberatory vehicle for escaping the confines of the body and/or repressive ideological discourses. If, as I have argued, ontology and metaphysics, discourse and figure, self and Other, are mutually constitutive and incommensurable, then an ethics of tattooed bodies and pleasures need be neither dogmatic nor nihilistic. Rather, it must concern itself with the ways in which identity and difference are constituted in culturally and historically specific ways, and at the same time, performatively affect the possibility of problematizing the material conditions of (un)becoming in and through processes that provoke further discussion. In short, to call this a conclusion is something of a misnomer since, despite the fact that I may be held accountable for the ways in which I have (re)read and (re)written the body of the subject in/of tattooing throughout this book, what I have demonstrated is that I can never have the last word. Like Nancy, I find my "self" in a double bind. I cannot produce a discourse on the tattooed body—at least not in any absolute sense—since this would consist of disavowing figuration, but, at the same time, I cannot *not* produce a discourse on it.

Bibliography

Bibliography

Agris, Joseph (1977) "Tattoos in Women", in *Plastic Reconstructive Surgery*, vol. 60, 22–37.

Allen, Jeffner (1988) "The Economy of the Body in a Post-Nietzschean Era", in *The Collegium Phaenomenologicum: The First Ten Years,* J. Sallis et al. (eds.), Boston and London: Kluwer Academic Publishers, 289–308.

Baden, M. (1973) "Symbols: Tattoos on Teenage Cadavers", in *Medical World News,* August, 14-15.

Barthes, Roland (1975) *Roland Barthes par Roland Barthes*, Paris: Seuil.

——— (1977) *Roland Barthes by Roland Barthes,* R. Howard (trans.), London: Macmillan Press.

——— (1982) *The Empire of Signs,* R. Howard (trans.), New York: Hill and Wang.

——— (1987) *Writer Sollers,* P. Thody (trans.), Minneapolis: University of Minnesota Press.

——— (1990a) "The Death of the Author", in *Modern Literary Theory,* P. Rice and P. Waugh (eds.), London and New York: Edward Arnold, 114–18.

——— (1990b) *A Lover's Discourse,* R. Howard (trans.), Harmondsworth: Penguin.

——— (1990c) "To Write: An Intransitive Verb?" in *Modern Literary Theory,* P. Rice and P. Waugh (eds.), London and New York: Edward Arnold, 42–51.

——— (1993) *Camera Lucida,* R. Howard (trans.), London: Vintage.

——— (1994) *The Pleasure of the Text,* R. Miller (trans.), New York: Hill and Wang.

——— (1995) *S/Z,* R. Miller (trans.), New York: Hill and Wang.

Bennahum, D. A. (1971) "Tattoos of Heroin Addicts in New Mexico", in *Rocky Mountain Medical Journal*, 68:9, 63–66.

Bennington, Geoffrey (1988) *Lyotard: Writing the Event,* New York: Columbia University Press.

Bernauer, James (1992) "Beyond Life and Death: On Foucault's Post-Auschwitz Ethic", in *Michel Foucault: Philosopher,* T. J. Armstrong (ed.), Brighton: Harvester Wheatsheaf.

——— (1994) "Michel Foucault's Ecstatic Thinking", in *The Final Foucault,* J. Bernauer and D. Rasmussen (eds.), Cambridge, MA: The MIT Press, 45–82.

Bersani, Leo (1995a) "Freud, Foucault, Fantasy and Power", in *GLQ: A Journal of Lesbian and Gay Studies*, 21:2, Spring, 11–33.

——— (1995b) "Is the Rectum the Grave?" in *Reclaiming Sodom,* J. Goldberg (ed.), New York: Routledge, 249–64.

Blanchard, Marc (1993) "Post-Bourgeois Tattoo Reflections on Skin Writing in Late Capitalist Societies", in *Visualizing Theory,* Lucien Taylor (ed.), New York: Routledge, 287–99.

Brain, Robert (1979) *The Decorated Body*, London: Hutchinson.

Bromberg, W. (1972) "Tattooing: Psychosexual Motivations", in *Sexual Behaviour,* vol. 2, 28–32.

Brown, Andrew (1992) *Roland Barthes: The Figures of Writing,* Oxford: Clarendon Press.

Brush, Pippa (1998) "Metaphors of Inscription: Discipline, Plasticity and the Rhetoric of Choice", in *Feminist Review,* no. 58, 22–43.

Bruss, Elizabeth (1982) *Beautiful Theories: The Spectacle of Discourse in Contemporary Criticism,* Baltimore and London: Johns Hopkins University Press.

Burke, Sean (1993) *The Death & Return of the Author: Criticism and Subjectivity in Barthes, Foucault, and Derrida,* Edinburgh: Edinburgh University Press.

Butler, Judith (1990) *Gender Trouble,* London and New York: Routledge.

Cadava, E., P. Connor, and J. Nancy (1991) *Who Comes after the Subject?* New York: Routledge.

Cadava, Eduardo (1998) *Words of Light: Theses on the Photography of History,* Princeton: Princeton University Press.

Califia, Pat (1983) "A Secret Side of Lesbian Sexuality", in *S and M: Studies in Sadomasochism,* T. Weinberg and G. W. Levi Kamel (eds.), Buffalo, NY: Prometheus, 129–36.

Chalmers, M. (1989) "Heroin, the Needle and the Politics of the Body", in *Zoot-Suits and Second Hand Dresses: An Anthology of Fashion and Music,* A. McRobbie (ed.), London: Macmillan, 150–55.

Chanter, Tina (1995) *Ethics of Eros: Irigaray's Rewriting of the Philosophers,* New York and London: Routledge.

Cixous, Helene (1975) "Sorties", in *The Newly Born Woman,* H. Cixous and C. Clément (eds.), B. Wing (trans.), Minneapolis: University of Minnesota Press, 63–132.

Clément, Catherine (1995) *Syncope: The Philosophy of Rapture,* Minneapolis: University of Minnesota Press.

Cohen, Andrea (1987) "Story of the Tattoo", in *Ploughshares,* 13:4, 29–30.

Copes, J., and C. J. Forsyth (1993) "The Tattoo: A Social Psychological Explanation", in *The International Review of Modern Sociology,* 23:2, Autumn, 83–89.

Crossley, Nick (1994) *The Politics of Subjectivity: Between Foucault and Merleau-Ponty,* Aldershot, UK: Avebury.

Culler, Jonathan (1974) "The Ever-Moving Finger", in *Times Literary Supplement,* 30, August.

——— (1983) *Barthes,* Glasgow: Fontana Modern Masters.

Curry, David (1993) "Decorating the Body Politic", *New Formations,* 19, 69–82.

Davidson, Theodore (1974) *Chicano Prisoners: The Key to San Quentin,* New York: Holt.

Davis, Colin (1996) *Levinas,* Cambridge: Polity Press.

Deleuze, G., and F. Guattari (1983) *Anti-Oedipus: Capitalism and Schizophrenia,* R. Hurley, M. Seem, and H. R. Lane (trans.), Minneapolis: University of Minnesota Press.

——— (1984) "Concrete Rules and Abstract Machines", C. J. Stivale (trans.), in *SubStance,* 13:3/4, 7–17.

——— (1987) *A Thousand Plateaus: Capitalism and Schizophrenia,* B. Massumi (trans.), Minneapolis: University of Minnesota Press.

Delio, Michelle (1993) *Tattoo: The Erotic Art of Skin Decoration,* Sydney: Pan Macmillan.

Derrida, Jacques (1986) *Margins of Philosophy,* A. Bass (trans.), Sussex: Harvester Press.

Descartes, Rene (1985) *"Discourse on Method", and the "Meditations",* Harmondsworth: Penguin.

Dews, P. (1992) "The Return of the Subject in Late Foucault", in *Radical Philosophy,* 51, Spring, 72–95.

Didi-Huberman, Georges (1984) "The Figurative Incarnation of the Sentence: Notes on the Autographic Skin", Caryn Davidson (trans.), in *Journal,* 47:5, 66–70.

Diprose, Rosalyn (1987) "The Use of Pleasure in the Constitution of the Body", in *Australian Feminist Studies,* 5, Summer, 95–104.

—— (1994) *The Bodies of Women: Ethics, Embodiment, and Sexual Difference,* London and New York: Routledge.

—— (forthcoming) *Corporeal Generosity: On Giving with Nietzsche, Merleau-Ponty, and Levinas,* New York: State University of New York Press.

Dollimore, Jonathan (1991) *Sexual Dissidence, Augustine to Wilde, Freud to Foucault,* Oxford: Clarendon Press.

Ebensten, Hanns (1953) *Pierced Hearts and True Love,* London: Derek Verschoyle.

Edgerton, R., and H. Dingman (1963) "Tattooing and Identity", in *The International Journal of Social Psychiatry,* 9, 143–53.

Evslin, Bernard (1975) *Gods, Demigods and Demons: An Encyclopedia of Greek Mythology,* New York and Sydney: Scholastic Book Services.

Eysenck, H. J., and S. B. G. Eysenck (1967) "On the Unitary Nature of Extraversion", in *Acta Psychologica,* 26, 383–90.

Falk, P. (1995) "On Inscriptions in the Flesh", in *Body & Society,* 1:1, 95–105.

Favazza, A. (1996) *Bodies Under Siege: Self-mutilation and Body Modification in Culture and Psychiatry,* 2nd ed., Baltimore: Johns Hopkins University Press.

Ferenczi, Sandor (1968) *Thalassa, A Theory of Genitality,* H. Alden Bunker (trans.), New York: Norton.

Ferguson-Rayport, S. M., R. M. Griffith, and E. W. Strauss (1955) "The Psychiatric Significance of Tattoos", in *Psychiatric Quarterly,* 29, 112–31.

Feury, Patrick, and Nick Mansfield (1997) *Cultural Studies and the New Humanities: Concepts and Controversies,* Melbourne: Oxford University Press.

Fiske, John (1989) *Understanding Popular Culture,* New York: Routledge.

Flew, Antony (ed.) (1984) *The Pan Dictionary of Philosophy,* London: Pan Books Limited.

Foucault, Michel (1965) *Madness and Civilization: A History of Insanity in the Age of Reason,* R. Howard (trans.), New York: Pantheon.

—— (1977) *Language, Counter-Memory, Practice: Selected Essays,* D. Bouchard (ed.), Oxford: Blackwell.

—— (1979) *Discipline and Punish: The Birth of the Prison,* A. Sheridan (trans.), Harmondsworth: Penguin.

—— (1980a) *Herculine Barbin, Being the Recently Discovered Memoirs of a Nineteenth Century French Hermaphrodite,* New York: Random House.

—— (1980b) *The History of Sexuality Volume One: An Introduction,* R. Hurley (trans.), New York: Vintage Books.

—— (1980c) *Power/Knowledge: Selected Interviews and Other Writings 1972–77,* C. Gordon (ed.), Brighton, Sussex: Harvester Press.

—— (1987) *The Use of Pleasure: The History of Sexuality Volume II,* R. Hurley (trans.), Harmondsworth: Penguin.

—— (1988) "Le Gai Savoir" (I), in *Mec Magazine* 5, June, 32–36.

—— (1990) *The Care of the Self: The History of Sexuality Volume III*, R. Hurley (trans.), Harmondsworth: Penguin.

—— (1991a) "On the Genealogy of Ethics: An Overview of a Work in Progress", in *The Foucault Reader*, Paul Rabinow (ed.), Harmondsworth: Penguin, 340–72.

—— (1991b) "What Is Enlightenment?" in *The Foucault Reader*, Paul Rabinow (ed.), Harmondsworth: Penguin, 32–50.

—— (1994) "The Ethic of Care for the Self as a Practice of Freedom", (1984 interview) J. D. Gauthier (trans.), in *The Final Foucault*, J. Bernauer and D. Rasmussen (eds.), Cambridge, MA: The MIT Press, 1–20.

—— (1997) "Sex, Power, and the Politics of Identity", in Paul Rabinow (ed.), R. Hurley (trans.), *Michel Foucault: Ethics, Subjectivity and Truth*, New York: New Press, 157–62.

Freud, Sigmund (1970) *The Future of an Illusion*, W. D. Robson-Scott (trans.), London: Hogarth Press.

—— (1973) *Civilization and Its Discontents*, J. Riviere (trans.), London: Hogarth Press.

—— (1984) "Beyond the Pleasure Principle", in *On Metapsychology: The Theory of Psychoanalysis*, J. Strachey (trans.), The Penguin Freud Library, vol. 11, Harmondsworth: Penguin.

Fuss, Diana (1989) *Essentially Speaking: Feminism, Nature, and Difference*, New York: Routledge.

Gallop, Jane (1988) *Thinking through the Body*, New York: Columbia University Press.

Gatens, Moira (1996) *Imaginary Bodies: Ethics, Power and Corporeality*, London and New York: Routledge.

Gittleson, N., G. Wallen, and K. Dawson-Butterworth (1969) "The Tattooed Psychiatric Patient", in *British Journal of Psychiatry*, 115, 1249–53.

Goldstein, Norman (1979) "Psychological Implications of Tattoos", in *Journal of Dermatology and Surgical Oncology*, 5, 883–88.

Great Performances (producers) (1995) *Marks*, New York.

Grimshaw, Jean (1993) "Practices of Freedom", in *Up against Foucault: Explorations of Some Tensions between Foucault and Feminism*, Caroline Ramazanoglu (ed.), London and New York: Routledge, 51–72.

Grognard, Catherine (1994) *The Tattoo: Graffiti for the Soul*, Sydney: Treasure Press.

Grosz, Elizabeth (1990a) "Inscriptions and Body-Maps: Representations and the Corporeal", in *Feminine Masculine and Representation*, T. Threadgold and A. Cranny-Francis (eds.), Sydney: Allen and Unwin, 62–74.

—— (1990b) *Jacques Lacan: A Feminist Introduction*, Sydney: Allen & Unwin.

—— (1994) *Volatile Bodies: Towards a Corporeal Feminism*, Sydney: Allen & Unwin.

Grumet, G. W. (1983) "Psychodynamic Implications of Tattoos", in *The American Journal of Orthopsychiatry*, 53:3, July, 482–92.

Halperin, David (1995) *Saint Foucault*, New York and Oxford: Oxford University Press.

Hambly, W. D (1925) *The History of Tattooing and Its Significance*, London: H. F. and G. Witherby.

Hamburger, E. (1966) "Tattooing as a Psychic Defense Mechanism", in *International Journal of Social Psychiatry*, 12, 60–62.

Hardy, Don Ed (ed.) (1992) *Forever Yes: Art of the New Tattoo,* Hawaii: Hardy Marks Publications.

Hebdige, Dick "(1997) "Posing . . . Threats, Striking . . . Poses: Youth, Surveillance, and Display", in *The Subcultures Reader,* K. Gelder and S. Thornton (eds.), London and New York: Routledge, 393–405.

Hegel, G.W.F. (1977) *Phenomenology of Spirit,* A. V. Miller (trans.), Oxford: Oxford University Press.

Hill, Leslie (1988) "Barthes's Body", in *Paragraph,* 11, 107–25.

Hopcke, Robert (1983) "S/M and the Psychology of Male Initiation: An Archetypal Perspective", in *S and M: Studies in Sadomasochism,* T. Weinberg and G. W. Levi Kamel (eds.), Buffalo, NY: Prometheus, 65–76.

Horn, David G. (1995) "This Norm Which Is Not One", in *Deviant Bodies,* J. Terry and J. Urla (eds.), Bloomington and Indianapolis: Indiana University Press, 109–28.

Hough, Graham (1977) "The Importation of Barthes", in *Times Literary Supplement,* 9 December.

Idexa, (1993) "Idexa: Radical Primitive She/Boy", in *Body Play and Modern Primitives Quarterly,* 2:2, Summer, 8–13.

Irigaray, Luce (1985) *This Sex Which Is Not One,* C. Porter (trans.), Ithaca, NY: Cornell University Press.

——— (1991) "Sexual Difference", in *The Irigaray Reader,* M. Whitford (ed.), London: Basil Blackwell.

——— (1993) *An Ethics of Sexual Difference,* C. Burke and G. Gill (trans.), Ithaca, NY: Cornell University Press.

Jaguer, Jeff (1990) *The Tattoo: A Pictorial History,* Hampshire: Milestone Publications.

Jefferson, Ann (1989) "Bodymatters: Self and Other in Bakhtin, Sartre and Barthes", in *Bakhtin and Cultural Theory,* K. Hirschop and D. Sheperd (eds.), Manchester: Manchester University Press, 152–77.

Jeffreys, Sheila (1994) "Sadomasochism, Art & the Lesbian Sexual Revolution", in *Artlink,* 14:1, 19–21.

Jones, C. P. (1987) "Stigmata: Tattooing and Branding in Greco Roman Antiquity", in *Journal of Roman Studies,* 17, 139–55.

Juno, Andrea, and V. Vale (1989) *Modern Primitives,* London: Re/Search Publications.

Kafka, Franz (1995) *The Judgement and In the Penal Colony,* Harmondsworth: Penguin.

Kristeva, Julia (1984) *Revolution in Poetic Language,* M. Waller (trans.), New York: Columbia University Press.

Lander, J., and A. Kohn (1943) "A Note on Tattooing among Selectees", in *American Journal of Psychiatry,* 100, 326–27.

Lavers, Annette (1982) *Roland Barthes: Structuralism and After,* London: Methuen.

Leitch, Vincent B. (1983) *Deconstructive Criticism: An Advanced Introduction,* New York: Columbia University Press.

Levinas, Emmanuel (1969) *Totality and Infinity,* A. Lingis (trans.), Pittsburgh: Duquesne University Press.

——— (1978) *Otherwise Than Being or Beyond Essence,* A. Lingis (trans.), The Hague, Boston, and London: Martinus Nijhoff.

——— (1986) "The Trace of the Other", in *Deconstruction in Context: Literature and Philosophy,* M. C. Taylor (ed.), Chicago: University of Chicago Press.

—— (1987a) *Collected Philosophical Papers,* A. Lingis (trans.), Dordrecht, Boston, and Lancaster: Martinus Nijhoff.

—— (1987b) "Diachrony and Representation", in *Time and the Other and Additional Essays,* R. A. Cohen (trans.), Pittsburgh: Duquesne University Press, 97–120.

Lingis, Alphonso (1978) "The Last Form of Will to Power", in *Philosophy Today,* 22, Fall, 193–205.

—— (1979) "Face to Face: A Phenomenological Meditation", in *International Philosophy Quarterly,* 19, 151–63.

—— (1983a) "The Rapture of the Deep", in *Excesses: Eros and Culture*, Albany: State University of New York Press, 1–16.

—— (1983b) "Savages", in *Excesses: Eros and Culture*, Albany: State University of New York Press, 17–46.

—— (1985) *Libido: The French Existentialist Theories,* Bloomington: Indiana University Press.

—— (1986) "The Sensuality and the Sensitivity", in *Face to Face with Levinas*, R. A. Cohen (ed.), New York: SUNY Press, 219–30.

—— (1989) *Deathbound Subjectivity,* Albany: State University of New York Press.

—— (1994a) *The Community of Those Who Have Nothing in Common,* Bloomington: Indiana University Press.

—— (1994b) *Foreign Bodies*, New York: Routledge.

—— (1994c) "The Society of Dismembered Body Parts", in *Gilles Deleuze and the Theatre of Philosophy*, C. V. Boundas and D. Olkowski (eds.), New York and London: Routledge, 289–304.

Lombroso, Cesare, Enrico Ferri, Raffaele Garofalo, and Giulio Fioretti (1886) *Polemica in Difesa Della Scuola Criminale Positiva*, Bologna: Zanichelli.

Lombroso-Ferrero, Gina (1972) *Criminal Man According to the Classification of Cesare Lombroso*, Montclair, NJ: Patterson Smith.

Loos, Adolf (1908) "Ornamentation and Crime", in *The Architecture of Adolf Loos,* New York: Arts Council, 100–103.

Lyotard, Jean-Francois (1971) *Discourse, Figure*, Paris: Klincksieck.

—— (1988) *The Differend: Phrases in Dispute*, G. Van den Abbeele (trans.), Minneapolis: University of Minnesota Press.

—— (1990) *Heidegger and "the jews"*, A. Michel and M. Roberts (trans.), Minneapolis and London: University of Minnesota Press.

—— (1993) *Libidinal Economies*, Iain Hamilton Grant (trans.), Bloomington and Indianapolis: Indiana University Press.

Lyotard, Jean-Francois, and Jean-Loup Thébaud (1985) *Just Gaming*, G. Godzich (trans.), Minneapolis: University of Minnesota Press.

McClintock, Anne (1993) "The Return of Female Fetishism and the Fiction of the Phallus", in *New Formations*, 19, Spring, 1–21.

McLane, Janice (1996) "The Voice on the Skin: Self-Mutilation and Merleau-Ponty's Theory of Language", in *Hypatia,* 11:4, 107–18.

Macey, David (1994) *The Lives of Michel Foucault,* London: Vintage.

Malloy, Ann B. (1996) *Tattoo Matters: The Materialization of the Body Through the Performance of Tattooing*, Indiana State University (unpublished master's thesis).

Mansfield, Nick (1997) *Masochism: The Art of Power,* Westport, CT: Praeger.

Marshall, Stuart (1990) "Picturing Deviancy", in *Ecstatic Antibodies: Resisting the AIDS Mythology,* T. Boffin and S. Gupta (eds.), London: Rivers Oram, 19–36.

Martin, L., H. Gutman, and P. Hutton (1988) *Technologies of the Self,* Amherst: University of Massachusetts Press.

Massumi, Brian (1993) "Everywhere You Want to Be: An Introduction to Fear", in *The Politics of Everyday Fear,* B. Massumi (ed.), Minneapolis: University of Minnesota Press.

Merleau-Ponty, Maurice (1962) *The Phenomenology of Perception,* C. Smith (trans.), London: Routledge and Kegan Paul.

––––– (1964) *The Primacy of Perception,* Evanston: Northwestern University Press.

––––– (1968) *The Visible and the Invisible,* A. Lingis (trans.), Evanston: Northwestern University Press.

Mifflin, Margot (1997) *Bodies of Subversion: A Secret History of Women and Tattoo,* New York: ReSearch Publications.

Moore, Joan, (1978) *Homeboys: Gangs, Drugs, and Prison in the Barrios of Los Angeles,* Philadelphia: Temple University Press.

Moriarty, Michael (1991) *Roland Barthes,* Oxford: Polity Press.

Mortimer, Armine Kotin (1989) *The Gentlest Law,* New York: Peter Laing Publishing.

Muecke, Stephen (1997) *No Road,* South Fremantle: Fremantle Arts Centre Press.

Musafar, Fakir (1996) "Body Play: State of Grace or Sickness?" in *Bodies Under Siege: Self-mutilation and Body Modification in Culture and Psychiatry,* A. R. Favazza, Baltimore and London: Johns Hopkins University Press, 325–34.

Nancy, Jean-Luc (1991) *The Inoperative Community,* P. Connor et al. (trans.), Minneapolis: University of Minnesota Press.

––––– (1993) *The Birth to Presence,* B. Holmes et al. (eds.), Palo Alto: Stanford University Press.

Nietzsche, Friedrich (1968a) *The Anti-Christ,* R. J. Hollingdale (trans.), Harmondsworth: Penguin.

––––– (1968b) *Will to Power,* W. Kaufman and R. J. Hollingdale (trans.), New York: Vintage.

––––– (1974) *The Gay Science,* W. Kaufmann (trans.), New York: Vintage Books.

––––– (1978) *Thus Spoke Zarathustra,* W. Kaufmann (trans.), Harmondsworth: Penguin.

––––– (1984) *Beyond Good and Evil,* R. J. Hollingdale (trans.), Harmondsworth: Penguin.

O'Farrell, Clare (1989) *Foucault: Historian or Philosopher?* London: Macmillan.

Olguín, B. V. (1997) "Tattoos, Abjection and the Political Unconscious: Towards a Semiotics of the *Pinto* Visual Vernacular", in *Cultural Critique,* 37, Fall, 159–214.

Parry, Albert (1933) *Tattoo: Secrets of a Strange Art as Practiced Among the Natives of the United States,* New York: Simon and Schuster.

––––– (1934) "Tattooing among Prostitutes and Perverts", in *Psychoanalytic Quarterly,* 3, 476–82.

Peters, F. E. (1967) *Greek Philosophical Terms; A Historical Lexicon,* New York: New York University Press.

Post, Richard S. (1968) "The Relationship of Tattoos to Personality Disorders", in *Journal of Criminal Law, Criminology, and Police Science,* 59, 516–24.

Probyn, Elspeth (1993) *Sexing the Self*, London and New York: Routledge.

Rabinow, Paul (ed.) (1997) *Michel Foucault: Ethics, Subjectivity, and Truth (Essential Works of Foucault, 1954–84, Volume One)*, New York: The New Press.

Readings, Bill (1991) *Introducing Lyotard: Art and Politics*, London and New York: Routledge.

Robbins, Jill (1995) "Tracing Responsibility in Levinas's Ethical Thought", in *Ethics as First Philosophy*, A. Peperzak (ed.), London: Routledge, 173–84.

Robbins, Tim (producer) (1995) *Dead Man Walking*, New York.

Rochlitz, Rainer (1992) "The Aesthetics of Existence: Post-conventional Morality and the Theory of Power in Michel Foucault", in *Michel Foucault Philosopher*, T. J. Armstrong (trans.), London and New York: Harvester Wheatsheaf, 248–59.

Saint-Amand, Pierre (1996) "The Secretive Body: Roland Barthes' Gay Erotics", in *Yale French Studies*, 90, 153–71.

Sanders, Clinton R. (1988) "Marks of Mischief: Becoming and Being Tattooed", in *The Journal of Contemporary Ethnography*, 16:4, January, 395–432.

——— (1989) *Customizing the Body: The Art and Culture of Tattooing*, Philadelphia: Temple University Press.

Schor, Naomi (1986) "Roland Barthes: Necrologies", in *SubStance*, 14:3, 27–33.

Scutt, R., and C. Gotch (1974) *Skin Deep: The Mystery of Tattooing*, London: Peter Davies.

Seaton, Elizabeth (1987) "Profaned Bodies and Purloined Looks: The Prisoner's Tattoo and the Researcher's Gaze", in *Journal of Communication Enquiry*, 11:1, Summer, 17–25.

Secomb, Linnell (1997) "Queering Community", in *Queerzone*, Nepean: University of Western Sydney Women's Research Centre.

——— (2000) "Fractured Community", in *Hypatia*, 15:2, 133–50.

Serres, Michel (1982) "Platonic Dialogue", in *Hermes: Literature, Science, Philosophy*, J. V. Harari and D. F. Bell (eds.), Baltimore and London: Johns Hopkins University Press, 65–70.

Skin and Ink (1994) July.

Smart, Barry (1991) "On the Subjects of Sexuality, Ethics and Politics in the Work of Foucault", in *boundary 2*, 18:1, 201–20.

——— (1998) "Foucault, Levinas and the Subject of Responsibility", in *The Later Foucault*, J. Moss (ed.), London: Sage Publications, 78–92.

Sontag, Susan (1983) "Writing Itself: On Roland Barthes", in *A Barthes Reader*, New York: Hill and Wang, vii–xxxviii.

Speake, Jennifer (ed.) (1979) *A Dictionary of Philosophy*, London: Pan Books.

Steward, Samuel M. (1990) *Bad Boys and Tough Tattoos*, New York: Harrington Park Press.

Tallon, A. (1995) "Nonintentional Affectivity, Affective Intentionality, and the Ethical in Levinas's Philosophy", in *Ethics as First Philosophy*, A. Peperzak (ed.), London: Routledge, 107–22.

Taylor, Mark C. (1987) *Altarity*, Chicago: University of Chicago Press.

——— (1997) *Hiding*, Chicago: University of Chicago Press.

Terry, Jennifer, and J. Urla (eds.) (1995) *Deviant Bodies: Critical Perspectives on Difference in Science and Popular Culture*, Indianapolis: Indiana University Press.

Thody, Philip (1977) *Roland Barthes: A Conservative Estimate*, Atlantic Highlands: New Jersey Humanities Press.

Tournier, Michel (1985) *Gemini*, A. Carter (trans.), London: Methuen.

Ulmer, Gregory (1978) "Fetishism in Roland Barthes's Nietzchean Phase", in *Papers on Language and Literature*, 14:3, Summer, 334–55.

Ungar, Steven (1978) "Doing and Not Doing Things with Barthes", in *Enclit*, 2:2, Autumn, 86–109.

Virel, Andre (1980) *Decorated Man: The Human Body as Art*, New York: Harry N. Abrams.

Walkerdine, Valerie (1986) "Video Replay: Families, Film and Fantasy", in *Formations of Fantasy*, V. Burgin, J. Donald, and C. Kaplan (eds.), London: Methuen.

Walsh, Barent, and Paul Rosen (1988) *Self-Mutilation: Theory, Research and Treatment*, New York: Guilford Press.

West, D. J., and D. P. Farrington (1977) *The Delinquent Way of Life*, New York: Crane Russak.

Westlake, Michael (1989) *Imaginary Women*, London: Paladin.

Westphal, Merold (1993) "Levinas and the Immediacy of the Face", in *Faith and Philosophy*, 10:4, October, 486–502.

Williams, James (1998) *Lyotard: Towards a Postmodern Philosophy*, Cambridge: Polity Press.

Winterson, Jeanette (1993) "The Poetics of Sex", in *The Penguin Book of Lesbian Short Stories*, M. Reynolds (ed.), Penguin: Harmondsworth, 412–22.

Wittig, Monique (1992) *The Straight Mind and Other Essays*, Boston: Beacon Press.

Wojcik, Daniel (1995) *Punk and Neo-Tribal Body Art*, Jackson: University Press of Mississippi.

Wroblewski, Chris (1988) *Modern Primitives*, Wien: Verlag Christian Brandstatter.

Wyschogrod, Edith (1990) *Saints and Postmodernism*, Chicago: University of Chicago Press.

Yamamoto, J., W. Seeman, and B. K. Lester (1963) "The Tattooed Man", in *Journal of Nervous and Mental Disorders*, 136, 365–67.

Youniss, Richard (1959) "The Relationship of Tattoos to Personal Adjustment among Enlisted Submarine School Scholars", in *U.S.N. Medical Research Report No. 319*, Westport, CT: New London.

Index

About the Author

NIKKI SULLIVAN is a lecturer in Critical and Cultural Studies at Macquarie University. She has published articles on body modification, self-mutilation, and queer theory.